VMware vSphere 5.1 Cookbook

Over 130 task-oriented recipes to install, configure, and manage various vSphere 5.1 components

Abhilash GB

BIRMINGHAM - MUMBAI

VMware vSphere 5.1 Cookbook

First published: July 2013

Production Reference: 1040713

Published by Packt Publishing Ltd.
Livery Place
35 Livery Street
Birmingham B3 2PB, UK.

ISBN 978-1-84968-402-6

www.packtpub.com

Cover Image by J.Blaminsky (milak6@wp.pl)

Credits

Author

Abhilash GB

Reviewers

Edvaldo Alessandro Cardoso

Christian Mohn

Chris Wahl

Acquisition Editors

Saleem Ahmed

Rukhsana Khambatta

Lead Technical Editor

Arun Nadar

Technical Editors

Ruchita Bhansali

Sampreshita Maheshwari

Nitee Shetty

Hardik B. Soni

Project Coordinator

Arshad Sopariwala

Proofreaders

Stephen Copestake

Dirk Manuel

Indexer

Hemangini Bari

Graphics

Abhinash Sahu

Production Coordinator

Arvindkumar Gupta

Cover Work

Arvindkumar Gupta

About the Author

Abhilash GB specializes in the area of Datacenter Virtualization and Cloud Computing. He is also a VMware Certified Advanced Professional in Datacenter Administration (VCAP-DCA #382).

He is currently working as a VMware Specialist at Hewlett-Packard, Bangalore.

He has nine years of IT experience, which includes over 6 years on VMware products and technologies.

His primary areas of interest include Datacenter Virtualization and Cloud Solutions using VMware technologies.

I would like to dedicate this book to my wife and my parents. Without their patience and support this book would not have been possible.

A big thanks to Dilip Venkatesh, Acquisition Editor, Packt Publishing, for giving me an opportunity to debut my first book. Special thanks to the Lead Technical Editors (Unnati Shah and Arun Nadar), the Project Coordinators (Vishal Bodwani and Arshad Sopariwala), and the Technical Reviewers (Christian Mohn, Chris Wahl, and Alessandro Cardoso) who helped me deliver this book.

About the Reviewers

Alessandro Cardoso is a virtualization and management enthusiast, author, and evangelist. He is a subject matter expert in cloud computing, virtualization, and management, and works at Insight as a Practice Manager for Cloud and Emerging technologies, leading award-winning IT projects in key areas involving Cloud, Virtualization, Security, Messaging, and Hosting within the IT, Health, and Government industries.

A VMware VCP and Microsoft Most Valuable Professional in virtualization since 2009, his product skill set includes Microsoft infrastructure technologies such as O365, Hyper-V, System Center, Windows Server, SQL Server, Active Directory, Exchange, SharePoint, IIS, and Forefront, and he also has sound knowledge of Quest Migration Manager, Linux Infrastructure, Networking, Security Solutions, and VMware in complex and large scenarios.

He is a well-known speaker at IT-related events and is the author of the book *System Center Virtual* Machine Manager 2012 and was the technical reviewer of the *Windows 2012 Hyper-V Cookbook*.

You can also check his personal blog where he talks about Microsoft Virtualization and System Center at `http://virtualisationandmanagement.wordpress.com` or can follow him on twitter at `@edvaldocardoso`.

I would like to thank my wife Daniele and my kids Matheus, Lucas, and Nicole for the support and for being my inspiration. I love you all.

Christian Mohn is currently employed as a senior consultant at EVRY Consulting AS in Norway, and is currently serving as Tech Champion for Server Virtualization.

He has a background as an IT-professional since 1997, and has worked both as a consultant and as an infrastructure manager for a large Norwegian shipping company.

He is also one of the co-hosts of the vSoup Virtualization Podcast. Christian was awarded the VMware vExpert title for both 2011 and 2012.

He wrote the foreword in *Building End-User Computing Solutions with VMware View*, which is available at `http://www.lulu.com/shop/mike-laverick-and-barry-coombs/building-end-user-computing-solutions-with-vmware-view/ebook/product-20368612.html`.

Chris Wahl has over 13 years of IT experience in enterprise infrastructure design, implementation, and administration within a diverse set of business and regulatory requirements, such as HIPPA, SOX, PCI-DSS, ITIL, and ePHI. He has held architect and engineer roles in a variety of virtualization, converged infrastructure, and private cloud based engagements, while working with high-performance technical teams in tiered data center environments.

He has over 30 active industry certifications, including the VMware Certified Design Expert (VCDX #104), and is a recognized VMware vExpert. Additionally, he holds an active "Master" rank on the VMware Technology Network (VMTN) as a contributor and forum moderator. Chris also volunteers as a Leader in the Chicago VMware User Group (VMUG) to help spread education and technical knowledge of VMware's products and related architecture.

As an Independent Blogger for the award winning "Wahl Network" Chris focuses on creating content that revolves around virtualization, converged infrastructure, and evangelizing products and services that benefit the technology community. Over the past three years, he has published over 200 articles and was voted the "Favorite Independent Blogger" by vSphere-Land.com for 2012. Chris also travels globally to speak at industry events, provide subject matter expertise, and offer insight as a technical analyst.

www.PacktPub.com

Support files, eBooks, discount offers and more

You might want to visit www.PacktPub.com for support files and downloads related to your book.

Did you know that Packt offers eBook versions of every book published, with PDF and ePub files available? You can upgrade to the eBook version at www.PacktPub.com and as a print book customer, you are entitled to a discount on the eBook copy. Get in touch with us at service@packtpub.com for more details.

At www.PacktPub.com, you can also read a collection of free technical articles, sign up for a range of free newsletters and receive exclusive discounts and offers on Packt books and eBooks.

http://PacktLib.PacktPub.com

Do you need instant solutions to your IT questions? PacktLib is Packt's online digital book library. Here, you can access, read and search across Packt's entire library of books.

Why Subscribe?

- Fully searchable across every book published by Packt
- Copy and paste, print and bookmark content
- On demand and accessible via web browser

Free Access for Packt account holders

If you have an account with Packt at www.PacktPub.com, you can use this to access PacktLib today and view nine entirely free books. Simply use your login credentials for immediate access.

Instant Updates on New Packt Books

Get notified! Find out when new books are published by following @PacktEnterprise on Twitter, or the *Packt Enterprise* Facebook page.

Table of Contents

Preface

Amid all the recent competition from Citrix and Microsoft, VMware's vSphere product line is still the most feature-rich product in the virtualization industry. Knowing how to install and configure VMware vSphere components is important to give yourself a head start towards datacenter virtualization using VMware.

VMware vSphere 5.1 Cookbook is a task-oriented, fast-paced practical guide to installing and configuring vSphere 5.1 components. This book was written with the intention of providing the reader with a visual walkthrough of the most common configuration tasks that an administrator will perform in a VMware vSphere environment. It takes you through all of the steps required to accomplish a task, with less reading required. The book concentrates more on the actual task rather than theory around it, making it easier to understand what really is needed to achieve the task. However, most of the concepts has been well described, to help the reader understand its background and working.

The main highlight of this book is the use of the new vSphere 5.1 Web Client to accomplish most of the tasks. Although a few tasks cannot be accomplished using web client with the current vSphere version, VMware will be integrating them into the web client in future product releases.

What this book covers

Chapter 1, Upgrading to vSphere 5.1, discusses the procedures involved in upgrading the current vSphere environment to vSphere 5.1. It covers upgrading the vCenter Server and the ESXi host.

Chapter 2, Performing a Fresh Installation of vSphere 5.1, explains how to deploy a new vSphere 5.1 environment. It covers the installation of vCenter 5.1 and ESXi 5.1.

Chapter 3, vSphere Auto Deploy, explains how to install and configure Auto Deploy in order to provision ESXi servers. It also covers stateless caching and stateful installation.

Chapter 4, ESXi Image Builder, explains how to create, manage, and apply Image Profiles to ESXi hosts.

Chapter 5, Creating and Managing VMFS Datastores, explains how to create, view, and manage VMFS datastores on an ESXi host. It also covers datastore clusters and storage DRS.

Chapter 6, Managing iSCSI and NFS Storage, explains how to configure iSCSI and NAS storage on an ESXi host.

Chapter 7, Profile-driven Storage and Storage I/O Control, explains how to use storage profiles to ensure that the VMs are placed in appropriate datastores, and how to use storage I/O control to manage queue bandwidth between VMs.

Chapter 8, Configuring the vSphere Network, explains how to set up and configure vSphere networking using vSphere standard switches and vSphere distributed switches. It also covers port mirroring, NetFlow, and PVLANs.

Chapter 9, Creating and Managing Virtual Machines, explains how to create and configure virtual machines in a vSphere environment.

Chapter 10, Configuring vSphere HA, explains how to configure High Availability for ESXi servers.

Chapter 11, Configuring vSphere DRS, DPM, and VMware EVC, explains how to enable and configure DRS on a cluster. It also covers vSphere Distributed Power Management (DPM) and VMware Enhanced vMotion Capability (EVC).

Chapter 12, Upgrading and Patching using VMware Update Manager, explains how to install and configure VMware Update Manager to manage patching and upgrading ESXi hosts. It also covers the installation and configuration of the Update Manager Download Service (UMDS).

Chapter 13, Using vSphere Management Assistant (vMA 5.1), explains how to deploy and configure vMA 5.1 to run commands/scripts with the need to authenticate every attempt.

What you need for this book

You will learn the software requirements for every vSphere component covered in this book, but to start with the basics you will need at least two ESXi servers, a vCenter Server, a domain controller, a DHCP server, a DNS server, and a TFTP server. For learning purposes, you don't really need physical machines to run ESXi. You can use VMware Workstation to set up a hosted lab on your desktop PC or laptop, provided the machine has adequate resources. For shared storage, you can use any of the free virtual storage appliances, such as the Celera UBER, the Openfiler, or a trial version of HP LeftHand (StoreVirtual) VSA.

  ▸ Celera UBER 3.2

    ```
    http://nickapedia.com/2010/10/04/play-it-again-sam-celerra-
    uber-v3-2/
    ```

▸ Openfiler

```
http://www.openfiler.com/
```

▸ Hp LeftHand (StoreVirtual) VSA

```
http://h18006.www1.hp.com/products/storage/software/vsa/index.
html
```

Who this book is for

This book is a guide for anyone who wants to learn how install and configure VMware vSphere components. It is an excellent handbook for support professionals, or for anyone looking for a head start in learning how to install and configure vSphere 5.1 components. It is also a good, task-oriented reference material for consultants who design and deploy vSphere environments.

Conventions

In this book, you will find a number of styles of text that distinguish between different kinds of information. Here are some examples of these styles, and an explanation of their meaning.

Code words in text, database table names, folder names, filenames, file extensions, pathnames, dummy URLs, user input, and Twitter handles are shown as follows: "The datamigration.zip file can located under the datamigration folder on root the vCenter installer ISO/ZIP/DVD."

A block of code is set as follows:

```
#
# Sample scripted installation file
#
# Accept the VMware End User License Agreement
vmaccepteula

# Set the root password for the DCUI and Tech Support Mode
rootpw mypassword

# Install on the first local disk available on machine
install --firstdisk -overwritevmfs

# Set the network to DHCP on the first network adapter
network --bootproto=dhcp --device=vmnic0

# A sample post-install script
%post --interpreter=python --ignorefailure=true
import time
stampFile = open('/finished.stamp', mode='w')
stampFile.write( time.asctime() )
```

When we wish to draw your attention to a particular part of a code block, the relevant lines or items are set in bold:

```
#
# Sample scripted installation file
#
# Accept the VMware End User License Agreement
vmaccepteula

# Set the root password for the DCUI and Tech Support Mode
rootpw mypassword

# Install on the first local disk available on machine
install --firstdisk -overwritevmfs

# Set the network to DHCP on the first network adapter
network --bootproto=dhcp --device=vmnic0

# A sample post-install script
%post --interpreter=python --ignorefailure=true
import time
stampFile = open('/finished.stamp', mode='w')
stampFile.write( time.asctime() )
```

Any command-line input or output is written as follows:

Set-ExecutionPolicy Unrestricted

New terms and **important words** are shown in bold. Words that you see on the screen, in menus or dialog boxes for example, appear in the text like this: "It can be enabled at the vCenter Server by navigating to **Administration | vCenter Server Settings | SSL Settings**, and selecting the **vCenter requires verified host SSL certificates** checkbox."

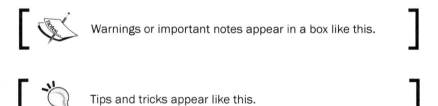

Warnings or important notes appear in a box like this.

Tips and tricks appear like this.

The numbered circle-pointers in the screenshots of the book do not always correspond to the numbered steps. The circle-pointers are used to provide navigational guidance.

Reader feedback

Feedback from our readers is always welcome. Let us know what you think about this book—what you liked or may have disliked. Reader feedback is important for us to develop titles that you really get the most out of.

To send us general feedback, simply send an e-mail to feedback@packtpub.com, and mention the book title via the subject of your message.

If there is a topic that you have expertise in and you are interested in either writing or contributing to a book, see our author guide on www.packtpub.com/authors.

Customer support

Now that you are the proud owner of a Packt book, we have a number of things to help you to get the most from your purchase.

Errata

Although we have taken every care to ensure the accuracy of our content, mistakes do happen. If you find a mistake in one of our books—maybe a mistake in the text or the code—we would be grateful if you would report this to us. By doing so, you can save other readers from frustration and help us improve subsequent versions of this book. If you find any errata, please report them by visiting http://www.packtpub.com/submit-errata, selecting your book, clicking on the **errata submission form** link, and entering the details of your errata. Once your errata are verified, your submission will be accepted and the errata will be uploaded on our website, or added to any list of existing errata, under the Errata section of that title. Any existing errata can be viewed by selecting your title from http://www.packtpub.com/support.

Piracy

Piracy of copyright material on the Internet is an ongoing problem across all media. At Packt, we take the protection of our copyright and licenses very seriously. If you come across any illegal copies of our works, in any form, on the Internet, please provide us with the location address or website name immediately so that we can pursue a remedy.

Please contact us at copyright@packtpub.com with a link to the suspected pirated material.

We appreciate your help in protecting our authors, and our ability to bring you valuable content.

Questions

You can contact us at questions@packtpub.com if you are having a problem with any aspect of the book, and we will do our best to address it.

1
Upgrading to vSphere 5.1

In this chapter we will cover the following:

- ▸ Carrying out pre-upgrade checks before performing a vCenter upgrade
- ▸ Performing an in-place upgrade of vCenter Server
- ▸ Creating a table space for SSO on a SQL instance
- ▸ Creating DB users for the SSO database
- ▸ Upgrading a 32-bit vCenter Server to vCenter 5.1
- ▸ Upgrading to ESXi 5.1
- ▸ Installing vSphere Web Client
- ▸ Upgrading VMware Tools
- ▸ Upgrading the virtual machine hardware

Introduction

In this chapter, we will focus on the steps required to upgrade your ESX servers to ESXi 5.1 and the vCenter Server to vCenter 5.1. If you are trying to rebuild or set up a new vSphere 5.1 environment then you should refer to *Chapter 2, Performing a Fresh Installation of vSphere 5.1*.

Always the rule of thumb is to upgrade the vCenter Server first, followed by the ESX server.

The upgrade is a three-step process:

1. Upgrade the vCenter Server to 5.1.
2. Upgrade the ESX/ESXi servers to 5.1.
3. Upgrade VMware Tools and then the virtual machine hardware.

It is recommended that you check the *VMware Compatibility Guide* web page for changes in the supportability of your current hardware. The hardware components may sometimes need a firmware upgrade to work as expected when used with a newer release of vSphere.

The *VMware Compatibility Guide* web page is available at www.vmware.com/go/hcl.

Upgrading the vCenter Server

VMware vCenter 5.1 is 64-bit; so the process of upgrading the vCenter Server to version 5.1 can be different, depending on whether you are already running your current vCenter on a 64-bit operating system or a 32-bit operating system.

There are two methods of upgrading your current vCenter to vCenter 5.1:

► The in-place upgrade method
► Migrating vCenter data using the vSphere Data Migration tool

The in-place upgrade is done by running the vCenter 5.1 installer on the machine where you have the existing vCenter Server, provided it is 64-bit. It is called in-place, because you are just letting the installer do the upgrade by automatically preserving the settings of the existing vCenter Sever. This procedure is discussed in the *Performing an in-place upgrade of vCenter Server* recipe.

If your existing vCenter is running on a 32-bit operating system, then you cannot install vCenter 5.1 on the same machine because it is a 64-bit application. You will need a machine running a 64-bit version of Windows. This is when you can choose to migrate the current vCenter data, using the vSphere **Data Migration** tool, from the 32-bit machine to a 64-bit machine where you intend to install vCenter 5.1. To learn how this is done, read the *Upgrading a 32-Bit vCenter Server to vCenter 5.1* recipe.

Upgrading the ESXi server

Unlike the vCenter Server, the process of upgrading the ESXi server to version 5.1 is pretty straightforward. It is important that you upgrade the vCenter Server prior to upgrading the ESXi servers. There are different methods to upgrade the ESX server to ESXi 5.1. Refer to the *Upgrading to ESXi 5.1* recipe for more information on how the upgrade is done using the ESX 5.1 installation DVD. References for other methods can be found in the same chapter.

vSphere Web Client

Starting with vSphere 5.1, VMware has introduced a Web Client component that can be used to manage the vSphere environment. Although, I will be using vSphere Web Client for most of the tasks in the chapters, you could still use the vSphere Client to perform the same tasks. But there are certain tasks that can only be done using the vSphere Client. For example, the VMware Update Manager plugin is not available for the vSphere Web Client. Having said that, VMware will be moving all of the vSphere management GUIs to the Web Client in the upcoming versions of vSphere. So it would be good to get used to the vSphere Web Client interface. For instructions on how to install the vSphere Web Client component, refer to the *Installing vSphere Web Client* recipe.

Carrying out pre-upgrade checks before performing a vCenter upgrade

Although running the installation wizard to upgrade the vCenter Server is a straightforward process, there are a few pre-upgrade steps that have to be performed so that you can finish the upgrade process without any issues.

How to do it...

The following are the steps that you have to perform before doing the upgrade:

1. Check the ESX server compatibility.
2. Run Host Agent Pre-Upgrade Checker.
3. Check database compatibility.
4. Back up the SSL certificates.
5. Enable the SSL certificate verification.
6. Uninstall non-default software and its corresponding vCenter plugins.

Checking the ESX server compatibility

This check is very critical, make sure that this is tagged as a mandatory step in your upgrade action plan.

It is again a best practice to check the *VMware Product Interoperability Matrixes* web page for verification:

```
http://www.vmware.com/resources/compatibility/sim/interop_matrix.php
```

vCenter Server 5.1 can be used to manage ESX/ESXi 4.x and ESX 5.0.

 Note that ESX/ESXi 3.5 or earlier versions cannot be managed using vCenter 5.1.

Running VMware vCenter Host Agent Pre-Upgrade Checker

The **VMware vCenter Host Agent Pre-Upgrade Checker** feature is run to generate a report showing issues detected on the ESX servers, which in turn would prevent a successful upgrade of the vCenter Host Agent software on the ESXi servers. The component is listed under the **Utilities** section of the vCenter Server's installer home screen. The following are the steps to run the pre-upgrade checker:

1. Click on **Install** to start the installation wizard. It will start downloading data from VMware's online repository to update its reference database.

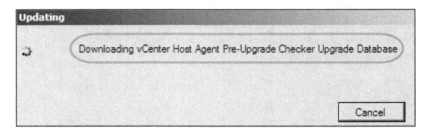

2. Once the database is upgraded, it will bring up the **VMware vCenter Host Agent Pre-Upgrade Checker** wizard. Click on **Next** to continue.

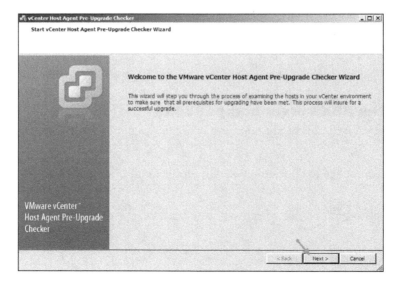

3. On the next screen, select the **DSN** value corresponding to the vCenter Server, choose the appropriate credentials, and Click on **Next**.

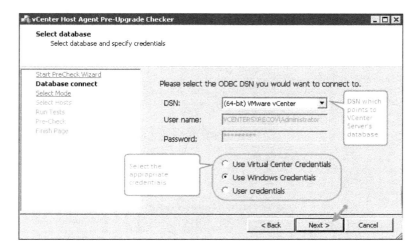

4. Once the connection to the vCenter Server has been successfully authenticated, then you will be prompted to choose preferred **Scan Mode**. There are two scan modes:

    ❏ **Standard Mode**: This will scan all the ESX hosts managed by the vCenter

    ❏ **Custom Mode**: This will let you choose the ESX hosts that you would like to scan

    I have chosen the **Custom Mode** radio button. Click on **Next** to continue.

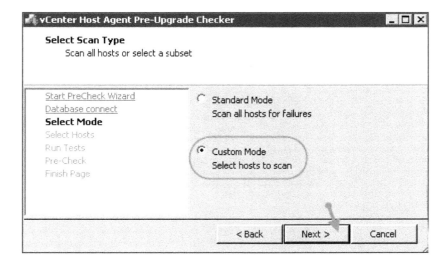

5. Select the ESX servers for a pre-upgrade check and click on **Next**.

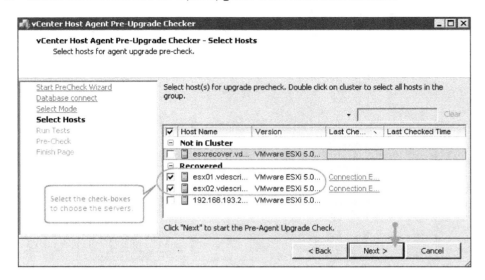

6. On the next screen, click on **Run precheck** to run the tests on the selected hosts. Then click on **Next**.

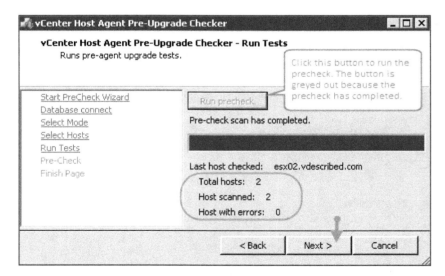

7. On the next screen, if the ESX hosts has passed the check, then the **Last Checked Status** value will be **Pass**.

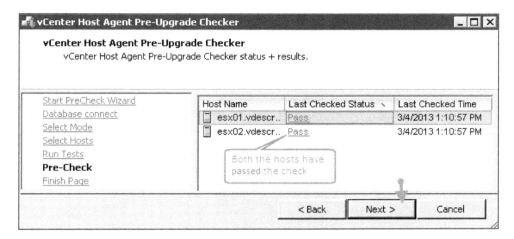

If any of the hosts failed the pre-check, then the issues reported should be addressed before you retry the upgrade.

Checking database compatibility

It is important that you verify whether the vCenter database in use is compatible with vCenter Server 5.

It is recommended to use the *VMware Product Interoperability Matrixes* page for verification. Also, refer to the table 4-6 in the *Supported Database Upgrades* section at page 51 in the *vSphere 5.1 Upgrade* guide for a complete list of supported database upgrades, available at the following link:

```
http://pubs.vmware.com/vsphere-51/topic/com.vmware.ICbase/PDF/
vsphere-esxi-vcenter-server-51-upgrade-guide.pdf
```

 The vCenter installation cannot be rolled back. So if the database is modified during a failed vCenter server installation, there is no going back. Thus, it is a good practice to back up the vCenter database before executing the installer. And, if you have vCenter installed on a VM, then you can back up the entire VM as well.

Backing up the SSL certificates

Make sure that you back up the Secure Sockets Layer (SSL) certificates from the folder:

- On Windows 2003: `%ALLUSERSPROFILE%\Application Data\VMware\VMware VirtualCenter\SSL`

- On Windows Vista or 2008 Server: `%ALLUSERSPROFILE%\VMWare\VMware VirtualCenter\SSL`

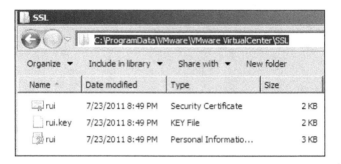

Enabling SSL certificate verification

By enabling SSL certificate verification, the vCenter Server will verify the validity of the SSL certificates of the ESX servers, when establishing SSL connections with them.

It can be enabled at the vCenter Server by navigating to **Administration | vCenter Server Settings | SSL Settings**, and selecting the **vCenter requires verified host SSL certificates** checkbox.

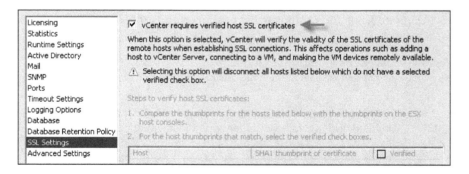

Uninstalling the non-default software and plugins

Since older versions of vCenter plugins will not be compatible with vCenter 5.1, it is recommended that you uninstall the non-default software and its corresponding plugins installed on the vCenter Server machine using **Add/Remove Programs** prior to the upgrade.

The non-default software and plugins include:

- ▸ vCenter Update Manager
- ▸ vCenter Converter
- ▸ vCenter Guided Consolidation

These plugins can be installed and re-enabled once their corresponding software versions are upgraded.

Performing an in-place upgrade of vCenter Server

An **in-place** upgrade can be performed only if the previous version of vCenter is already running on a 64-bit machine. If the previous version of vCenter is running on a 32-bit machine then you should migrate the vCenter Server's data using the vSphere Data Migration tool.

Only three releases of vCenter Server are eligible for an in-place upgrade:

- ▸ vCenter Server 4.0, if installed on a 64-bit machine
- ▸ vCenter Server 4.1
- ▸ vCenter 5.0

Here is a list of supported 64-bit operating systems vCenter 5.1 can be installed on:

- ▸ Windows Server 2003 Service Pack 2
- ▸ Windows Server 2003 R2
- ▸ Windows 2008 Service Pack 1 and Service Pack 2
- ▸ Windows 2008 R2
- ▸ Windows 2008 R2 Service Pack 1

 Starting with vCenter 5.0, Microsoft® Windows XP is no longer supported to host a vCenter Server. Hence, vCenter 5.1 also doesn't support it.

With vCenter 5.1, we now have more than one component involved in the vCenter Server configuration:

- ► vCenter Single Sign On
- ► vCenter Inventory Service
- ► vCenter Server

vCenter Server and the vCenter Single Sign On component's hardware requirements are as follows:

- ► Intel/AMD x64 with multiple logical cores clocked at minimum 2 GHz each
- ► A minimum of 3 GB memory and 2 GB disk space
- ► A network adapter with a minimum speed of 1 Gbps

The vCenter Inventory Service component's hardware requirements are as follows:

- ► Intel/AMD x64 with multiple logical cores clocked at a minimum 2 GHz each
- ► A minimum of 3 GB memory
- ► 60 GB disk space for medium- to large-sized inventories
- ► A network adapter with a minimum speed of 1 Gbps

 If the vCenter Single Sign On, Inventory Service, and vCenter Server components are installed on the same machine, then the recommended memory is 10 GB.

The vCenter Server installation bundle can be downloaded from VMware vSphere's downloads page, available at the following link:

```
https://my.vmware.com/web/vmware/info/slug/datacenter_cloud_
infrastructure/vmware_vsphere/5_1
```

The download item will be listed as **VMware vCenter Server 5.1.0 and modules**, which is available in both ISO and ZIP archives.

Once done, run the `AutoRun.exe` file, which should bring up the VMware vCenter installer's home screen.

How to do it...

In this section, I will show you how to perform an in-place upgrade of the vCenter Server. This process requires a downtime of the vCenter Server but the VMs hosted on the ESX server will continue to run. It is important that you read the *Carrying out pre-upgrade checks before performing a vCenter upgrade* recipe, before you proceed:

1. At the vCenter installation home screen, select **vCenter Server Simple Install** and click on the **Install** button to start the installation wizard.

2. At the **InstallShield vCenter Single Sign On** wizard screen, click on **Next** to continue.

3. At the **End User License Agreement** screen, select **I accept the terms in the license agreement** and click on **Next**.

4. Provide a new password for the Single Sign On (SSO) administrator account `admin@System-Domain` and click on **Next**.

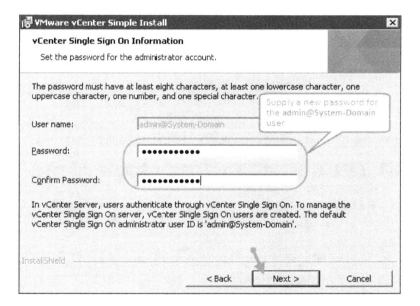

5. On the next screen, you will be prompted to either install a SQL 2008 R2 Express instance on the same machine or use an already existing supported database. Generally, in case of an upgrade you will already have an existing database server and all you would need to do is run the SQL script to create a database.

6. If you choose **Install a local Microsoft SQL Server R2 Express Instance** then supply a new password for the sa user and click on **Next**.

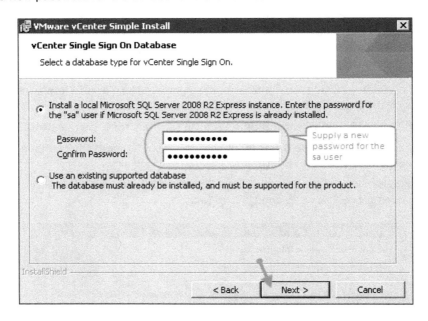

7. If you choose **Use an existing supported database**, then you will have to create a table space for the SSO database by running the SQL script suggested by the installer.

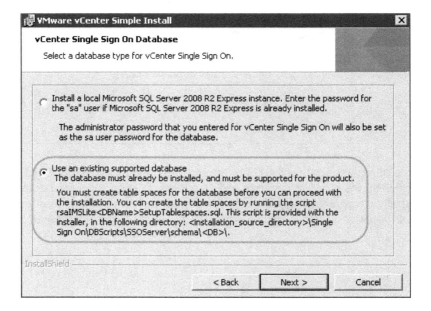

For instructions on creating a table space refer to the *Creating a table space for SSO on a SQL Instance* recipe. Once the table space has been created, click on **Next** to continue.

8. Next on the **Database Information** screen, provide the values, so that Single Sign On can create a JDBC connection to the SSO database.

   The database information includes: the database type (**Mssql**, **Oracle**, and **DB2**), the database name RSA, the database server's IP address, and the authentication credentials. The JDBC connection should be authenticated using the security login credentials RSA_USER and RSA_DBA, which are created using the SQL scripts provided by VMware. For instructions on how to manually create the DB users, refer to the *Creating DB users for the SSO database* recipe.

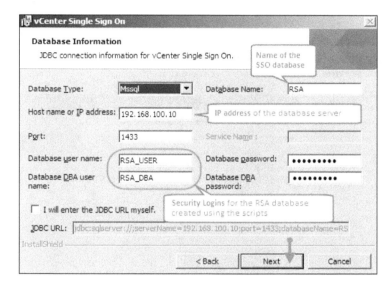

You also have an option to specify the JDBC connection URL yourself, by enabling the **I will enter the JDBC URL myself** checkbox. But you don't really have to go that route, because the installer will generate the JDBC connection URL based on the information you provide.

9. Once the database information has been supplied, click on **Next** to continue.

 In case the connection to the database fails, refer VMware KnowledgeBase article 2039092 to enable static port for the database instance.

10. Provide the **fully qualified domain name** (**FQDN**) of the machine where the installer is being executed. Make sure that the host record at the DNS server has a corresponding reverse DNS entry, else the installation will not succeed. Click on **Next** to continue.

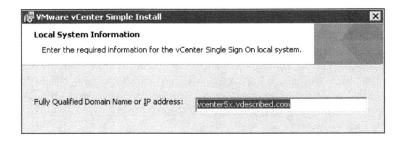

11. You will now be prompted to choose an administrator user for the **Security Support Provider Interface service** (**SSPI**) account. I have used the default selection **Use network service account** and click on **Next** to continue.

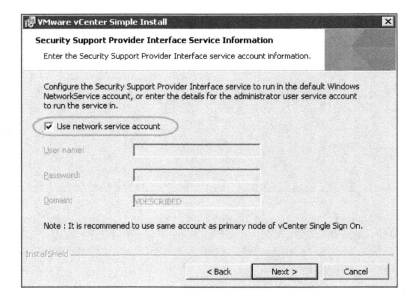

 For more details on what SSPI is, please refer to the following wiki URL:
`http://en.wikipedia.org/wiki/Security_Support_`
`Provider_Interface`

12. Modify the destination folder (install location) of the vCenter Simple Install if required by hitting the **Change** button. Click on **Next** to continue.

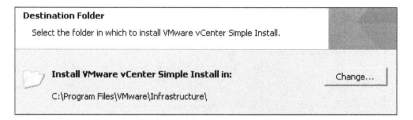

13. The next screen displays the **HTTPS port** number that will be used by SSO. Modify only if required. The default port is `7444`. Click on **Next** to continue.

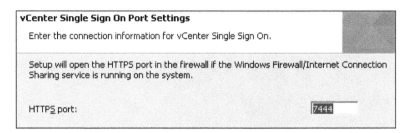

14. On the **Ready to Install** wizard screen, click on **Install** to begin the installation.

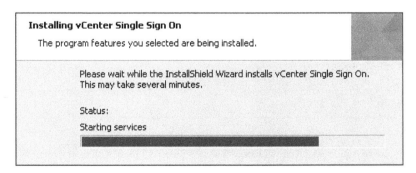

15. Once done it will automatically start the vCenter Inventory Service installer and will prompt you whether to **Do not overwrite. Leave my existing database in place**, or **Replace my existing database with an empty one** with regard to the inventory service database.

Since we are performing an upgrade, we generally do not intend to replace (overwrite) any of the databases. Hence, we will choose **Do not overwrite. Leave my existing database in place** and click on **Next** to continue.

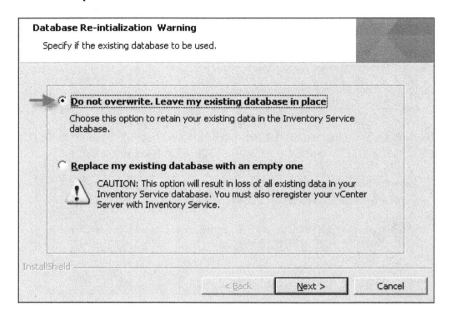

16. On the next screen, click on **Install** to begin installation of the VMware vCenter Inventory Service.

17. Once done, it will automatically start the vCenter Server installer and prompt for a license key. Enter a license key if available or just click on **Next** to install in evaluation mode:

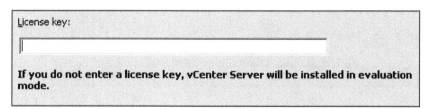

18. On the next screen it will detect the already available DSN information. Click on **Next** to continue.

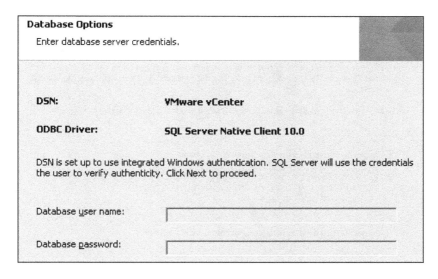

It will throw a warning if it detects an incompatible plugin/extension. Click on **OK**.

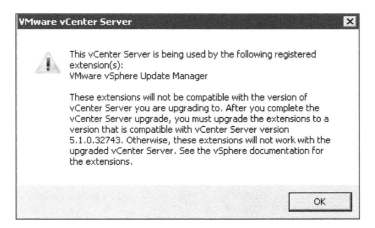

19. On the next screen, choose **Upgrade the existing vCenter Server database** and click on **Next** to continue.

20. Since we have already backed up the SSL folder, select the checkbox acknowledging the same.

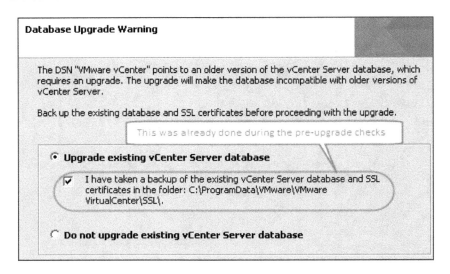

21. On the next screen, choose an intended vCenter Agent upgrade method. For the sake of this example, we will choose **Automatic**.

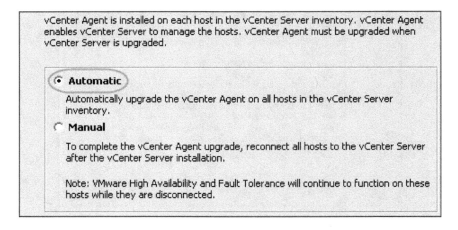

22. On the next screen, the installer prompts for the password of the detected administrator user. In this example, vcadmin is a domain user who has been added to the machine's local "Administrators" group.

23. Enter the password for the user and click on **Next** to continue.

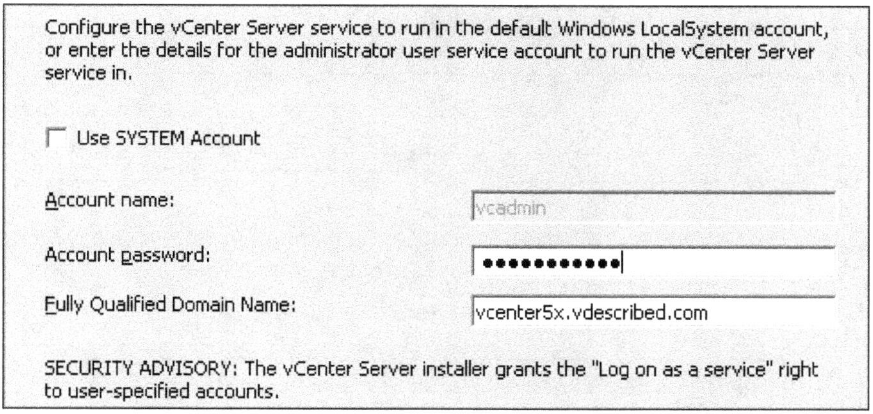

> Configure the vCenter Server service to run in the default Windows LocalSystem account, or enter the details for the administrator user service account to run the vCenter Server service in.
>
> ☐ Use SYSTEM Account
>
> Account name: vcadmin
>
> Account password: ••••••••••
>
> Fully Qualified Domain Name: vcenter5x.vdescribed.com
>
> SECURITY ADVISORY: The vCenter Server installer grants the "Log on as a service" right to user-specified accounts.

24. The next screen will show the ports that will be in use. Change it *only* if a change is necessary for your environment; otherwise leave the settings at their defaults.

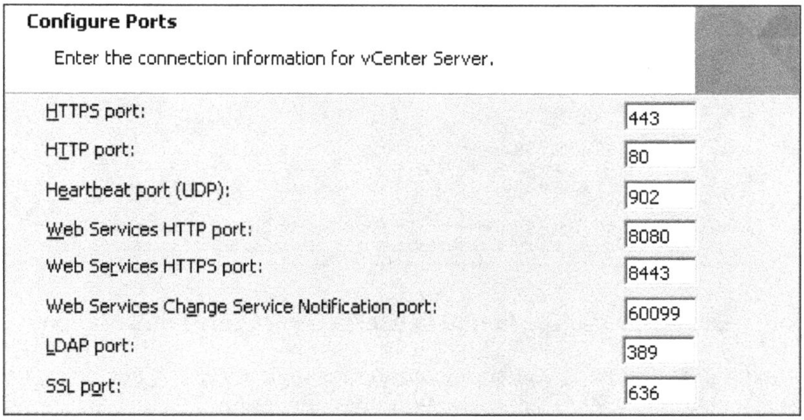

> **Configure Ports**
> Enter the connection information for vCenter Server.
>
> | | |
> |---|---|
> | HTTPS port: | 443 |
> | HTTP port: | 80 |
> | Heartbeat port (UDP): | 902 |
> | Web Services HTTP port: | 8080 |
> | Web Services HTTPS port: | 8443 |
> | Web Services Change Service Notification port: | 60099 |
> | LDAP port: | 389 |
> | SSL port: | 636 |

On the same screen you could also choose to increase the number of ephemeral ports. Ephemeral ports are ports on the dvSwitch to which the VMs connect, without any binding. Choosing to increase the number of available ephemeral ports will not set a total count on the number of ports configured. The count will be set to zero and you will be allowed to connect as many VMs as possible, with the total number of the ports on the dvSwitch being the limit.

In this example, we will leave it *unchecked*. Click on **Next** to continue.

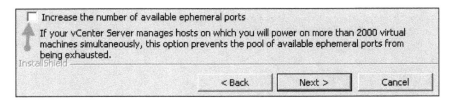

25. On the next screen, we will have to choose the planned inventory size, which will in turn determine the vCenter Server's JVM memory requirement.

26. Select the inventory size and click on **Next** to continue.

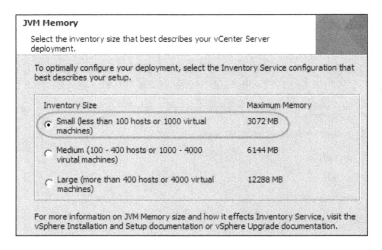

27. On the next screen, click on **Install** to begin vCenter Server installation.

Once the installation is complete you should get a message informing successful completion and the server needs to reboot to fully complete the installation.

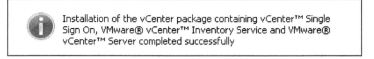

How it works...

A simple install will set up components in the following order:

- ▸ vCenter Single Sign On
- ▸ vCenter Inventory Service
- ▸ vCenter Server

If these components need to be installed separately, it is recommended that you follow the same order of installation as followed during the simple install.

Single Sign On, once installed, can be used with other vCenter installations in the vSphere environment. Meaning you wouldn't need more than one instance of Single Sign On server. A newly deployed vCenter can be connected to the same authentication server (Single Sign On server).

Unlike the previous upgrades wherein both the local and Active Directory users needed to be registered to the vCenter prior to the upgrade, an upgrade to 5.1 doesn't have this prerequisite.

There's more...

If vCenter's Single Sign On is being installed on a machine that is already added to a domain and is logged in using a domain user with administrator rights on the local machine then the Single Sign On install process will discover the domain and add that as an **identity source**.

An identity source can be of the following types:

- ▸ Active Directory
- ▸ Open LDAP
- ▸ The name of the local operating system identity source will be:
  - ❑ `localOS` if Linux
  - ❑ `hostname of the machine` if Windows
- ▸ System
  - ❑ The default being `System-Domain`

If the machine is not added to the domain then you could add the domain as an identity source after the installation is complete.

It is possible to add a local operating system identity source to the SSO server. The local operating system identity source will hold the local users on the machine where SSO is installed. For instance, if SSO is installed on a machine other than the one on which vCenter Server is installed, then the local identity source will hold the users from SSO machine and not the vCenter Server.

Creating a table space for SSO on a SQL instance

During the installation of Single Sign On, if you choose to use an existing supported database then you would have to manually create a table space for the SSO server's database.

By creating a table space, we are not creating a database schema (logical structure of the database). Instead, we are just creating storage locations of the database's primary and secondary data files and its transaction logfile.

In this recipe, I will show you the steps required to create a table space on an existing SQL Server database instance.

How to do it...

The following procedure will help you create a table space for the SSO server's database:

1. Copy the `rsaIMSLiteMSSQLSetupTablespaces.sql` script from the vCenter installation DVD to the database server. The location of the file is as follows:

   `CD/DVD ROM :\Single Sign On\DBScripts\SSOServer\schema\mssql`

2. At the database server machine, start the Microsoft SQL Server Management Studio and make sure that you are connected to the correct database server instance.

3. Drag-and-drop the `rsaIMSLiteMSSQLSetupTablespaces.sql` file to the SQL Server Management Studio.

4. Enter the hard disk location(s) for the database's primary data file (`RSA_DATA.mdf`), secondary data file (`RSA_INDEX.ndf`), and the transaction logfile (`translog.ldf`).

```
CREATE DATABASE RSA ON PRIMARY(
    NAME='RSA_DATA',
    FILENAME='C:\CHANGE ME\RSA_DATA.mdf',
    SIZE=10MB,
    MAXSIZE=UNLIMITED,
    FILEGROWTH=10%),
FILEGROUP RSA_INDEX(
    NAME='RSA_INDEX',
    FILENAME='C:\CHANGE ME\RSA_INDEX.ndf',
    SIZE=10MB,
    MAXSIZE=UNLIMITED,
    FILEGROWTH=10%)
LOG ON(
    NAME='translog',
    FILENAME='C:\CHANGE ME\translog.ldf',
    SIZE=10MB,
    MAXSIZE=UNLIMITED,
    FILEGROWTH=10% )
GO

-- Set recommended perform settings on the database
EXEC SP_DBOPTION 'RSA', 'autoshrink', true
GO
EXEC SP_DBOPTION 'RSA', 'trunc. log on chkpt.', true
GO

CHECKPOINT
GO
```

Supply a hard disk location to store the database's MDF, NDF and LDF files

Although the location(s) you specify is in a local location format, the files are created on the actual database server machine and not on the machine running the SQL Server Management Studio. In this example, I have used the location C:\SSO; you need to make sure that the SSO folder is already created on the database server's C:\.

Here is how the script would look after specifying the location for the files:

```
CREATE DATABASE RSA ON PRIMARY(
    NAME='RSA_DATA',
    FILENAME='C:\SSO\RSA_DATA.mdf',
    SIZE=10MB,
    MAXSIZE=UNLIMITED,
    FILEGROWTH=10),
FILEGROUP RSA_INDEX(
    NAME='RSA_INDEX',
    FILENAME='C:\SSO\RSA_INDEX.ndf',
    SIZE=10MB,
    MAXSIZE=UNLIMITED,
    FILEGROWTH=10)
LOG ON(
    NAME='translog',
    FILENAME='C:\SSO\translog.ldf',
    SIZE=10MB,
    MAXSIZE=UNLIMITED,
    FILEGROWTH=10)
GO

-- Set recommended perform settings on the database
EXEC SP_DBOPTION 'RSA', 'autoshrink', true
GO
EXEC SP_DBOPTION 'RSA', 'trunc. log on chkpt.', true
GO

CHECKPOINT
GO
```

Hard disk locations specified (Examples)

5. Click on **Execute** to run the script on the database server instance.

How it works...

Once the query has executed successfully, there will be a database RSA listed under databases in the SQL Server Management Studio's inventory.

On the database server you will see three files created under the specified directory:

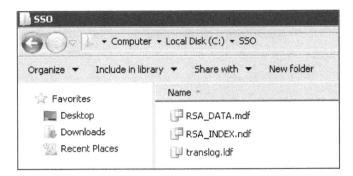

If you see three files (RSA_DATA.mdf, RSA_INDEX.mdf, and translog.ldf) at the specified location on the database server, then you have successfully created the table space for SSO.

Creating DB users for the SSO database

During the installation of the Single Sign On component, once the table space has been created, the installer would need a database username and password to generate a JDBC connection URL.

This user has to be manually created using the SQL script, rsaIMSLiteMSSQLSetupUsers.sql, available on the vCenter's installation DVD.

How to do it...

The following steps will help you create a DB user using the SQL script rsaIMSLiteMSSQLSetupUsers.sql:

1. Copy the rsaIMSLiteMSSQLSetupUsers.sql script from the vCenter's installation DVD to the database server. The location of the file is as follows:

   CD/DVD ROM :\Single Sign On\DBScripts\SSOServer\schema\mssql

2. On the database server machine, start the Microsoft SQL Server Management Studio and make sure that you are connected to the correct database server instance.

3. Drag-and-drop the rsaIMSLiteMSSQLSetupUsers.sql file to the SQL Server Management Studio.

4. Enter new passwords for the RSA_DBA and RSA_USER users.

```
USE MASTER
GO

CREATE LOGIN RSA_DBA WITH PASSWORD = '<CHANGE DBA PASSWORD>', DEFAULT_DATABASE = RSA
GO
CREATE LOGIN RSA_USER WITH PASSWORD = '<CHANGE USER PASSWORD>', DEFAULT_DATABASE = RSA
GO

USE RSA
GO

ALTER AUTHORIZATION ON DATABASE::RSA TO [RSA_DBA]
GO

CREATE USER RSA_USER FOR LOGIN [RSA_USER]
GO

CHECKPOINT
GO
```

Supply new passwords for the users "RSA_DBA" and "RSA_USER"

Here is how the script would look after the passwords have been supplied:

```
USE MASTER
GO

CREATE LOGIN RSA_DBA WITH PASSWORD = 'abhipass_123@great', DEFAULT_DATABASE = RSA
GO
CREATE LOGIN RSA_USER WITH PASSWORD = 'abhipass_123@great', DEFAULT_DATABASE = RSA
GO

USE RSA
GO

ALTER AUTHORIZATION ON DATABASE::RSA TO [RSA_DBA]
GO

CREATE USER RSA_USER FOR LOGIN [RSA_USER]
GO

CHECKPOINT
GO
```

New passwords supplied

5. Click on **Execute** to run the script on the database server instance.

How it works...

On a successful execution of the query, it creates two security login accounts, RSA_DBA and RSA_USER. It also creates two security users, dbo and RSA_USER, for the RSA database. The dbo user is mapped to the RSA_DBA login and RSA_USER will be mapped to the RSA_USER login.

Upgrading a 32-bit vCenter Server to vCenter 5.1

An in-place upgrade is not possible if the vCenter Server that you are trying to upgrade is installed on a 32-bit machine. This is because vCenter Server 5.1 is a 64-bit application. All the vCenter versions prior to vCenter 4.1.x were 32-bit, with vCenter 4.0 being an exception because it could be installed either on a 32-bit or a 64-bit machine.

For an upgrade to vCenter 5.0, we had an option to use the Data Migration tool. Unfortunately, vCenter 5.1 does not support the use of it. You can work around this limitation by using the Data Migration tool to migrate the data first to a 64-bit Windows machine, then install vCenter 5.0 on it, and finally perform an in-place upgrade to vCenter 5.1.

The Data Migration tool can be used to migrate data from the following versions of vCenter:

▶   Virtual Center 2.6 Update 6 or later

▶   vCenter Server 4.0 and its updated releases

The Data Migration tool is not supported for migrating vCenter 4.1 configurations or databases, because vCenter 4.1 is 64-bit; hence, it would be already installed on a 64-bit machine. It is only used to migrate vCenter data from a 32-bit machine.

The Data Migration tool can migrate the following configuration settings:

▶   Port settings for HTTP and HTTPS

▶   Port settings for vCenter Heartbeat and vCenter Web Services

▶   LDAP data

▶   Port settings for LDAP and LDAP SSL ports

▶   SSL certificates from the SSL folder

▶   License data

▶   Database data, for SQL Express database only

> The Data Migration tool can only be used to migrate a SQL Express database. A non-SQL express database should be backed up manually.

How to do it...

Migrating the vCenter data and database is a two-step procedure:

1.   Back up the setting from the 32-bit vCenter Server.

2.   Restore the settings on to the new 64-bit machine.

Backing up the settings from a 32-bit vCenter Server

The following steps are required to back up the settings on the 32-bit vCenter Server using the Data Migration tool:

1. Stop the vCenter Server service.

2. Extract the contents of the ZIP file, `datamigration.zip`, available on the vCenter installer ISO/ZIP/DVD to a hard disk location on the same machine. The `datamigration.zip` file can located under the `datamigration` folder on root the vCenter installer ISO/ZIP/DVD. The location for the file can be as follows:

   `DVD/CDROM:\datamigration\datamigration.zip`

   The following screenshot shows the contents of the `datamigration.zip` file once it is extracted:

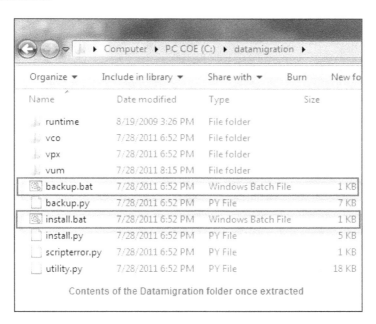

Contents of the Datamigration folder once extracted

3. Once the `datamigration.zip` archive is extracted, use the Windows command line and navigate to the `datamigration` folder; then run the `backup.bat` batch file to initiate the backup process.

   For example, if the ZIP archive was extracted to `C:\`, then at the command line, change to the `C:\Datamigation` directory, type `backup.bat` and hit *Enter*.

Restoring the configuration on the new machine

Now that you have backed up the needed data, it needs to be transferred to the intended destination machine (64-bit):

1. Once the `backup.bat` file is finished with its job, it will dump all the backed up data to the `./data/vc/` folder. To initiate a restore, copy the entire `datamigration` folder to the 64-bit machine.

2. Make sure that you have the vCenter Server's installation DVD in the DVD drive or the ISO mounted to the VM (if the destination vCenter Server is virtual machine).

3. Navigate to the `datamigration` folder using the Windows command prompt, and run the `install.bat` batch script.

How it works...

In this section, I will explain how the `backup.bat` and `install.bat` batch scripts work, when run on the 32-bit source and the 64-bit destination machines respectively.

What happens when you run the `backup.bat` batch script on the 32-bit vCenter Server?

When you run this script on the machine running the 32-bit vCenter Server, it will first check the vCenter Server's version and the database's compatibility with the Data Migration tool, and then backs up the configuration setting files. Subsequently, it will upgrade the database schema to Version 5. This is a four-step process:

1. The original database is backed up.

2. The database schema is upgraded to Version 5.0.

3. The upgraded database is backed up.

4. Restore the original database from the backup that was taken earlier.

```
C:\Datamigration>backup.bat
[INFO] Starting vSphere configuration backup script...

[INFO] Checking prerequisites...

[INFO] Checking vCenter Server version...
[INFO] vCenter Server installation version 4.0.0.27153
[INFO] vCenter Server installation version 4.0.0.27153
[INFO] Checking for DB type
[INFO] VMware vCenter Server DB type: bundled
[INFO] VMware vCenter Server DB instance: SQLEXP_VIM
[INFO] Checking for  VMware vCenter Server and VMware vSphere Update Manager database coexistence.
[INFO] Connecting to DB...
[INFO] Connected to  VMware vCenter Server database, checking version
[INFO] Found version in the database.
[INFO] Connecting to DB...
[INFO] Connected to  VMware vCenter Server database, checking VMware vSphere Update Manager version
[INFO]  VMware vCenter Server and VMware vSphere Update Manager use different databases.
[INFO] Validating vCenter Server inventory...
[INFO] VMware vCenter Server installation satisfies migration prerequisite

[INFO] Checking VMware vSphere Update Manager version...
[WARNING] VMware vSphere Update Manager is not installed or its version cannot be determined.
[WARNING] VMware Update Manager does not satisfy migration prerequisite
    Do you want to continue backup...? y|n: _
```

It will also try to detect the version of VMware Update Manager installed. If it encounters a version that is not supported then it would let you know that the Update Manager's version prerequisite is not met and it will seek your confirmation to continue with the backup. Such a backup will not include the Update Manager data. It does the same if it does not detect the presence of Update Manager.

Next, the backup script will start backing up the vCenter data (configuration files) and then the database.

```
[INFO] Successfully backed up vCenter Server installed data information  ◄───
[INFO] Backing up vCenter Server DB...
[INFO] Checking vCenter Server DB configuration...
[INFO] vCenter Server DB type: bundled
[INFO] vCenter Server DB instance: SQLEXP_VIM
[INFO] vCenter Server DB instance: SQLEXP_VIM
[INFO] Backing up DB...  Please do not stop this program.
[INFO] DB logs: Processed 9920 pages for database 'VIM_VCDB', file 'VIM_VCDB_dat' on file 1.
Processed 1 pages for database 'VIM_VCDB', file 'VIM_VCDB_log' on file 1.
BACKUP DATABASE successfully processed 9921 pages in 4.848 seconds (16.764 MB/sec).

Processed 1 pages for database 'VIM_VCDB', file 'VIM_VCDB_log' on file 1.
BACKUP DATABASE successfully processed 9921 pages in 4.848 seconds (16.764 MB/sec).

[INFO]
[INFO] Processed 10088 pages for database 'VIM_VCDB', file 'VIM_VCDB_dat' on file 1.
Processed 1 pages for database 'VIM_VCDB', file 'VIM_VCDB_log' on file 1.
BACKUP DATABASE successfully processed 10089 pages in 4.466 seconds (18.506 MB/sec).

[INFO] Processed 9920 pages for database 'VIM_VCDB', file 'VIM_VCDB_dat' on file 1.
Processed 1 pages for database 'VIM_VCDB', file 'VIM_VCDB_log' on file 1.
RESTORE DATABASE successfully processed 9921 pages in 6.653 seconds (12.215 MB/sec).

[INFO] Successfully backed up vCenter Server DB  ◄───

[INFO] vCenter Orchestrator configuration was successfully backed up

[INFO] Summary Information :
VMware vCenter Server data has been backed up successfully.  ◄───
Failed to backup data for VMware Update Manager.
VMware vCenter Orchestrator data has been backed up successfully.

[INFO] vSphere configuration backup script completed successfully

C:\Datamigration>
```

The backed-up information will be stored at the `DataMigration\Data\vc` location, as shown in the following screenshot:

Name ▲	Size	Type	Date Modified	Attrib
📁 vc_ssl		File Folder	1/31/2012 6:08 AM	
📄 vc_data	24 KB	File	1/31/2012 6:58 AM	A
📄 vc_source_orig_db	79,538 KB	File	1/31/2012 6:58 AM	A
📄 vc_upgraded_db	80,882 KB	File	1/31/2012 6:59 AM	A

Address: C:\Datamigration\data\vc

Contents of the Datamigration folder

What happens when you run the `install.bat` batch script on the 64-bit Windows machine where you intend to install vCenter 5.1?

On invoking the migration installer script `install.bat`, it would access the data from the `datamigration` directory and start verifying it.

If the machine has a different system name when compared to the source machine, then it will indicate the same and will seek your confirmation to continue. In such cases, once the installation is complete, you will have to modify the `<url>` tag in the XML file to supply a new system name and re-enable the plugins in the vCenter Plugin Manager. The location of the XML file is as follows:

```
c:\Program files\VMware\Infrastructure\VirtualCenter Server\
extensions\plugin-name
```

```
Administrator: Command Prompt - install.bat
c:\Datamigration>install.bat
[INFO] Starting vSphere 5.0 migration installer script...
[INFO] Checking prerequisites...
[INFO]   Migration data directory: c:\Datamigration\data
[INFO] Checking vCenter Server migration data...
      The name of this machine is different than backup system name ABHILASH-8C2EKP
      Do you want to continue install ...? y|n: y
[INFO] vCenter Server DB migration data present: choose installer bundled DB for restore
Enter path to vCenter Server 5.0 install media: D:
[INFO] vCenter Server install media found
[INFO]   vCenter Server migration data successfully verified
```

Once the data migration has been successfully verified it will call the vCenter Server installer with the backed-up installation data configuration.

Upgrading to ESXi 5.1

After vCenter Server is upgraded to 5.1, the next step is to upgrade the ESX servers to Version 5.1. There are five different methods to upgrade the ESX server:

▶   Use VMware Update Manager

▶   Use the ESXi installation CD/DVD

▶   Scripted upgrade

▶   Use the vSphere Auto Deploy server

▶   Use the `esxcli` commands

> Note that the `esxupdate` and `vihostupdate` utilities are not supported for ESXi 5.1 upgrades.

Although there are different methods, I will be discussing the method using the ESXi Installer ISO or disk in this chapter. For information on how to perform a host upgrade using the Update Manager read *Chapter 12, Upgrading and Patching using VMware Update Manager*.

And for information on using the vSphere Auto Deploy server read *Chapter 3, vSphere Auto Deploy*, and *Chapter 4, ESXi Image Builder*.

Before you decide to upgrade the ESX server to Version 5.1, it is recommended that you verify whether the host hardware is compatible with ESX 5.1. Use the *VMware Compatibility Guide* web page to verify (`www.vmware.com/go/hcl`).

Similar to the vCenter upgrade, the ESX upgrade also requires a few pre-checks:

- The server hardware should support 64-bit and Intel VT (Virtualization Technology) should be enabled in the BIOS.
- The upgrade requires 50 MB of free space on the local VMFS volume.
- It is recommended to disconnect the SAN LUNs hosting VMFS volumes prior to the upgrade. This is to prevent the possibility of you unintentionally selecting one of the SAN LUNs for ESX installation. This recommendation, however, made more sense with the older versions of ESX server. With the newer versions, the installer will categorize the storage devices detected as `local` or `remote`. So the chance that you might choose a remote SAN volume is reduced.
- Make sure that the server's hardware clock in the BIOS is set to UTC.

How to do it...

1. Boot the ESX server with the ESXi 5.1 CD/DVD, choose the ESXi standard installer, and press *Enter*.

```
          ESXi-5.1.0-799733-standard Boot Menu
ESXi-5.1.0-799733-standard Installer
Boot from local disk
```

2. This will load the ESXi 5.1 installer and take you to the installer's welcome screen prompting for a confirmation. Press *Enter* to continue.

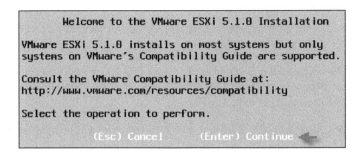

3. The next screen will prompt you to accept the EULA. Press *F11* to accept and continue. It will then scan for devices and prompt for a storage device selection:

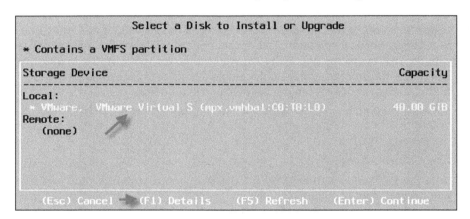

4. Select **Local** or **Remote** (if booted from SAN) disk and press *F1* to verify the details of the selected disk.

```
                      Disk Details
Model/Vendor:    VMware, VMware Virtual S
Full Disk Name: mpx.vmhba1:C0:T0:L0
LUN ID:          0
Target ID:       0
Capacity:        40.00 GiB
Path:            /vmfs/devices/disks/mpx.vmhba1:C0:T0:L0
ESX(i) Found:    ESXi 5.0.0
Datastores:      datastore1 (1)

                    (Enter) OK
```

5. Hit on **OK** and then press *Enter* to continue. Because the machine already has an older version of ESX running, the installer will detect the same and will by default suggest an upgrade.

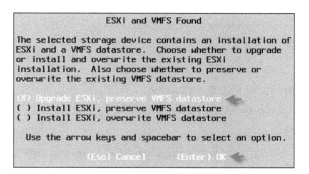

6. Since we are doing an upgrade, select the first option to upgrade ESXi and preserve the VMFS datastore.

7. The installer then will prompt you to confirm the upgrade. Press *F11* to confirm and initiate the upgrade.

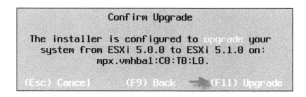

8. The installer now will begin the upgrade and proceed to completion.

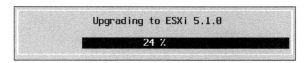

9. Once the upgrade is complete, press *Enter* to reboot the server.

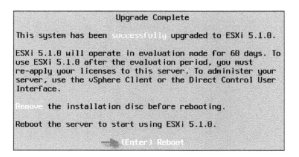

This upgrades the ESX server to ESXi 5.1.

How it works...

During the installation, the installer will detect the presence of an existing installation and provide the following options:

▶ **Upgrade ESX, preserve VMFS datastore**

▶ **Install ESXi, preserve VMFS datastore**

▶ **Install ESXi, overwrite VMFS datastore**

If you were upgrading an ESX/ESXi 4.x server instead of 5.x, and if it had custom VIBs that are not included in the installer ISO, then the **Upgrade ESX, preserve VMFS datastore** option will be replaced by **Force Migrate ESX, preserve VMFS datastore**.

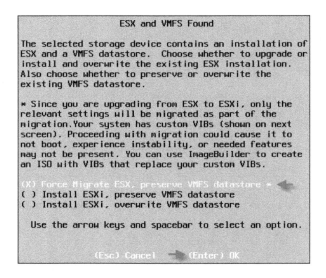

Unless you choose to overwrite the VMFS datastore, you are not forming a VMFS 5 volume. The **Install ESXi, preserve VMFS datastore** option will also retain the VMFS 3 filesystem structure.

You will also receive a warning message listing the custom VIBs.

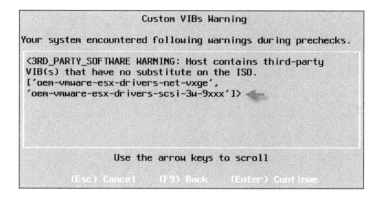

This is not the case when you migrate from ESXi 5.0, because the custom VIB will also be migrated.

Install ESXi, preserve VMFS datastore will do a fresh install of the ESXi 5.1 server but will retain the data in the VMFS datastore.

Install ESXi, overwrite VMFS datastore will do a fresh install of ESXi 5.1 and will also overwrite the contents of the VMFS volume.

The following is a list of configuration files that will be migrated:

- ▶ /etc/sfcb/sfcb.cfg
- ▶ /var/lib/sfcb/registration/repository/root/interop/*
- ▶ /etc/ntp.conf
- ▶ /etc/ntp.drift
- ▶ /etc/ntp.keys
- ▶ /etc/syslog.conf (This is migrated only for ESXi)
- ▶ /etc/security/access.conf
- ▶ /etc/sysconfig/network (vswifs are converted to vmknics)
- ▶ /etc/sysconfig/static-routes
- ▶ /etc/sysconfig/static-routes-ipv6
- ▶ /etc/sysconfig/network-scripts/route-$device
- ▶ /etc/nsswitch.conf
- ▶ /etc/krb.conf
- ▶ /etc/krb.realms
- ▶ /etc/krb5.conf

- `/etc/krb5.acl`
- `/etc/krb5.keytab`
- `/etc/krb5.log`
- `/etc/krb5.mkey`
- `/etc/pam.d/*` (Partially migrated)
- `/etc/snmp/snmpd.conf` (Migrated to `/etc/vmware/snmp.xml`)
- `/etc/motd` (Migrated, appends a note mentioning that it was upgraded to ESX 5.1)
- `/etc/vmware/vmiscsid/*`
- `/etc/vmware/esx.conf`
- `/etc/vmware/hostd/*`
- `/etc/vmware/vmauth/authentication.conf`
- `/etc/hosts`
- `/etc/resolv.conf`
- `/etc/fstab` (Only NFS entries will be migrated)
- `/etc/passwd` (Only root password will be saved)
- `/etc/shadow`

Installing vSphere Web Client

In this recipe, I will discuss the steps required to install vSphere Web Client.

The vSphere Web Client is an independent server component that is installed and then accessed via the web browser. It is independent because, unlike the older web client or the vSphere Client based on C#, you no longer have to connect the client to the vCenter Server. It connects to its own server and this server component is installed from the vSphere 5.1 installation's welcome screen.

The vSphere Web Client will let you add multiple vCenter Servers to its web-based GUI. Although, I will be using vSphere Web Client for most of the tasks in the chapters, you could still use the vSphere Client based on C# to perform the same tasks. Having said that, there are certain tasks that can only be done using the vSphere Client. For example, the VMware Update Manager plugin is not available for the vSphere Web Client.

How to do it...

1. At the VMware vCenter 5.1 installer home screen, select **VMware vSphere Web Client** and click on **Install** to bring up the **vSphere Web Client Installation** wizard. Click on **Next** to continue.

2. Accept the EULA and click on **Next** to continue.

3. On the next screen, you can choose to change the installation location if necessary and click on **Next** to continue.

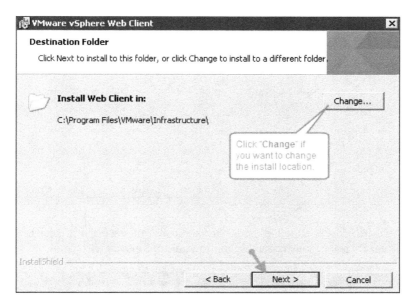

4. The next screen will show you the ports that will be used by the vSphere Web Client. You can change them if required and click on **Next** to continue.

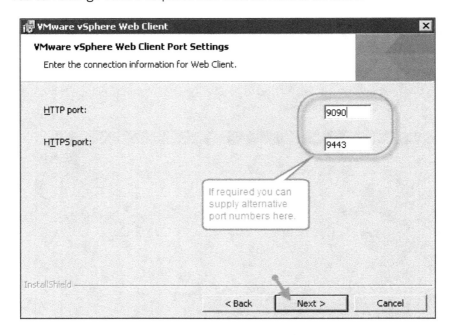

5. On the next screen, supply the SSO administrator password and click on **Next** to continue. Do not modify the value in the **Lookup Service URL** field:

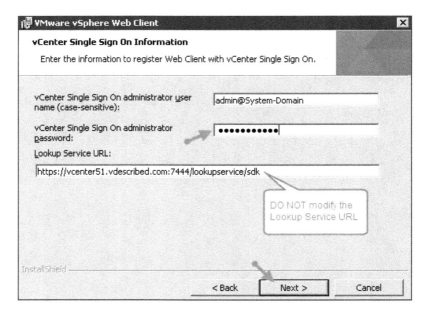

6. On the next screen, click on **Install** to begin the installation.

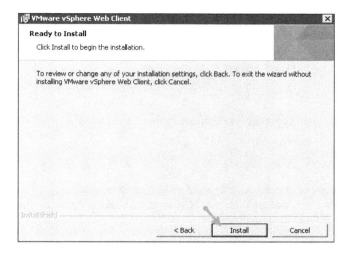

7. Once the installation is complete, click on **Finish** to exit the installation wizard.

The following syntax and URL will help you to connect to the vSphere Web Client server:

- **Syntax**: `https://<IP address or FQDN of the server where vSphere Web Client is installed>/vsphere-client`

- **Example**: `https://192.168.193.50:9443/vsphere-client/`

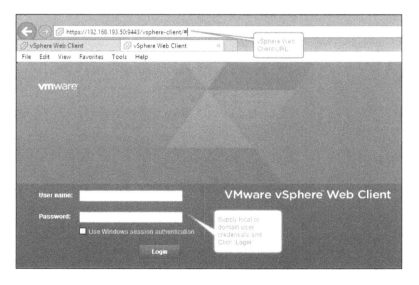

Upgrading VMware Tools

Once the server has been upgraded to ESXi 5.1, you can now start running virtual machines on the server. But not everything has been migrated to Version 5.1 yet. VMware Tools running inside the virtual machines need to be upgraded as well.

VMware Tools include the following:

▸ VMware device drivers for the virtual machine hardware

▸ VMware Tools control panel

▸ VMware balloon driver (`memctl`)

VMware Tools are available in specific type of ISOs (guest-operating type) packed with the ESX server. For Linux, they are also available as **VMware Operating Specific Packages** (**OSPs**) for download from the following repository URL:

```
http://packages.vmware.com/tools
```

In this recipe, we will learn how to upgrade the VMware Tools on the virtual machines.

How to do it...

The VMware Tools upgrade can be either done using vSphere Web Client or the vSphere Client. I will show you how to perform the task using the vSphere Web Client:

 The virtual machine requires a reboot for a successful completion of the VMware Tools upgrade. So, plan for a scheduled downtime to perform this task on the production virtual machines.

1. Connect to the vCenter Server using the Web Client.

2. Navigate to the **VMs and Templates Inventory** view.

3. Locate the VM and make sure it is powered-on and running.

4. Right-click on the VM and navigate to **All vCenter Actions | Guest OS | Install/Upgrade VMware Tools**.

5. Choose the **Automatic Upgrade** option and then click on **Upgrade** to initiate the upgrade.

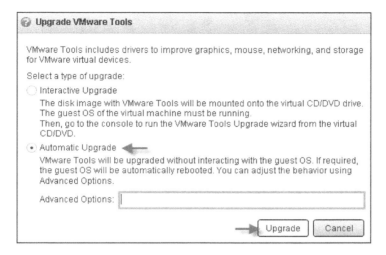

How it works...

The **Automatic Upgrade** option requires no user interaction. It will:

▸ Automatically uninstall the older version of VMware Tools

▸ Install the new version from the ISO that gets mounted

▸ Reboot the **guest operating system** (**GOS**) to finish the tools upgrade

To verify whether the tools upgrade is successfully completed, log on to the guest operating system then right-click on the system tray icon for VMware Tools, and click on **About VMware Tools**, which should show you the version of the VMware Tools.

On clicking the **About VMware Tools** menu item, it should bring up a dialog box showing the tools' version.

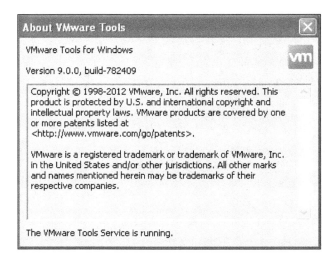

You can also check the virtual machine's tools version by navigating to **vCenter Servers | Clusters | Related Objects | Virtual Machines**. This will list all the virtual machines and its VMware Tools version status. The VMware Tools version status column is not enabled by default, you will have to enable it manually.

There's more...

Since we generally upgrade the virtual machine hardware or VMware Tools after a host upgrade, you will have to perform the upgrade on many virtual machines. Following the procedure we learned so far when dealing with hundreds of VM is always a tedious task. Fortunately we have an alternative method:

1. Once you are at the vSphere Web Client interface for vCenter, select the datacenter/cluster for the VMs and navigate to the **Related Objects** tab.

2. On the **Related Objects** tab, select the **Virtual Machines** subtab.

3. Highlight all or the needed VMs from the list and click on the **Actions** gear icon to navigate to the **Compatibility and the Tools upgrade** menu item.

4. Since you have multiple VMs selected, which may be running on different version of ESX server, you will get an option to choose between the compatible versions of the virtual machine hardware and the number of virtual machines to which the changes will be applied.

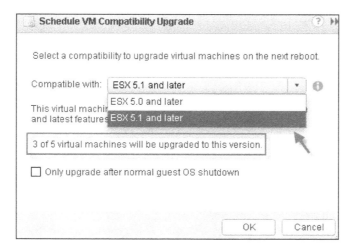

Upgrading the virtual machine hardware

Once VMware Tools have been upgraded, you can then upgrade the virtual hardware for the virtual machines. The virtual hardware will determine the BIOS/EFI used, CPU and memory maximums for the virtual machine, and other features. The virtual hardware version released with ESX 5.1 is 9. In this recipe, I will discuss the steps required to upgrade the virtual machine hardware. Once you upgrade the virtual hardware version to the current, you cannot downgrade it. If you have a multi-version ESX cluster, then make sure that the VM version (virtual hardware version) is at a level supported by all the participating hosts in the cluster. Also, for the upgrade to complete, the virtual machine requires a downtime.

How to do it...

The virtual hardware upgrade can be either done using vSphere Web Client or the vSphere Client. I will show you how to perform the task using the vSphere Web Client:

1. Connect to the vCenter Server using the Web Client.
2. Navigate to the **VMs and Templates Inventory** view.
3. Locate the VM and power off if you intend to perform the upgrade now.

4. Right-click on the VM and navigate to **All vCenter Actions | Compatibility | Upgrade VM Compatibility**.

5. Click on **Yes** in the conformation prompt.

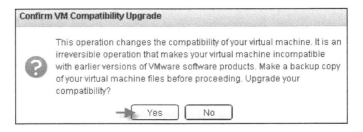

6. On the **Configure VM Compatibility** dialog box, select the ESX version you had upgraded the server to and click on **OK** to finish reconfiguring the VM.

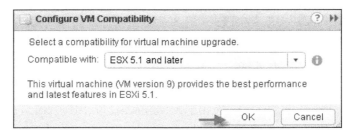

How it works...

We cannot finish the virtual hardware upgrade while the virtual machine is powered on. Hence, we need to power off the virtual machine for an immediate upgrade. If you have a large number of virtual machines, then you can schedule the virtual hardware upgrade to happen during the next reboot of the virtual machine.

Click on **Yes** to confirm scheduling an upgrade and then select an appropriate version. Click on **OK** to schedule the upgrade.

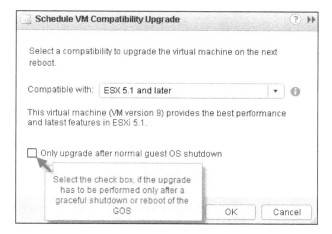

2

Performing a Fresh Installation of vSphere 5.1

In this chapter we will cover the following:

- ▶ Installing vCenter 5.1

- ▶ Deploying a VMware vCenter Server Appliance (vCSA)

- ▶ Preparing vCenter Server Appliance for first use

- ▶ Installing the vCenter Server Appliance update

- ▶ Upgrading the vCenter Server Appliance

- ▶ Installing ESXi 5.1

- ▶ Performing a scripted Install of the ESXi server

Introduction

Starting with vSphere 5.0, VMware doesn't offer the ESX classic version, but the ESXi hypervisor version. The classic version of the ESX server had a Linux-based Service Console. One of the most evident benefits of removing the Service Console is that ESX hypervisor version (ESXi) will have a smaller installation footprint. It can even be embedded on the server boards or USB drives. Because of the smaller footprint, the installation is faster. Historically, most of the security updates that VMware released were for the Service Console and not for the hypervisor component. Meaning, as we move ahead we will require less frequent patching to be done on the ESXi servers.

The vCenter Server is the component that provides centralized management of your vSphere environment. Most of the administrative tasks on a single ESXi server can be done by using the vSphere Windows Client software. As in most cases, however, when you have an environment that has multiple ESXi servers, managing each of them by making individual vSphere Client connections will be cumbersome. This is where the vCenter Server would come in handy. It would let you add more than one ESXi server to its management interface, so that all the servers can be managed using just a single vSphere Client connection to the vCenter Server. Furthermore, with ESXi servers added to the vCenter Server, could use the vSphere features such as cluster, High Availability (HA), Distributed Resource Scheduler (DRS), VMware Update Manager (VUM), and vSphere Data Recovery.

VMware vCenter Server Appliance (vCSA)

The VMware vCenter Appliance is a Linux appliance with the all necessary modules and a built-in database. This appliance comes in handy when you want to deploy a vCenter instance without having to go through the installation procedure. Since it is a Linux VM, you don't have to install a compatible Windows OS (VM/physical machine) and license it. For information on how to deploy vCSA read the *Deploying a VMware vCenter Server Appliance (vCSA)* recipe.

In this chapter, I will focus on the steps required to install and configure the ESXi server, the vCenter Server Windows version, and the VMware vCenter Server Appliance.

Installing vCenter 5.1

This recipe will focus on the steps needed to perform a fresh/new installation of vCenter Server 5.1 on a Windows machine.

Getting ready

Let's take a look at the pre-install checks that need to be performed:

1. Check the vCenter Server software requirements.
2. Check the ESX server compatibility.
3. Check the database compatibility.
4. Back up the SSL certificates.

We won't be discussing these checks here since these were discussed in the *Upgrading vCenter Server* section in *Chapter 1, Upgrading to vSphere 5.1*.

You could download the vCenter Server installation bundle from the following download page:

```
https://my.vmware.com/web/vmware/info/slug/datacenter_cloud_
infrastructure/vmware_vsphere/5_1
```

The download item would be listed as **VMware vCenter Server 5.1 and modules**. The download is available in both ISO and ZIP archives.

If you start the installation on a Windows machine that already has a previous version of vCenter Server installed, then the installation wizard will not provide you with an option to perform a fresh/new installation of the vCenter Server. It will always be an upgrade, unless you manually uninstall the existing version the vCenter Server.

To uninstall the existing version of vCenter Server from your machine, perform the following steps:

1. Stop the vCenter and component services.

2. Uninstall the vCenter Server using **Add/Remove Programs**. (In Windows 2008 it is **Control Panel | Programs | Programs and Features**.)

With vSphere 5.1 we now have a new component called **vCenter Single Sign On**, which is an authentication server. It is a requirement to have vCenter Single Sign On installed, to perform a vCenter Server install/upgrade.

How to do it...

The following step-by-step procedure will help you perform a fresh installation of vCenter 5.1:

1. Start the simple install, which will begin with vCenter Single Sign On installation. For the Single Sign On installation procedure, read steps 1 through 14 of the *Performing an in-place upgrade of vCenter Server* recipe in *Chapter 1, Upgrading to vSphere 5.1*.

2. Once the vCenter Single Sign On component is successfully installed, the installer will then begin the installation of the vCenter Inventory Service and then the vCenter Server component. The installer would need you to configure access to a database it will use, which can be an existing one (a precreated one) or a new install of MS SQL Server 2008 Express database.

   ❏ If you have SQL Server already installed, then you should create a new database and then create a 64-bit DSN using the SQL Native Client driver.

 ODBC data sources snap-in is located at:
Start | Administrative Tools | Data Sources (ODBC)

❏ When you create the DSN make sure that the default database selected is the vCenter database.

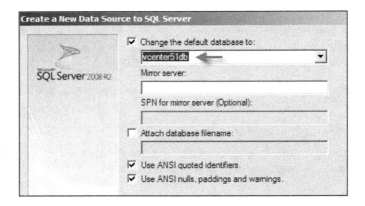

3. Choose the **Use an existing supported database** option, select the DSN that points to the pre-created database, and click on **Next**.

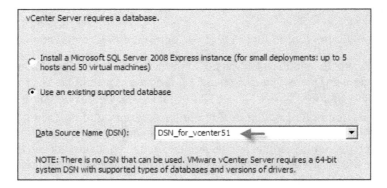

4. On the next screen authenticate the **sa** user, and click on **Next** to continue.

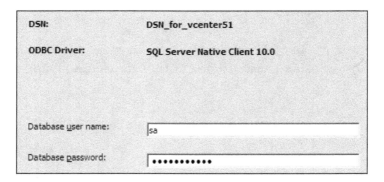

Although I have used the **sa** user for the DSN, you could use Windows NT authentication. If your database uses NT authentication, then the username and password fields will be disabled.

5. On the next screen you can choose which administrator user (generally a domain user) will be granted with the **Log on as a service** right. It is best practice to leave this option unedited, which would grant the right to the LocalSystem administrator.

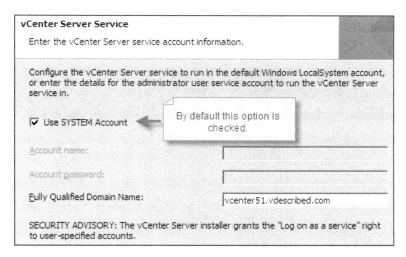

6. On the next screen, change the default ports if required. In this example, we will leave them at their default values and click on **Next** to continue.

Configure Ports

Enter the connection information for vCenter Server.

HTTPS port:	443
HTTP port:	80
Heartbeat port (UDP):	902
Web Services HTTP port:	8080
Web Services HTTPS port:	8443
Web Services Change Service Notification port:	60099
LDAP port:	389
SSL port:	636

☐ Increase the number of available ephemeral ports

If your vCenter Server manages hosts on which you will power on more than 2000 virtual machines simultaneously, this option prevents the pool of available ephemeral ports from being exhausted.

InstallShield

7. Subsequent to this, the wizard will prompt you to choose the inventory size. A maximum of 1 GB is required for a small inventory of 100 ESX servers or 100 VMs; for a large inventory of 400 ESX servers and 4,000 VMs, you would need a maximum of 3 GB. The memory requirement being referred to here is the JVM memory.

8. On the final **Ready to Install** screen you get an option to increase the number of ephemeral ports available. Choose to increase the number of ephemeral ports if you plan to manage more than 2,000 VMs.

9. And finally, click on **Install** to begin the installation. Note that it upgrades the vCenter database prior to installing the vCenter Server.

Deploying a VMware vCenter Server Appliance (vCSA)

The vCenter Server Appliance (vCSA) can be either downloaded as a single package (OVA); or the OVF, system disk, and data disk can be downloaded separately.

At the time of writing this book, the following were the names of the appliance files:

```
VMware-vCenter-Server-Appliance-5.1.0.5100-799730_OVF10.ova
```

Or

```
VMware-vCenter-Server-Appliance-5.1.0.5100-799730_OVF10.ovf
```

```
VMware-vCenter-Server-Appliance-5.1.0.5100-799730-system.vmdk
```

```
VMware-vCenter-Server-Appliance-5.1.0.5100-799730-data.vmdk
```

These names could possibly change when VMware releases the next update. I have included the file names only to give you a sense of what files have to be downloaded.

 Before you deploy the appliance, create a DNS entry for the hostname that is given to the appliance.

How to do it...

In this recipe we will learn how to deploy the vCSA appliance in your infrastructure:

1. In order to deploy the appliance you would need to use the **Deploy OVF Template** wizard using vSphere Client. Navigate to **File** | **Deploy OVF Template**, and browse to select the OVF file.

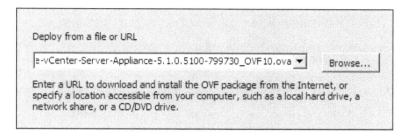

2. The next screen will show you the summary of the appliance; notice the differences in the download size and the size on disk values. Click on **Next** to continue.

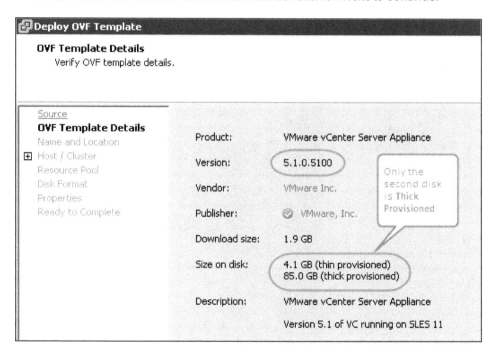

3. On the next screen you will need to supply a display name for the appliance VM and click on **Next** to continue.

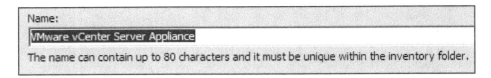

4. Then, choose a datastore where you would like to place the appliance VM.

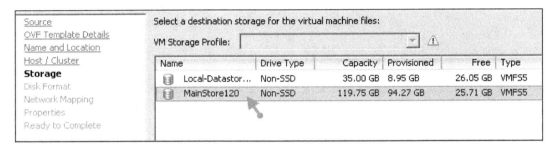

Once you highlight the datastore needed, click on **Next** to continue.

5. The next screen will let you select the VMDK format. The default selection is **Thick Provision Lazy Zeroed**, because the second disk is thick provisioned. You can choose **Thin Provision** if you don't want to create a VMDK committing 85 GB disk usage.

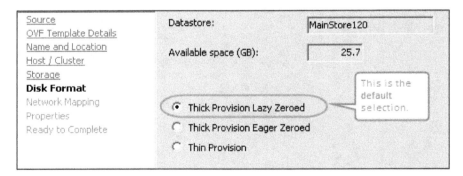

6. On the next screen, select the port group that the appliance's vNIC will be connected to. The port groups will be listed under the **Destination Networks** drop-down menu.

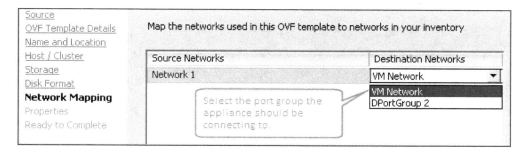

7. Subsequent to this is the **Ready to Complete** screen, which will show you a summary of all configuration selections that you made during the wizard. Click on **Finish** at this screen to deploy.

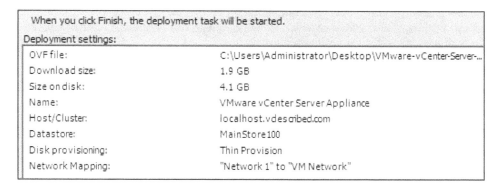

How it works...

By default the appliance VM is configured to use two vCPUs, 8 GB of memory, and 2 VMDKs of sizes 25 GB and 60 GB.

The Linux version in the appliance is SUSE Linux Enterprise Server 11 SP1 for VMware 11.1.1-1.4. The following is the screenshot from the postinstall.log file (/root/postinstall.log) showing the SLES version:

```
# | Alias                                                      | Name
                                          | Enabled | Refresh | Type
--+---------------------------------------------------------+----------+---------+----------------
                                          +----------+---------+--------
1 | SUSE-Linux-Enterprise-Server-11-SP1-for-VMware 11.1.1-1.4 | SUSE-Linux-Enter
prise-Server-11-SP1-for-VMware 11.1.1-1.4 | Yes      | Yes     | yast2
2 | studio-repo1                                              | studio-repo1
                                          | Yes      | No      | yast2
3 | studio-repo2                                              | studio-repo2
```

There's more...

If vCSA is configured to use the embedded database, then it cannot be used to manage more than 5 ESX servers or 50 virtual machines. This is because the embedded PostGreSQL database is sized that way. This limitation should not looked at as limitation with the vCSA. The default SQL Express database, which is included with the Windows-based vCenter, has the same limitation. The other limitations are:

► It cannot be configured to use MS SQL Server

► It does not support vCenter Linked Mode configuration

► It does not support the use of IPv6

 The embedded database used is PostGreSQL and can only be used as an embedded database.

Preparing vCenter Server Appliance for first use

Just deploying the appliance wouldn't just make it available for use. The appliance has to be prepared so that it can be made available on the network and can be used to manage ESXi servers.

Getting ready

Power on the appliance virtual machine. The first screen after the boot is shown in the following screenshot:

```
VMware vCenter Server Appliance 5.1.0.5100 Build 799730

To manage your appliance please browse to https://192.168.193.200:5480/

Welcome to VMware vCenter Server Appliance

Quickstart Guide: (How to get vCenter Server running quickly)
    1 - Open a browser to: https://192.168.193.200:5480/
    2 - Accept the EULA
    3 - Select the desired configuration mode or upgrade
    4 - Follow the wizard

    The configured appliance will be ready to use.
    In case of upgrade the appliance will reboot and may change
    its network address.


  *Login
   Set Timezone (Current:UTC)          Use Arrow Keys to navigate
                                       and <ENTER> to select your choice
```

At this screen you could select **Login** to log in to the appliance.

 The default username and password for the appliance are root and vmware.

The **Quickstart Guide** section of the first screen will show you the URL that should be used to connect to the web interface of vCenter Server Appliance. This web interface is not used to manage the ESXi server, but to configure the vCenter Server Appliance. The *How to do it...* section of this recipe will help you configure and prepare the appliance for its first use.

How to do it...

In this recipe we will learn how to perform the initial configuration and prepare the appliance for first use:

1. Connect to the web interface of the appliance using the URL provided at the welcome screen of the appliance.

The URL will be of the `https://ip-address-of-the-appliance:5480/` format.

2. Log in using the **root** user credentials and, when prompted for accepting the license agreement, select the checkbox **Accept license agreement**, and click on **Next** to go to the next screen or click on **Cancel** to cancel the wizard.

3. At the appliance's web interface, navigate to **Network | Address** and then change the **IPv4 Address Type** value from **DHCP** to **Static**. It is recommended that you use a static IP address for the appliance. This is because, if the DNS server is down for some reason, then you as an administrator will know the IP address, which can used to reach the vCenter Server.

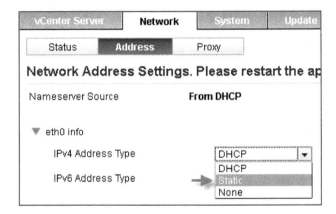

The moment you click on **Static**, it will then prompt you to enter the static configuration. Supply a hostname or the FQDN, the IPv4 address and Netmask. Make sure that a DNS record corresponding to the hostname entry is already created.

The default gateway and the DNS server information will be already prefilled with the information it received from the DHCP server.

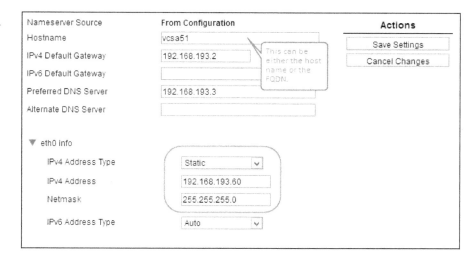

4. Once done click on **Save Settings**. It might just take a while to save the network settings. If successful, it should terminate the current session and take you back to the appliance's login page.

5. Relogin to the appliance and launch the setup wizard located at **Summary | Utilities**.

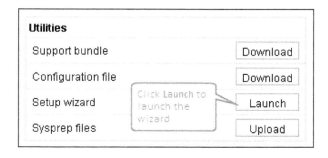

6. The vCenter Server setup wizard will first prompt you to choose a configuration method. Use **Configure with default settings**, if you don't want to customize any options. Use **Upgrade from previous version**, if you are upgrading the appliance; **Set custom configuration** will let you customize every option. I have selected **Set custom configuration** so that we can review the options available.

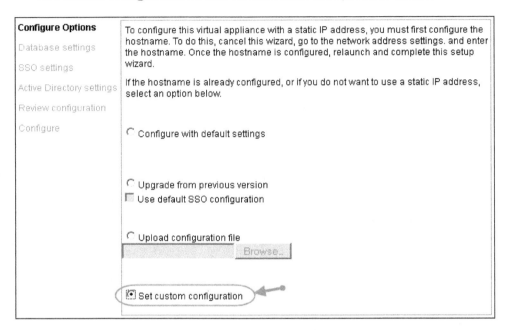

7. On the next screen choose the database type. You could use either **embedded** or **oracle**. We have chosen to use the embedded `PostGreSQL` database.

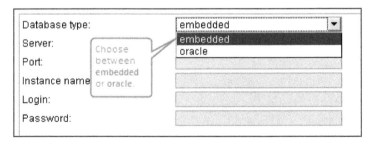

8. Next, you will be prompted to configure SSO deployment type and database type. If there is an existing SSO environment you could use the **External** option to supply the values. In this case we will continue with the default embedded deployment type and embedded database.

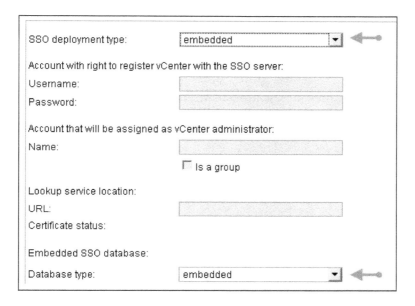

9. If you want the vCenter Server to be part of the Active Directory then you could select the option to enable Active Directory.

10. On the next screen, review the supplied configuration and click on **Start** for the wizard to start configuring the database, SSO, and the Active Directory.

Installing the vCenter Server Appliance update

Unlike the Windows version of vCenter, the vCSA will let you check for updates from within the appliance. This is different from upgrading the appliance. For upgrade instructions read the *Upgrading a vCenter Server Appliance* recipe.

In this recipe, I will show you how to install an available update.

This option is available under the **Update** tab, which has two subtabs, **Status** and **Settings**. The **Status** subtab will display the current appliance version. You can install any available updates to the appliance on this page.

How to do it...

The following procedure will guide you through the steps required to update the vCenter Server appliance:

1. Log in to the vCenter Server Appliance's web page as **root**.
2. Go to the **Update** tab.
3. Under the **Status** subtab, click on the **Check Updates** button to check for an available update.
4. If an update is available it will show the new appliance version under **Available Updates**. Click on **Install Updates**.

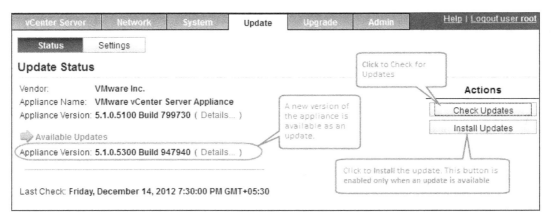

5. At the **Install Update** dialog box, click on **OK** to start the installation.

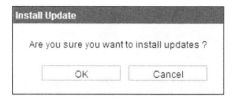

Once you confirm to install the update, it will show a message indicating the update is in progress.

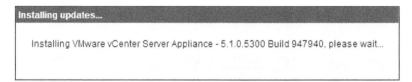

6. It will take a while to perform the update; once the update is complete, reboot the appliance.

How it works...

By default automatic updates are disabled. The **Settings** tab would let you configure the update settings. We can modify and choose to set **Automatic check for updates** or **Automatic check for updates and install updates**. You also do have the option to schedule a frequency for the update checks. By default it uses VMware's online update repository, available at the following link:

```
http://vapp-updates.vmware.com/vai-catalog/valm/vmw/8e70f769-fd50-
4a7a-bee2-2c0d945e23b0/5.1.0.5100.latest
```

You could also choose to perform an update from a CD ROM or another custom repository:

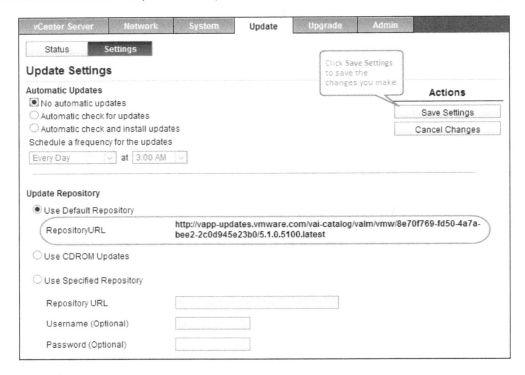

Upgrading a vCenter Server Appliance

The **Upgrade** tab is used when you have deployed a new version of the appliance and you want to migrate the settings to the new appliance. The upgrade is not in-place you will be deploying a new vCSA appliance and will migrate the settings from the old appliance to the newly deployed one.

How to do it...

The following procedure will guide you through the steps required to upgrade a vCenter Server Appliance:

1. Deploy and power on the new appliance and accept the EULA at the web interface.
2. Navigate to the **Upgrade** tab of the new appliance and under the **Prepare** subtab select the appliance role as **Destination**.
3. Navigate to the **Upgrade** tab of the old appliance and under the **Prepare** subtab select the appliance role as **Source**.

4. Navigate to the **Establish Trust** subtab on the new appliance and copy the **local appliance** key.

5. Navigate to the **Establish Trust** subtab on the old appliance and paste the local key from the new appliance into the **Remote Appliance Key** field and click on **Import Remote Key**.

6. Navigate to the **Import** subtab on the new appliance and click on **Start Import**.

How it works...

The newly deployed appliance will import all the configuration data from the old appliance. Once the import is complete it will shut down the old appliance.

Installing ESXi 5.1

ESXi 5.1 does not have a graphical installer. A new installation of ESXi 5.1 will now use a **GUID Partition Table** (**GPT**) instead of MBR, hence enabling the use of disks greater than 2 TB for installation.

 A new installation of ESXi 5.1 will create a **4 GB scratch partition** and the remainder of the disk space will be formatted using VMFS.

Installation of ESXi 5.1 is pretty straightforward. It is recommended that you refer to the *VMware Compatibility Guide* web page to verify whether the server hardware is compatible with ESXi 5.1, available at the following link:

```
http://www.vmware.com/resources/compatibility/search.php
```

For a complete list of hardware requirements, please refer to page 26 of the *ESX Server Installation and Setup* guide, available at the following link:

```
http://www.vmware.com/support/pubs/vsphere-esxi-vcenter-server-pubs.
html
```

You could download the ESXi 5.1 ISO from the following link:

```
https://my.vmware.com/web/vmware/info/slug/datacenter_cloud_
infrastructure/vmware_vsphere/5_1
```

You will be prompted to log in to your **My VMware** account to download the ISO.

How to do it...

The following procedure will guide you through the steps required to perform a new installation of the ESXi server using the ESXi 5.1 installation DVD:

1. Configure the boot device order in the server BIOS, in such a way that the server will attempt to boot from the CD/DVD ROM drive first.

2. Once you boot the server using the ESXi installation DVD, the ESXi standard boot menu will provide you with options to either start the ESXi 5.1 installer or to boot from the local disk.

3. Select the ESXi installer entry and press the *Enter* key to start the text-based installer.

4. After the installer is done with loading all the necessary modules into memory, it displays the **Welcome to the VMware ESXi 5.1.0 Installation** screen. Press the *Enter* key to continue.

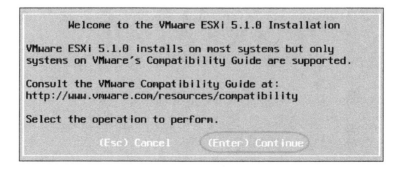

5. You will then be presented with the VMware's **End User License Agreement (EULA)** screen. Press the function key *F11* to accept and continue.

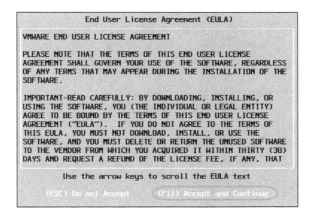

6. The next screen will show that the installer is scanning for available devices:

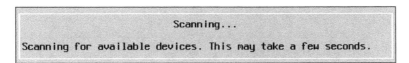

Wait until it detects the devices and prompt you for a storage device selection.

7. At the **Select a Disk to Install or Upgrade** screen, choose the intended storage device and press the *Enter* key to continue to the next screen. If it detects more than one storage device, then you can use the up and down arrow keys on the keyboard to make the needed selection. The **Local** and **Remote** (SAN) storage devices will be listed under separate categories.

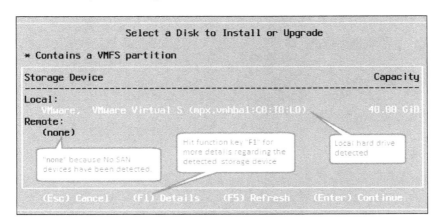

8. On the next screen, make a keyboard layout selection. The default is **US Default**. Use the up and down arrow keys on the keyboard to make a needed selection and press the *Enter* key to continue to the next screen.

```
            Please select a keyboard layout

 Swiss French
 Swiss German
 Turkish
 US Default
 US Dvorak
 Ukrainian
 United Kingdom

            Use the arrow keys to scroll.

 (Esc) Cancel      (F9) Back      (Enter) Continue
```

9. Next, you will be prompted to configure a password for the **root** login. Supply the password and press the *Enter* key to continue.

```
        Please enter a root password (recommended)

    Root password: ***********
 Confirm password: ***********_

              Passwords match.

  (Esc) Cancel      (F9) Back      (Enter) Continue
```

10. The next screen will indicate that it is scanning the system for additional information. Wait at this screen until you see the **Confirm Install** message.

```
                  Scanning system...

 Gathering additional system information. This may take a few moments.
```

11. At the **Confirm Install** message, press the function key *F11* to start the installation.

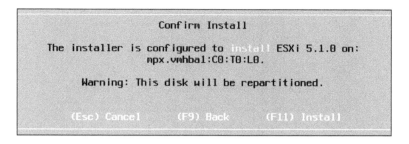

12. You will now see the **Installing ESXi 5.1.0** screen, showing the progress of the installation. This will take a few minutes to complete.

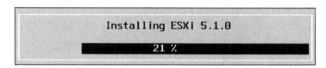

13. Once the installation completes successfully, you will be presented with an **Installation Complete** message. At this point eject the CD/DVD ROM drive to remove the ESXi 5.1 installation DVD and press the *Enter* key to reboot the ESX server.

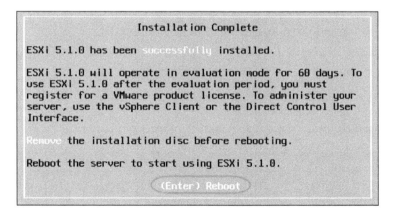

14. At the subsequent screen, prior to the reboot, a message **Rebooting Server** is displayed. You don't have to do anything at this screen:

```
                    Rebooting Server

The server will shut down and reboot.

The process will take a short time to complete.
```

15. Once the reboot is complete, you will be at the main screen for ESXi 5.1.0.

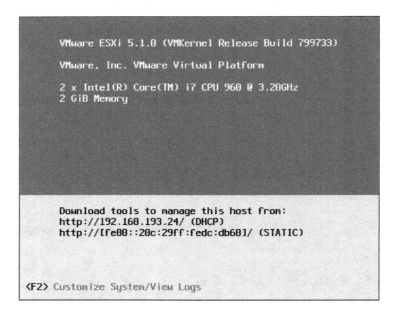

```
VMware ESXi 5.1.0 (VMKernel Release Build 799733)

VMware, Inc. VMware Virtual Platform

2 x Intel(R) Core(TM) i7 CPU 960 @ 3.20GHz
2 GiB Memory




Download tools to manage this host from:
http://192.168.193.24/ (DHCP)
http://[fe80::20c:29ff:fedc:db68]/ (STATIC)


<F2> Customize System/View Logs
```

16. At this screen, press the function key *F2* for the login prompt.

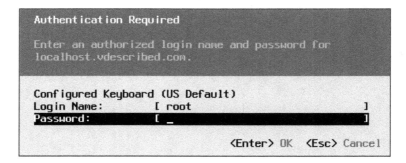

```
Authentication Required

Enter an authorized login name and password for
localhost.vdescribed.com.


Configured Keyboard (US Default)
Login Name:      [ root                              ]
Password:        [ _                                 ]

                            <Enter> OK   <Esc> Cancel
```

Performing a scripted install of the ESXi server

With the help of the *Installing ESXi 5.1* recipe, you should now be familiar with the regular interactive installation of the ESXi server. Although the interactive installation is an easy task, it becomes a tedious one when you are deploying servers in a larger environment. This is where a scripted installation could come in handy.

The *How to do it...* section will guide you through the steps required to perform a scripted installation.

How to do it...

The following are the steps involved in a scripted-installation process:

1. Boot the server with the ESXi installation CD in the CD/DVD ROM drive.
2. At the ESXi installer's **Loading ESXi installer** screen, press *Shift + O*.

3. On pressing *Shift + O*, you would see the default command the installer uses: `runweasel`.

4. At this prompt, specify the location of the install script. I have used an FTP location. Local CD ROM, USB driver, HTTP/HTTPS, or NFS are other supported script locations.

```
<ENTER: Apply options and boot>
> runweasel ks=ftp://admin:pass@192.168.0.102/forbook.cfg
```

The `ks` script will then locate and load the specified configuration file and proceed with the installation.

5. Once the installation is complete, it will prompt for a reboot. Press *Enter* to reboot.

Note that all the commands in the script file should be in lowercase. In this example we have created an install script with the name `forbook.cfg` and saved it onto an FTP server.

How it works...

An installation script is a plain text file with a `.cfg` extension and can only contain supported commands.

The ESXi installer has a default install script, `ks.cfg`, that performs a standard installation on the first detected disk. This file is located in the initial RAM disk at `/etc/vmware/weasel/ks.cfg`. The following is the default script file:

```
#
# Sample scripted installation file
#
# Accept the VMware End User License Agreement
vmaccepteula

# Set the root password for the DCUI and Tech Support Mode
rootpw mypassword

# Install on the first local disk available on machine
install --firstdisk -overwritevmfs

# Set the network to DHCP on the first network adapter
network --bootproto=dhcp --device=vmnic0

# A sample post-install script
%post --interpreter=python --ignorefailure=true
import time
stampFile = open('/finished.stamp', mode='w')
stampFile.write( time.asctime() )
```

When you install an ESXi server using the `ks.cfg` script, the default password is `mypassword`.

A single script can be used to install ESXi on multiple machines. Some modifications might be needed if you choose to install ESXi on a different hard drive, because by default it would install on the first local hard drive.

A scripted install has two stages. In the first stage, we create a custom script with needed commands or edit the script if it needs to be unique for a specific host. In the second stage we will redirect the installer to use the script file.

At the `runweasel` prompt, use the postfix `ks=location of the script`. This boot option will call the install script with additional boot parameters, if supplied. If we do not specify the `ks=` boot option, then the standard-text installation will proceed. The following is the script being used:

```
forbook.cfg - Notepad
File   Edit   Format   View   Help
#
# Sample scripted installation file
#
# Accept the VMware End User License Agreement
vmaccepteula

# Set the root password for the DCUI and Tech Support Mode
rootpw bookpassword

# Install on the first local disk available on machine
install --firstdisk --overwritevmfs

# Set the network to DHCP on the first network adapter
network --bootproto=dhcp --device=vmnic0

# A sample post-install script
%post --interpreter=python --ignorefailure=true
import time
stampFile = open('/finished.stamp', mode='w')
stampFile.write( time.asctime() )
```

On successfully locating the configuration file (forbook.cfg in this case), the scripted install will begin. The following screenshot shows all the phases the installer would go through during the scripted install:

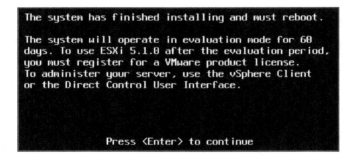

```
Preliminary checks ( 0 / 1 )

Writing binary to boot partition. ( 0 / 10 )

Partitioning disk for ESXi ( 5 / 10 )

Writing binary to boot partition. ( 0 / 10 )

Writing GUIDs to the bootbanks. ( 0 / 2" )

Caching the required files for ESXi ( 63 / 67 )

Configuring network settings ( 3 / 10 )

Writing the first-boot scripts ( 0 / 5 )
```

Once the installation is complete, it will indicate that the server must be rebooted:

```
The system has finished installing and must reboot.

The system will operate in evaluation mode for 60
days. To use ESXi 5.1.0 after the evaluation period,
you must register for a VMware product license.
To administer your server, use the vSphere Client
or the Direct Control User Interface.




                 Press <Enter> to continue
```

There's more...

The ks= boot option supports the following syntaxes:

- ks=cdrom:/path
- ks=usb:/path
- ks=file://path
- ks=protocol://serverpath

There are many more commands than what you see in the default script, and those commands can be used to create scripts to install ESXi servers as per your requirement.

Starting with ESXi 5.0, you can use the script to perform upgrades on the server. The following is the list of commands:

- `vmaccepteula`
- `clearpart`
- `dryrun`
- `install`
- `installorupgrade`
- `keyboard`
- `network`
- `paranoid`
- `part` or `partition`
- `reboot`
- `rootpw`
- `upgrade`
- `%include`
- `%pre`
- `%post`
- `%firstboot`

 Note that there are a few commands with a `%` prefix; those are multiline commands.

For more information on each of these commands refer the vSphere installation guide at the following link:

`http://www.vmware.com/support/pubs/vsphere-esxi-vcenter-server-pubs.html`

3
vSphere Auto Deploy

In this chapter we will cover the following:

- ► Installing Auto Deploy server
- ► Configuring a TFTP server with Auto Deploy files
- ► Configuring a DHCP server for PXE boot
- ► Testing the PXE boot configuration
- ► Preparing VMware PowerCLI for first use
- ► Downloading an ESXi Offline Bundle
- ► Adding the Offline Bundle to the Auto Deploy server
- ► Choosing an ESXi Image to deploy
- ► Creating a Host Profile
- ► Creating a deploy rule
- ► Activating a deploy rule
- ► Testing Auto Deploy
- ► Enabling Stateless Caching
- ► Performing an Auto Deploy stateful install

Introduction

VMware Auto Deploy helps an administrator to fast-provision multiple **ESXi servers** without having the need to insert the **ESXi Image** DVD to the server's local DVD ROM drive.

In this chapter, we will learn how to setup an auto deployed virtual infrastructure. The new features in vSphere 5.1, such as the stateless caching and stateful install, will further ease the work of an administrator.

VMware **Auto Deploy** doesn't work on its own. It needs a PXE environment configured for the server to boot up, talk to the Auto Deploy server, and use an appropriate image.

PXE (**Preboot Execution Environment**) is an environment to boot computers using the network interface on them, without the need for a local/remote data storage or a preinstalled operating system.

We need the following components configured for an ESXi server to be auto deployed.

  ▸ An Auto Deploy server

  ▸ Servers with PXE-enabled BIOS

  ▸ A DHCP server

  ▸ A TFTP server

  ▸ Host Profiles configured at the vCenter Server

Installing the Auto Deploy server

The Auto Deploy server software component is available on the **vCenter Server** installation DVD. The installation can be initiated from the installation **Welcome** screen.

How to do it...

The following procedure will guide you through the steps required to install Auto Deploy server.

You can start the installation wizard by clicking on the **Install** button on the vSphere installation DVD welcome screen, to bring up the **vSphere Auto Deploy** install wizard. Click on **Next** to continue.

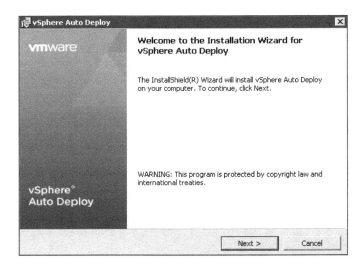

1. Accept the EULA.

2. Choose the destination install folder, `Auto Deploy Repository` directory, and the planned maximum size of the Auto Deploy repository and click on **Next**.

 The default size of the Auto Deploy repository is 2 GB, which is as per the best practice to allow enough room in the repository for four (4) Image Profiles. Each Image Profile requires approximately 350 MB of free repository space.

By default, the installer will dump the files into the following directory:

`c:\Program Files(x86)\VMware\VMware vSphere Auto Deploy\`

And the default Auto Deploy Repository directory will be:

`C:\Program Data\VMware\VMware vSphere Auto Deploy\Data`

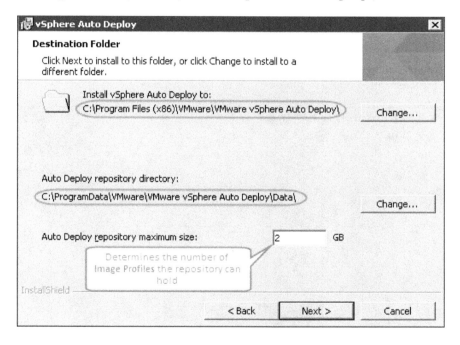

3. Supply vCenter Server's IP address/FQDN, the administrator credentials, and click on **Next**.

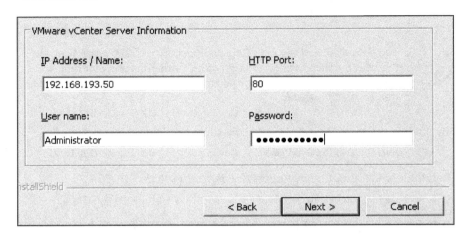

4. If you are prompted to trust the SSL certificate then click on **Yes**.

5. The default **Server Port** and **Management Port** numbers can be modified if required; otherwise, leave them at their default and click on **Next**.

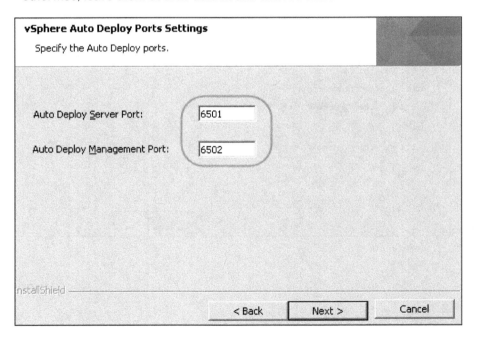

6. Specify how vSphere Auto Deploy should be identified on the network. You can choose between the IP address or FQDN of the vCenter Server. Choosing the IP address would make sense only if it is a static IP address. Click on **Next** to continue.

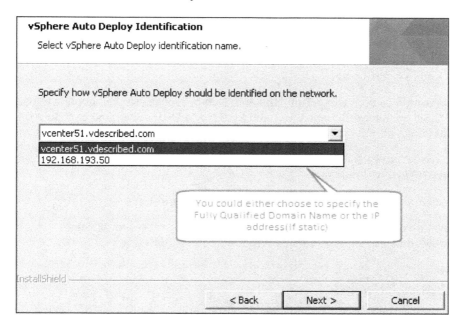

7. On the next screen, click on **Install** to begin the installation.
8. Once the installation is complete connect to the vCenter Server using the vSphere Client. The Inventory Home screen will show **Auto Deploy** under **Administration**.

 Note that Auto Deploy cannot be accessed from the vSphere 5.1 Web Client.

Configuring a TFTP server with Auto Deploy files

A TFTP server is a remote storage that will be used to store configuration or boot files. The **TFTP (Trivial File Transfer Protocol)** requires no authentication. More details and a protocol walkthrough is available at its wiki page: http://en.wikipedia.org/wiki/Trivial_ File_Transfer_Protocol.

A **TFTP server** will be contacted during the Auto Deploy process for PXE-booting the server on which ESXi will be deployed. Hence we need to deploy a TFTP server and configure it with a **gPXE boot** image and the configuration files.

There are many freeware TFTP servers on the internet to choose from. I have deployed **WinAgents** TFTP server manager.

http://www.winagents.com/en/products/tftp-server/

The installation of the TFTP server manager is pretty straightforward. Make sure it is installed on a Windows machine and the service is started before you begin.

How to do it...

The following steps will help you configure the TFTP server to facilitate PXE booting:

1. Deploy the WinAgents TFTP server, by installing it on a Windows machine.

2. Click on the **Auto Deploy** icon to bring up the configuration screen at the vCenter Inventory Home.

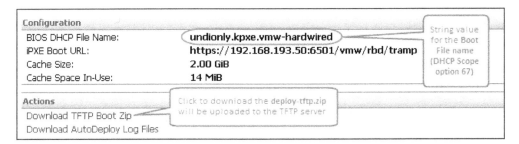

3. Make a note of the BIOS DHCP file name undionly.kpxe.vmw-hardwired that will be used as the string value to the DHCP scope option-67 (boot file name) and then download the TFTP boot ZIP (deploy-tftp.zip) file.

If there is a security alert not letting you download the file then enable **File Download** in the security settings.

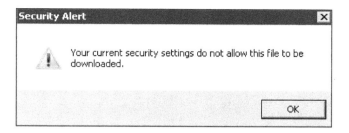

Here are the steps to enable file download and retry downloading the TFTP boot ZIP.

1. Go to **Control Panel**.
2. Bring-up the **Internet Options**.
3. Navigate to the **Security** tab.
4. Select the appropriate **Zone**. In most cases, it is the Internet.
5. Click on the **Custom Level** button and scroll down to the **Downloads** category.
6. Enable **File download** and retry the download of the **TFTP Boot Zip** file.

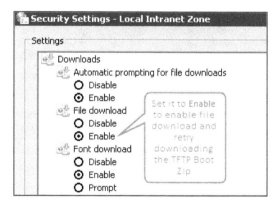

The following screenshot shows the contents of the TFTP boot ZIP file:

Name ^	Type	Compressed size
snponly64.efi	EFI File	90 KB
snponly64.efi.vmw-hardwired	VMW-HARDWIRED File	90 KB
tramp	File	1 KB
undionly.0	0 File	67 KB
undionly.kpxe	KPXE File	67 KB
undionly.kpxe.debug	DEBUG File	74 KB
undionly.kpxe.debugmore	DEBUGMORE File	78 KB
undionly.kpxe.vmw-hardwired	VMW-HARDWIRED File	67 KB

7. Extract `deploy-tftp.zip` and then drag-and-drop its contents onto the TFTP server Virtual root (\) folder of the WinAgents TFTP server.

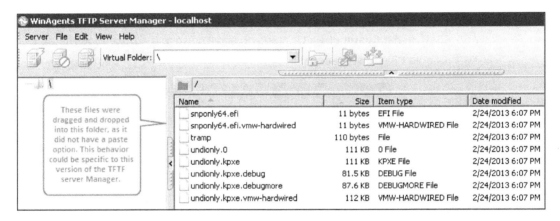

How it works...

The TFTP server is used to configure the gPXE boot image and the configuration files. The TFTP server will be contacted during the Auto Deploy process for PXE-booting the server.

There's more...

For more information on the TFTP server, PXE, and gPXE refer to *Page: 20* in the *vSphere Installation and Setup Guide* `http://pubs.vmware.com/vsphere-51/topic/com.vmware.ICbase/PDF/vsphere-esxi-vcenter-server-51-installation-setup-guide.pdf`.

Configuring the DHCP server for PXE boot

You need a DHCP server available in the same subnet as that of the machines on which ESX server will be Auto Deployed.

There are three ways you can set the IP addressing for the Auto Deployed hosts via DHCP:

1. Create a DHCP scope for the subnet to which the ESXi servers will be connecting.
2. If there is already an existing DHCP server with a scope for subnet then edit the scope options 66 and 67 accordingly.
3. Create a reservation using the MAC address of the host.

Creating a scope is the most common method, since the whole purpose of Auto Deploy is to spawn a considerably large number of servers. The *How to do it...* section will guide you through the steps required to create a DHCP scope.

How to do it...

The following steps will help you create a new DHCP scope and configure it with the TFTP information. However, if you already have an existing scope servicing the subnet then you could start with step 12, to configure the scope options.

1. Bring up the **DHCP Snap-in**, right-click on **IPv4**, and click on **New Scope**.

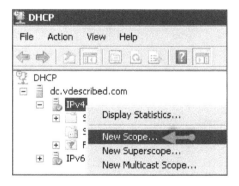

2. At the **New Scope** Wizard, click on **Next**, specify a name and an optional description, and click on **Next**.

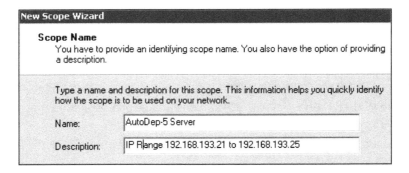

3. On the next screen, choose the **IP address** range for the scope by specifying the start and the end IP address of the range.

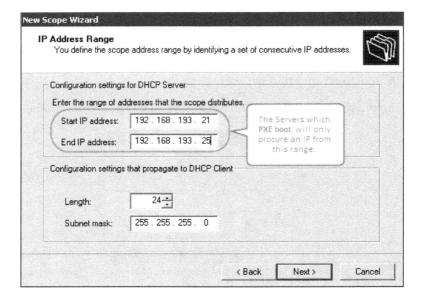

4. On the next screen, add an optional exclusion range or a DHCPOFFER delay, if required. Otherwise, just click on **Next** to continue.

5. Choose a **DHCP lease duration** and click on **Next**.

6. The **New Scope** wizard will now prompt you to choose whether to configure the additional information such as the Default gateway, DNS servers, and so on. Select **Yes, I want to configure these options now** and click on **Next**.

7. At the **Router (Default Gateway)** wizard page, add the IP address of the default gateway.

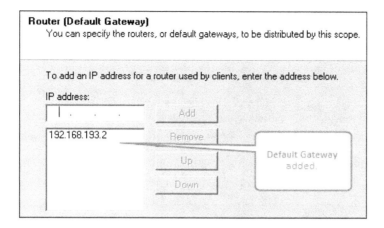

8. On the next screen, specify the parent domain, resolve the DNS servers IP address, and add it.

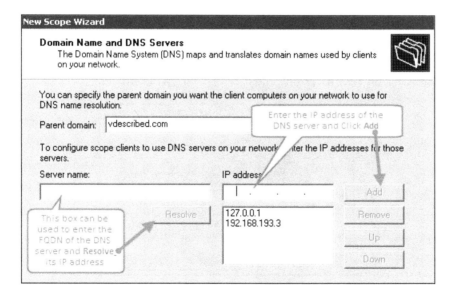

9. On the next screen, specify the WINS sever details if needed and click on **Next**.

10. Choose to activate the scope and click on **Next**.

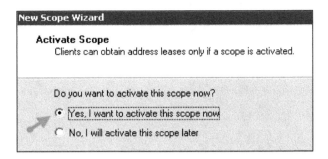

11. Then, click on **Finish** to create and activate the scope. Once done, the scope will be listed in the inventory.

12. Right-click on **Scope Options** and click on **Configure Options**.

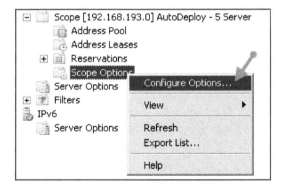

13. Under the **General** tab of the **Scope Options** window, scroll-down and select the check box against the option **066 Boot Server Host Name**; supply the string value with the FQDN or IP address of the TFTP server.

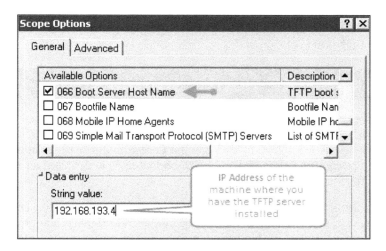

14. Next, select **067 Bootfile Name** and supply the string value `undionly.kpxe.vmw-hardwired`, which we made a note of from the Auto Deploy plugin page at the vCenter Server.

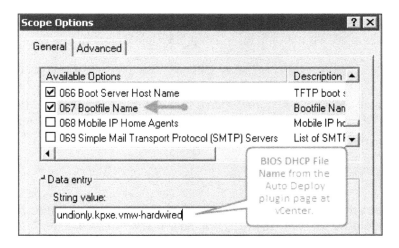

How it works...

When a machine is chosen to be provisioned with ESXi and is powered-on, it does a PXE boot by fetching an IP address from the DHCP server. The DHCP scope configuration option 66 and 67 will direct the server to contact the TFTP server and load the bootable gPXE image and an accompanying configuration file.

Testing the PXE boot configuration

Once you have configured the TFTP and the DHCP servers, it is a best practice to verify whether the servers can PXE boot successfully. If you haven't already configured the TFTP and DHCP severs then follow the instructions in the *Configuring a TFTP server with Auto Deploy files* and *Configuring DHCP Server for PXE boot* recipes in this chapter before proceeding with testing the PXE Configuration.

Although we don't specify the ESXi Image the server should boot from, while configuring the TFTP or DHCP servers, the PXE boot process should be able to reach a point to confirm that the PXE boot is working and all it would need is an ESXi Image to proceed further.

The *How to do it...* section of this recipe will guide you through the procedure required to test the PXE Boot Configuration.

How to do it...

The following procedure will help you test the PXE boot configuration:

1. Configure the BIOS of the server so that it will attempt a network boot (PXE boot) during every boot-up.
2. Make sure the server is connected to a segment that has an active DHCP scope. The DHCP scope options 66 and 67 should already be configured correctly.
3. Boot-up the server to check if its network boots.

How it works...

On the first screen during the PXE boot (network boot) process, note that the server does procure an IP address 192.168.193.25 from the scope we created at the DHCP server. The scope that we defined was of the range 192.168.193.21 to 192.168.193.27.

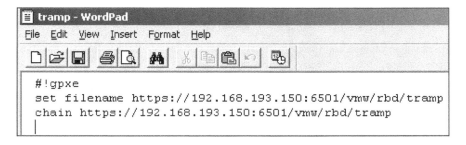

```
Network boot from Intel E1000
Copyright (C) 2003-2008   VMware, Inc.
Copyright (C) 1997-2000   Intel Corporation

CLIENT MAC ADDR: 00 0C 29 31 E1 44   GUID: 564D038F-E52C-326A-5168-A9C17F31E144
CLIENT IP: 192.168.193.21  MASK: 255.255.255.0  DHCP IP: 192.168.193.3
GATEWAY IP: 192.168.193.2
PXE->EB:  !PXE at 9E95:0070, entry point at 9E95:0106
          UNDI code segment 9E95:0BDE, data segment 98FF:5960 (611-638kB)
          UNDI device is PCI 02:01.0, type DIX+802.3
          611kB free base memory after PXE unload        IP Configuration procured from the DHCP server.
iPXE initialising devices...ok

VMware Build: 756170 undionly.kpxe.vmw-hardwired
iPXE 1.0.0+ -- Open Source Network Boot Firmware -- http://ipxe.org
Features: HTTP HTTPS iSCSI DNS TFTP AoE bzImage COMBOOT ELF MBOOT PXE PXEXT

net0: 00:0c:29:31:e1:44 on UNDI (open)
  [Link:up, TX:0 TXE:0 RX:0 RXE:0]
DHCP (net0 00:0c:29:31:e1:44).... ok                     The TFTP Boot image being loaded
net0: 192.168.193.21/255.255.255.0 gw 192.168.193.2
Next server: 192.168.193.4
Filename: tramp
tftp://192.168.193.4/tramp.https://192.168.193.50:6501/vmw/rbd/tramp./vmw/rbd/ho
st-register?bootmac=00:0c:29:31:e1:44..........._
                                                          "IP Address : Server Port" of the Auto
                                                                   Deploy Server
```

Since we had supplied `option 66` and `option 67` to the DCHP scope, it knows the IP address of TFTP server and the UNDI driver to be used. Subsequently, it boots using the `tramp` file, located on the virtual root of TFTP server. It is part of the `deploy-tftp.zip` bundle. If you examine the contents of the `tramp` file, you will see that it has the IP address of the machine where Auto Deploy was installed.

```
tramp - WordPad
File  Edit  View  Insert  Format  Help

#!gpxe
set filename https://192.168.193.150:6501/vmw/rbd/tramp
chain https://192.168.193.150:6501/vmw/rbd/tramp
```

Now, an `HTTP Boot Request` (*with the machine attributes*) is sent to the Auto Deploy server. Since the Auto Deploy server doesn't have any **Image Profile** or rule created to match the attributes, the PXE boot doesn't proceed any further.

```
* However, there is no ESXi image associated with this host.
*
* Detail: No rules containing an Image Profile match this host.
* You can create a rule with the New-DeployRule PowerCLI cmdlet
* and add it to the rule set with Add-DeployRule or Set-DeployRuleSet.
* The rule should have a pattern that matches one or more of the
* attributes listed below.
*
* Machine attributes:
* . asset=No Asset Tag
* . domain=vdescribed.com                    These are the machine
* . hostname=                              attributes that can be used
* . ipv4=192.168.193.21                    when creating Auto Deploy
* . mac=00:0c:29:31:e1:44                            Rules
* . model=VMware Virtual Platform
* . oemstring=[MS_VM_CERT/SHA1/27d66596a61c48dd3dc7216fd715126e33f59ae7]
* . oemstring=Welcome to the Virtual Machine
* . serial=VMware-56 4d 03 8f e5 2c 32 6a-51 68 a9 c1 7f 31 e1 44
* . uuid=564d038f-e52c-326a-5168-a9c17f31e144
* . vendor=VMware, Inc.
*
* Sleeping for 5 minutes and then rebooting...
*******************************************************************************
```

Preparing VMware PowerCLI for first use

All the tasks performed on the Auto Deploy server are done using **VMware PowerCLI** commands. Hence, it is a requirement to have VMware vSphere PowerCLI installed and configured for use.

At the time of writing this book, the latest available version was VMware-PowerCLI-5.0.1-581491. Download and install VMware PowerCLI from the following URL:

`www.vmware.com/go/powercli`

The installation of PowerCLI is pretty straight-forward. Just go through the wizard defaults and finish the installation. Once the installation is complete, it needs to be configured so that it can be used in your environment.

How to do it...

The following procedure will help you configure VMware PowerCLI for first use and also add the vCenter Server that will be used to manage the ESXi servers which you plan to deploy in your environment:

1. If VMware PowerCLI is being installed for the first time, you need to make sure that you issue the command to set the execution policy to either `RemoteSigned` or `Unrestricted`, by issuing any of the following commands:

    `Set-ExecutionPolicy Unrestricted`

    Or

    `Set-ExecutionPolicy RemoteSigned`

2. Close the PowerCLI window and re-open it. You should see vSphere PowerCLI welcome screen.

3. Connect the vCenter Server to VMware PowerCLI, by issuing the following command:

    Syntax:

    `Connect-VIServer FQDN or IP address of the vCenter`

    Example:

    `Connect-VIServer vcenter51.vdescribed.com`

```
PowerCLI C:\Program Files (x86)\VMware\Infrastructure\vSphere PowerCLI>
 Connect-VIServer vcenter51.vdescribed.com

Name                           Port  User
----                           ----  ----
vcenter51.vdescribed.com       443   Administrator


PowerCLI C:\Program Files (x86)\VMware\Infrastructure\vSphere PowerCLI>
PowerCLI C:\Program Files (x86)\VMware\Infrastructure\vSphere PowerCLI> _
```

How it works...

VMware PowerCLI is a set of cmdlets based on Microsoft Power Shell.

The **Set-Execution** policy cmdlet will determine what type of PowerCLI commands/scripts are allowed to run from the computer where VMware PowerCLI is installed. There are four types of execution policy, such as `Restricted`, `AllSigned`, `RemoteSigned`, and `Unrestricted`.

The default execution policy is `Restricted`, which does not allow running any scripts.

- Setting it to `RemoteSigned` will allow running scripts/cmdlets signed by a trusted publisher, in this case VMware Inc.
- Setting it to `Unrestricted` will impose no restrictions.

The **Connect-VIServer** cmdlet can be used to connect either the vCenter Server or the ESXi host. But for you to be able to address Clusters, Folders, and Host Profiles when creating a deploy rule, you will need vCenter level access. Therefore, you will need to connect to the vCenter Server and not the ESXi server.

Downloading an ESXi Offline Bundle

To Auto Deploy an ESXi server, we need to have the **ESXi Offline Bundle** ready. The vanilla version of the offline bundle can be downloaded from the VMware's website. Customized Offline Bundles from the server vendors are available for download from the vendor's website. It is also available at VMware's download page. It is under the **Drivers & Tools** tab and listed under the category **OEM Customized Installer CDs**.

How to do it...

You can download the ESXi 5.1 Offline Bundle from VMware's downloads page: `https://my.vmware.com/web/vmware/details?downloadGroup=VCL-VSP510-ESXI-510-EN&productId=285&rPId=3361`.

See the following screenshot that shows the bundle name and details.

VMware-ESXi-5.1.0-799733-depot.zip File size:298M File type: zip Release Date:2012-09-10 Build Number:799733	ESXi 5.1 Offline Bundle Contains VIB packages, and image profiles for ESXi, including VMware Tools. Use the image profiles and the VIB packages with VMware Image Builder and VMware Auto Deploy to create custom image/ISO generation for ESXi deployments. The VIB packages and image profiles may also be used with the new VMware ESXCLI MD5SUM:e1e0af718719ab680e04a75a62e983ff SHA1SUM:943a5035ade07d9618a3d41908a29b20ac5fa88c

Copy the downloaded Offline Bundle ZIP into the machine where vSphere PowerCLI will be Installed. That is, we have to copy it in to a directory `C:\AutoDeploy-VIBS`.

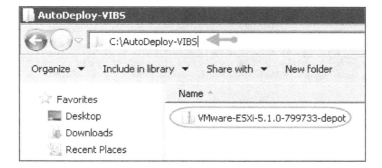

Adding the Offline Bundle to the Auto Deploy server

Once we have the Offline Bundle downloaded on the VMware PowerCLI machine, the next step is to present the Offline Bundle to the Auto Deploy server. This step is performed using the VMware PowerCLI. It is a requirement that the Offline Bundle should be accessible on the machine where PowerCLI is installed.

How to do it...

To present the ESXi 5.1 Offline Bundle to the Auto Deploy server, issue the following command:

```
Add-EsxSoftwareDepot "C:\AutoDeploy-VIBS\ VMware-ESXi-5.1.0-799733-depot.
zip"
```

```
PowerCLI C:\Program Files (x86)\VMware\Infrastructure\vSphere PowerCLI>
 Add-EsxSoftwareDepot "C:\AutoDeploy-VIBS\VMware-ESXi-5.1.0-799733-depot.zip"

Depot Url
--------
zip:C:\AutoDeploy-VIBS\VMware-ESXi-5.1.0-799733-depot.zip?index.xml

PowerCLI C:\Program Files (x86)\VMware\Infrastructure\vSphere PowerCLI> _
```

How it works...

A successful execution of the command basically informs the Auto Deploy server of the location of the Offline Bundle from where to fetch the Image Profiles.

Choosing an ESXi Image to deploy

The Offline Bundle presented to the Auto Deploy server, using the `Add-ESXSoftwareDepot` command, may contain more than one image of ESXi. We need to identify the required image and select it for use.

How to do it...

The following steps will help you list all the available Image Profiles and assign them to different variables:

1. Display all the images currently detected by the Auto Deploy server by issuing the following command:

   ```
   Get-EsxImageProfile
   ```

```
PowerCLI C:\Program Files (x86)\VMware\Infrastructure\vSphere PowerCLI>
  Get-EsxImageProfile

Name                         Vendor          Last Modified     Acceptance Level
----                         ------          -------------     ----------------
ESXi-5.1.0-799733-no-tools   VMware, Inc.    8/2/2012 3:0...   PartnerSupported
ESXi-5.1.0-799733-standard   VMware, Inc.    8/2/2012 3:0...   PartnerSupported

PowerCLI C:\Program Files (x86)\VMware\Infrastructure\vSphere PowerCLI> _
```

2. The Image Profile list generated by the `Get-ESXImageProfle` command can be assigned to a VMware PowerCLI array variable by issuing the following command:

   ```
   $imageprofile=Get-EsxImageProfile
   ```

3. The array variable `imageprofile` now holds an array of ESXi Image Profile elements. Each of the elements in the array can be individually addressed using the array element number starting with zero(0).

The following command will display array elements 0 and 1:

```
$imageprofile[0].name
$imageprofile[1].name
```

```
PowerCLI C:\Program Files (x86)\VMware\Infrastructure\vSphere PowerCLI>
   $imageprofile=Get-EsxImageProfile
PowerCLI C:\Program Files (x86)\VMware\Infrastructure\vSphere PowerCLI>
   $imageprofile[0].name
ESXi-5.1.0-799733-no-tools
PowerCLI C:\Program Files (x86)\VMware\Infrastructure\vSphere PowerCLI>
   $imageprofile[1].name
ESXi-5.1.0-799733-standard
PowerCLI C:\Program Files (x86)\VMware\Infrastructure\vSphere PowerCLI> _
```

From the output of the preceding command, we now know the names of the images available. Here they are:

- ESXi-5.1.0-799733-no-tools
- ESXi-5.1.0-799733-standard

How it works...

The variable created can hold array of image names. The VMware Auto Deploy PowerCLI cmdlets can use these variables to perform version operations.

Creating a Host Profile

Before we create a deploy rule to deploy any of the ESXi Images, we need to create a configuration template that is then applied to the ESXi server deployed using the Auto Deploy. The template is created from an existing host in the cluster that meets all the virtual infrastructure configuration requirements. Such a configuration template is called a **Host Profile**.

How to do it...

The following procedure will help you create a Host Profile using an existing ESXi server:

1. Navigate to the Inventory Home. **Host Profiles** is listed under the **Monitoring** section.

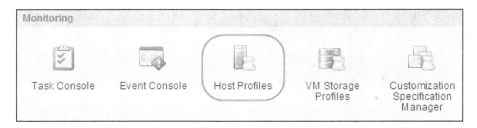

2. At the **Host Profiles** page, click on the **+** sign to bring-up the **Extract Host Profiles Wizard**.

3. At the **Extract Host Profile** wizard screen, select the **reference host** from the list and click on **Next** to continue.

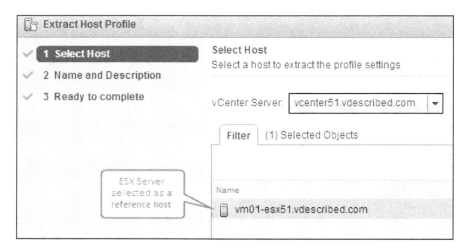

4. On the next screen enter a name of the Host Profile and an optional **Description**; click on **Next**.

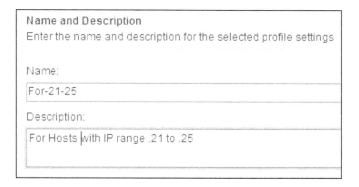

5. At the **Ready to Complete** screen, click on **Finish** to generate the profile.

This will generate a profile and list it under the Host Profile objects.

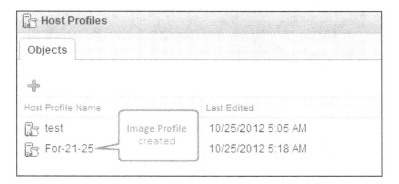

Creating a deploy rule

A deploy rule is created to deploy a chosen ESXi Image onto a server or group of servers chosen based on a supported pattern. Without a deploy rule, Auto Deploy server will not be able to associate an ESXi Image with a server to boot.

The pattern used to choose a server for deploying ESXi uniquely identifies the machine or a group of machines. The pattern can be an IPv4 address range, a MAC address, hardware vendor name, Asset tag, domain name, server model, serial number, and so on.

How to do it...

The following procedure will help you create a new deploy rule.

To create a new deploy rule issue the following command:

```
New-DeployRule -Name "RuleIP-21-25" -Item $imageprofile[1],
"Cluster-21-25" -pattern "ipv4=192.168.193.21-192.168.193.25"
```

Here, `RuleIP-21-25` is the name of the deploy rule; `$imageprofie[1]` is ESXi-5.0.0-20111104001-standard; `Cluster-21-25` is the name of the cluster at the vCenter Server; pattern `ipv4=192.168.193.21-192.168.193.25` is the IP scope we created at the DHCP server, for the subnet to which the ESXi servers will be connected.

We could also attach a Host Profile to the ESXi server being deployed, when we create a rule.

Here is the command:

```
New-DeployRule -Name New-01 -Item $img[1],"Cluster-21-25",
"For-21-25" -Pattern "ipv4=192.168.193.21-192.168.193.24"
```

```
PowerCLI C:\Program Files (x86)\VMware\Infrastructure\vSphere PowerCLI>
 New-DeployRule -Name New-01 -Item $img[1],"Cluster-21-25","For-21-25" -Pattern
"ipv4=192.168.193.21-192.168.193.24"


Name         : New-01
PatternList  : {ipv4=192.168.193.21-192.168.193.24}
ItemList     : {ESXi-5.0.0-20111104001-standard, Cluster-21-25, For-21-25}


PowerCLI C:\Program Files (x86)\VMware\Infrastructure\vSphere PowerCLI> _
```

Host Profile

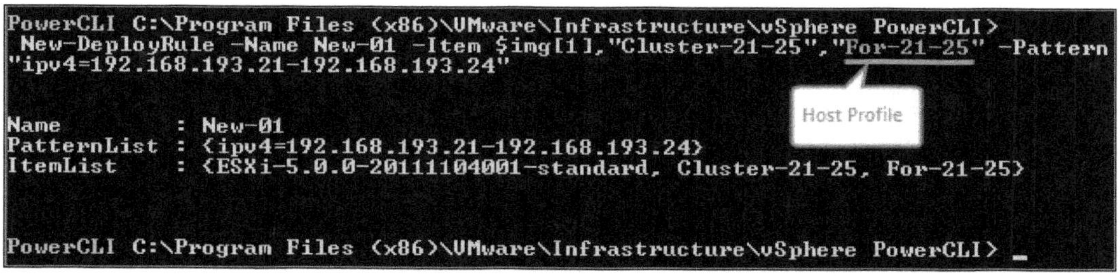

Here, `For-21-25` is the name of the Host Profile. Host Profiles are used to apply configuration templates to an ESXi server.

How it works...

When the command to create a new deploy rule is executed, it starts uploading the **VIBs** (**vSphere Installation Bundles**) in the image onto the Auto Deploy's `cache` folder.

The `cache` folder location is as follows:

```
C:\ProgramData\VMware\VMware vSphere Auto Deploy\Data\cache
```

The following screenshot shows the Auto Deploy's `cache` folder:

cache					_ □ ×
⊙ ⊙ ▽ 📁	C:\ProgramData\VMware\VMware vSphere Auto Deploy\Data\cache	▼ ⟳	Search c...		🔎
Organize ▼ Include in library ▼ Share with ▼ New folder		▦ ▼ ▯ ②			
☆ Favorites	0a	6d	19	73	ab	df
🖳 Desktop	0b	6f	24	75	ac	e1
📥 Downloads	01	7f	36	80	b8	e9
🗺 Recent Places	1c	9a	40	85	c2	ea
	02	9b	48	86	c8	ec
📚 Libraries	3a	9c	52	93	cd	ef
🗎 Documents	4f	9d	56	99	d3	f7
🎵 Music	5c	9e	58	a1	dc	fd
🖼 Pictures	5d	11	62	a3	dd	
🎞 Videos						

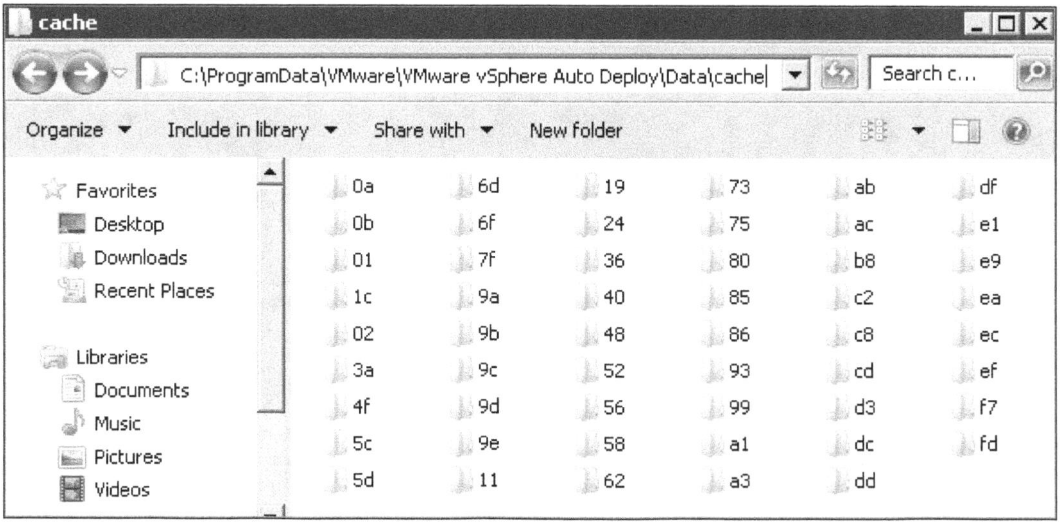

Once it is done with the uploading of VIBs, it will finish and summarize the operations.

```
Downloading scsi-megaraid-sas 4.32-1vmw.500.0.0.469512
Download finished, uploading to AutoDeploy...
Upload finished.

Name        : RuleIP-21-25
PatternList : {ipv4=192.168.193.21-192.168.193.25}
ItemList    : {ESXi-5.0.0-20111104001-standard, Cluster-21-25}


PowerCLI C:\Program Files (x86)\VMware\Infrastructure\vSphere PowerCLI>
```

Activating a deploy rule

The Auto Deploy rules that you create will become part of a rule set.

There are two types of rule sets:

▶ Active rule set
▶ Working rule set

For a newly created deploy rule to be used, it must be added to the active rule set.

How to do it...

To add the deploy rule to an active rule set, issue the following command:

```
Add-DeployRule -DeployRule "RuleIP-21-25"
```

```
Add-DeployRule –DeployRule "New01"
```

```
PowerCLI C:\Program Files (x86)\VMware\Infrastructure\vSphere PowerCLI>
  Add-DeployRule -DeployRule "RuleIP-21-25"


Name        : RuleIP-21-25
PatternList : {ipv4=192.168.193.21-192.168.193.25}
ItemList    : {ESXi-5.1.0-799733-standard, Cluster-21-25}


PowerCLI C:\Program Files (x86)\VMware\Infrastructure\vSphere PowerCLI>
  Add-DeployRule -DeployRule "New01"


Name        : RuleIP-21-25
PatternList : {ipv4=192.168.193.21-192.168.193.25}
ItemList    : {ESXi-5.1.0-799733-standard, Cluster-21-25}

Name        : New01
PatternList : {ipv4=192.168.193.21-192.168.193.25}
ItemList    : {ESXi-5.1.0-799733-standard, Cluster-21-25, For-21-25}
```

How it works...

Only rules in the active rule set are referenced by the Auto Deploy server when it receives an `HTTP Boot Request`. The `Add-DeployRule` command, by default, adds the deploy rule to both the working and active rule sets. When a machine boots for the first time, the Auto Deploy servers select the Image Profile based on a deploy rule in the active rule set. Once the Image Profile has been identified, it will be cached at the Auto Deploy server and reused during the future reboots.

There's more...

A common problem with Auto Deployed servers is that the servers sometimes boot from a wrong image or an image that doesn't contain the latest update. This happens when an Image Profile/deploy rule corresponding to an Auto Deployed server has been changed, but since the server is booting from the Auto Deploy cache, it remains unaware of the changes. We can resolve this issue by verifying the Auto Deploy cache against the active deploy rule to make sure that the cache is up-to-date and remediate it if necessary.

To verify the Auto Deploy cache against the deploy rule, use the cmdlet `Test-DeployRuleSetCompliance`. To remediate a host or a set of hosts with the updated Image Profile, use the cmdlet `Repair-DeployRuleSetCompliance`.

Read the recipe *Applying an Image Profile to the Host* recipe in *Chapter 4, ESXi Image Builder*, to learn how to use these commands.

Testing Auto Deploy

Now that we have deploy rules created, let's boot up an ESX Server in the subnet and check if it is able to fetch and load the image from the Auto Deploy server.

How to do it...

Start the machine intended to host the ESXi server. If everything has been configured correctly then it will PXE-boot and will start loading the VIBs into from the cache to the server's memory.

```
                         Loading VMware ESXi

Loading /vmw/cache/02/d9675438b52b6942bbd146092a09d6/tboot.2cbadfb6e2567af9f09150a898840cc0
Loading /vmw/cache/cd/73ddb7d5b7ccadd4e29327546eddbb/b.db6e3683f212fa6732a9a735ba8fe16e
Loading /vmw/cache/cd/73ddb7d5b7ccadd4e29327546eddbb/useropts.db6e3683f212fa6732a9a735ba8fe16e
Loading /vmw/cache/cd/73ddb7d5b7ccadd4e29327546eddbb/k.db6e3683f212fa6732a9a735ba8fe16e
Loading /vmw/cache/02/d9675438b52b6942bbd146092a09d6/a.2cbadfb6e2567af9f09150a898840cc0
Loading /vmw/cache/6f/5f7b82a710c2b39b5ee487a2411c45/ata-pata.de670812b0d8072121a4fae955f48cb1
Loading /vmw/cache/3a/711e9c462eb337aa24824da0b21f7d/ata-pata.086eb2d336e38516c245bd08e6cf3548
```

Once it is done, it will load all the VIBs to the memory and it will finish booting up the ESXi server.

```
VMware ESXi 5.1.0 (VMKernel Release Build 799733)

VMware, Inc. VMware Virtual Platform

2 x Intel(R) Core(TM) i7 CPU 960 @ 3.20GHz
2 GiB Memory




Download tools to manage this host from:
http://192.168.193.21/ (DHCP)
http://[fe80::20c:29ff:fe31:e144]/ (STATIC)
```

As per the deploy rule, it should add the host to the Cluster-21-25 cluster. You should also, see it applying the Host Profile to the ESX Server.

How it works...

Now that we learned how to Auto Deploy an ESXi server, it will be beneficial to understand what happens in the background during the first and the subsequent server boot-up operations.

First boot

When a machine chosen to be provisioned with ESXi is powered-on, it does a PXE boot by fetching an IP address from the DHCP server. The DHCP scope configuration option 66 and 67 will direct the server to contact the TFTP server and load the bootable gPXE image and an accompanying configuration file. The configuration will direct the server to send an HTTP Boot Request to the Auto Deploy server. The HTTP Boot Request will contain the server attributes such as the IP address, MAC address, vendor details, and so on.

On receipt of the HTTP Boot Request, the Auto Deploy server will check its rule engine to see if there are any rule criteria that match with the host attributes. If it finds a corresponding rule then it would use that rule from the active rule set to load an appropriate ESXi Image from an Image Profile.

Subsequent boot

After the host is provisioned and added to the vCenter Server, the vCenter Server holds the details of the Image Profile and the Host Profile associated with the host object, in its database. Hence during a subsequent reboot, the Auto Deploy server doesn't have to leverage its **Rule Engine** again. Instead, it would use the information from the vCenter database.

If for whatever reason the vCenter Server is unavailable then the Auto Deploy Rule Engine is engaged to determine the Image Profile and the Host Profile to be used. Since vCenter is unavailable, the Host Profile cannot be applied to the server.

Enabling Stateless Caching

ESXi servers deployed using `AutoDeploy` require the Auto Deploy server to be available and reachable every time the host reboots. Prior to vSphere 5.1, if the network boot fails, the server did not have a source to continue the boot process. Now with vSphere 5.1, you can enable **Stateless Caching** that will add a level resiliency in case the network boot (PXE boot) fails. The Stateless Caching mode is enabled by editing the Host Profile associated to the ESX server.

How to do it...

The following procedure will help you enable Stateless Caching:

1. Select the Host Profile and navigate to **Actions | Edit Host Profile**.

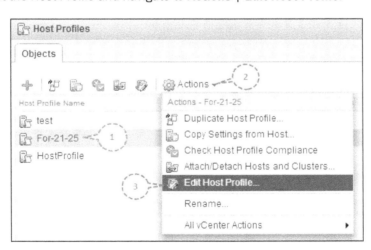

2. At the **Edit Host Profile** wizard, click on **Next** to go to the **Edit Host Profile** page of the wizard.

3. Expand **Advanced Configuration Settings** and then check the **System Image Cache Configuration** checkbox.

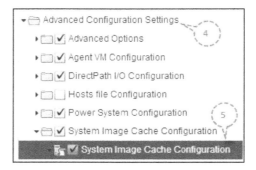

4. On the right-pane, use the **System Image Cache Profile Settings** drop-down menu to select **Enable stateless caching on the host** from the list.

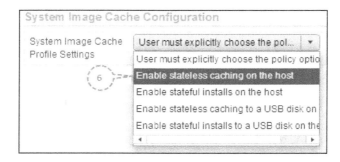

5. Once selected, it will show the arguments for the first local disk.

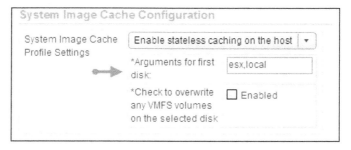

 Note that usually there is no need to change the argument, because it auto detects the first local disk available.

6. If intended you could also choose to overwrite the VMFS volumes on the selected disk.

7. Click on **Finish** to close the Edit Host Profile wizard.

8. Change the boot order in the BIOS of the ESXi machine in a way that it would always attempt a network boot first and then fall back to hard drive if network boot fails.

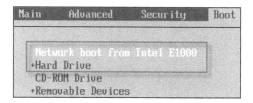

9. Reboot the ESX Server.

How it works...

Once you have enabled Stateless Caching on the associated Host Profile and configured the BIOS to always do a network boot first and then during the next reboot of the ESX machine, it performs a network boot and loads the ESXi Image from the Auto Deploy server. The server finishes booting and applies (remediation) the Host Profile. Remediation will dump the ESXi Image running in memory to the first disk (the local disk by default) selected during the Stateless configuration.

Subsequent to this, if an attempt to network-boot the server fails, it will load the image that was cached to the local disk during the previous successful network boot.

Performing an Auto Deploy stateful install

An Auto Deployed ESXi server, will always have to PXE-boot, engage the Auto Deploy server or the vCenter database (if it has the information Image Profile and Host Profile information). This is because the ESXi Image is not stored on the machine but is loaded directly into the server's volatile memory. So every reboot requires the server to go through the PXE boot procedure to load an ESXi Image into its memory. Starting with vSphere 5.1 you can use Auto Deploy to install the ESXi Image onto the local disk of the chosen server. This process if referred to as a **stateful install**.

How to do it...

The following procedure will help you prepare a host for a stateful install.

1. Extract a Host Profile from a reference host and edit the settings.

2. Expand **Advanced Configuration Settings** and then check the **System Image Cache Configuration** checkbox.

3. On the right-pane, use the **System Image Cache Profile Settings** drop-down menu to select **Enable stateful installs on the host**.

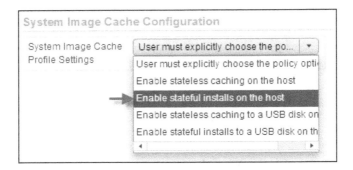

4. Configure an Auto Deploy rule for the intended hosts to use the Host Profile you created.

5. At the BIOS of a machine on which you intend to perform stateful installs, make sure the boot order is configured in a way so that the server attempts to boot from the local hard drive first and should fall back to network boot if that fails.

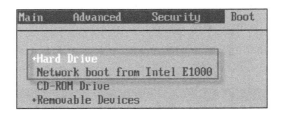

6. Boot the machine. Once the server is booted, it will be automatically placed in **Maintenance Mode**.

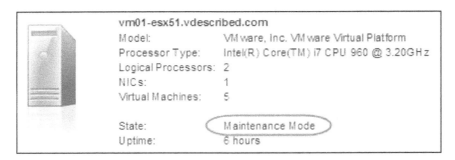

7. Navigate to the **Actions** menu for the server, then to **All vCenter Actions | Host Profiles | Remediate**.

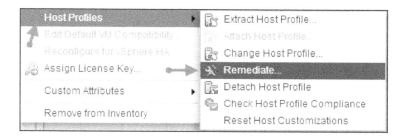

8. It will prompt you for host customization. Supply the needed information and click on **Next** to review the remediation tasks and then click on **Finish** to begin remediation.

9. Reboot the server to load from the local hard disk.

How it works...

With stateful install configured correctly, when you boot a server for the first time, it attempts to boot from the hard drive. Since there is no image on the local disk, it does a network boot and loads the ESXi Image from the Auto Deploy server. The rule configured at the Auto Deploy server will attach the Host Profile to the ESX Server. The ESXi server deployed will be automatically put in maintenance mode.

Now, you will have to manually remediate the hosts, to apply the changes made to the Host Profile. Remediation will save the ESXi Image from the memory to the local hard disk of the ESXi machine. Keep in mind that, even though remediation dumps the image to the local hard drive, the server is still running an image loaded from the memory. The server will have to be rebooted so that a boot from the local hard disk succeeds.

4

ESXi Image Builder

In this chapter we will cover the following:

- ▶ Creating an Image Profile by cloning an existing one
- ▶ Removing an Image Profile
- ▶ Adding a VIB (software package) to an Image Profile
- ▶ Exporting an Image Profile as an ISO or Offline Bundle
- ▶ Creating an Image Profile from scratch
- ▶ Applying an Image Profile to the host

Introduction

As the name suggests, the **ESXi Image Builder** is used to build ESXi bootable images. It is particularly useful when there is a need to custom-build an ESXi Image. For example, it can be used to custom-build ESXi Images with an updated device driver, for use in your **vSphere Environment**. VMware Auto Deploy leverages this ability of the ESXi Image Builder, to deploy stateless ESXi hosts.

The Image Builder requires the following data to proceed:

- ▶ An ESXi Offline Bundle
- ▶ Driver/Software Offline Bundles from the vendor-partners
- ▶ VMware PowerCLI

Once you have all the required data, you can use ESXi Image Builder cmdlets to create an Image Profile using the ESXi offline depot.

The following task-flow is generally used to form an Image Profile:

1. Add the ESXi and the Driver/Software Offline Bundles to the software depot.
2. Clone a base profile and custom add/remove the VIBs.
3. Save or export the Image Profile to an ISO file, which can then be used to install/AutoDeploy new ESXi hosts.

The ESXi Image builder doesn't need a separate installation. The vSphere PowerCLI has the Image Builder snap-in built into it. You should be ready to go once you have **VMware vSphere PowerCLI** 5.1 installed.

Offline Bundle

An **Offline Bundle** is an archive that is available for download from VMware or from the OEM's website for use with ESXi Image Builder. The bundle can either be the entire ESXi Image or it can be a driver bundle. It is a collection of VIBs. This is the first thing that the Image Builder will need to perform any of its tasks. It is also referred to as a **Software Depot**.

VIB (vSphere Installation Bundle)

A VIB or a vSphere Installation Bundle is a packaged archive that contains a file archive, an XML configuration file and a signature file. Most of the hardware OEMs package their device driver bundles as VIBs.

Image Profiles

An Image Profile is a predefined or custom-defined set of VIBs that can be addressed as a package. All the VMware ESXi Offline Bundles will have more than one VMware-defined Image Profiles. The Image Profiles are used to deploy, upgrade, and patch Auto Deployed ESXi servers. Read *Chapter 3, vSphere Auto Deploy*, to learn how to Auto Deploy ESXi servers.

All the recipes discussed in this chapter will be performed using vSphere PowerCLI 5.1

Creating an Image Profile by cloning an existing one

All the predefined Image Profiles available from an Offline Bundle are read-only. To customize such Image Profiles, you will need to clone them to form new Image Profiles. In this recipe we will learn how to create a new Image Profile by cloning an existing one.

How to do it...

The following procedure will guide you through the steps required to clone a predefined ESXi Image Profile available from an ESXi Offline Bundle.

It is a four step process:

1. Verifying the existence of a Software Depot in the current session.
2. Adding a Software Depot.
3. Listing available Image Profiles.
4. Cloning an Image Profile to form a new one.

Verifying the existence of a Software Depot in the current session

To verify whether there are any existing Software Depots defined in the current PowerCLI session, issue the following command:

```
$DefaultSoftwareDepots
```

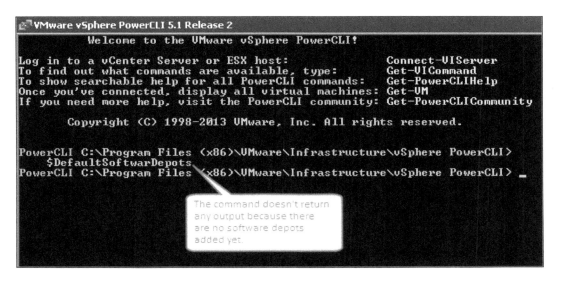

Note that the command has not returned any values. Meaning, there are no Software Depots defined in the current session. If the needed Software Depot was already added then the command output will list the depot. In that case, you can skip step 2, Add a Software Depot, and start with step 3, List available Image Profiles.

Adding a Software Depot

Before you add a Software Depot, make sure that you have the Offline Bundle saved on to your local disk. The Offline Bundle can be downloaded from VMware's website or from the OEM's website. The bundle can either be an ESXi Image or a device driver bundle.

We already have the Offline Bundle downloaded to the `C:\AutoDeploy-VIBS` directory.

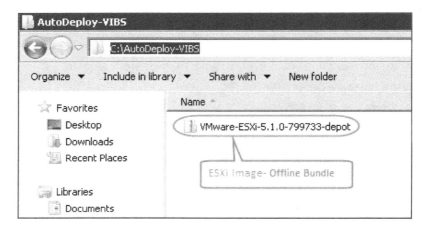

Now, let's add this to the current PowerCLI session.

To add the downloaded Software Depot, issue the following command:

```
Add-EsxSoftwareDepot -DepotUrl C:\AutoDeploy-VIBS\ESXi500-201111001.zip
```

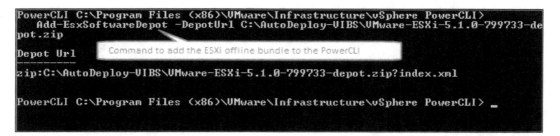

Once the Software Depot has been successfully added to the PowerCLI session, the command `$DefaultSoftwareDepots` should list the newly added Software Depot.

```
PowerCLI C:\Program Files (x86)\VMware\Infrastructure\vSphere PowerCLI>
    $DefaultSoftwareDepots
Depot Url                          Now displays the newly added software depot
---------
zip:C:\AutoDeploy-VIBS\VMware-ESXi-5.1.0-799733-depot.zip?index.xml

PowerCLI C:\Program Files (x86)\VMware\Infrastructure\vSphere PowerCLI>
```

You could also just issue the command `Get-EsxSoftwareDepot` to list all the added depots (Offline Bundles).

```
PowerCLI C:\Program Files (x86)\VMware\Infrastructure\vSphere PowerCLI>
    Get-EsxSoftwareDepot          Command to list all the added software depots(offline bundles)
Depot Url
---------
zip:C:\AutoDeploy-VIBS\VMware-ESXi-5.1.0-799733-depot.zip?index.xml
file://custom/depot/index.xml
zip:C:\AutoDeploy-VIBS\DriverVIBS\be2net-4.4.231.0-offline_bundle-1028063.zi...

PowerCLI C:\Program Files (x86)\VMware\Infrastructure\vSphere PowerCLI> _
```

Listing available Image Profiles

Once the Software Depot has been added, the next step will be to list all the currently available Image Profiles from the depot by issuing the following command:

`Get-EsxImageProfile`

```
PowerCLI C:\Program Files (x86)\VMware\Infrastructure\vSphere PowerCLI>
    Get-EsxImageProfile

Name                          Vendor        Last Modified     Acceptance Level
----                          ------        -------------     ----------------
ESXi-5.1.0-799733-no-tools    VMware, Inc.  8/2/2012 3:0...   PartnerSupported
ESXi-5.1.0-799733-standard    VMware, Inc.  8/2/2012 3:0...   PartnerSupported

PowerCLI C:\Program Files (x86)\VMware\Infrastructure\vSphere PowerCLI> _
```
Two Image Profiles are available

We see that there are two image profiles that the ESXi Offline Bundle offers. One is an ESXi Image, with no VMware Tools ISOs bundled with it, and the other is the standard image, with the VMware Tools ISOs bundled with it.

Cloning an Image Profile to form a new one

Now that we know there are two Image Profiles available, the next step will be to clone a needed Image Profile to form a new one. This is done by using the `New-ESXImageProfile` cmdlet. The cmdlet can be supplied with the name of the Image Profile as an argument. However, in most cases remembering the names of the Image Profiles available would be difficult. So the best way to work around this difficulty is to define an array variable to hold the names of the Image Profiles and then the array elements (Image Profile names) can be easily and individually addressed in the command.

In this example, we will be using a user defined array variable `$profiles` to hold the output of the command `Get-EsxImageProfile`.

The following expression will save the output of the `Get-ESXImageProfile` command to a variable `$profiles`.

```
$profiles = Get-EsxImageProfile
```

The `$profiles` variable now holds the two Image Profile names as array elements `[0]` and `[1]` sequentially.

The following command can be issued to clone the array element `[1]` `ESXi-5.1.10-799733-standard` to form a new Image Profile, with a user defined name `Profile001`.

```
New-EsxImageProfile -CloneProfile $profiles[1] -Name "Profile001"

-Vendor VMware
```

Once the command has been successfully executed, you can issue the `Get-EsxImageProfile` command to list the newly created Image Profile.

```
PowerCLI C:\Program Files (x86)\VMware\Infrastructure\vSphere PowerCLI>
New-EsxImageProfile -CloneProfile $profiles[1] -Name "Profile001" -Vendor VMware

Name                      Vendor        Last Modified    Acceptance Level
----                      ------        -------------    ----------------
Profile001                VMware        8/2/2012 3:0...  PartnerSupported

PowerCLI C:\Program Files (x86)\VMware\Infrastructure\vSphere PowerCLI>
   Get-EsxImageProfile

Name                      Vendor        Last Modified    Acceptance Level
----                      ------        -------------    ----------------
ESXi-5.1.0-799733-no-tools  VMware, Inc.  8/2/2012 3:0...  PartnerSupported
Profile001                  VMware        8/2/2012 3:0...  PartnerSupported
ESXi-5.1.0-799733-standard  VMware, Inc.  8/2/2012 3:0...  PartnerSupported

PowerCLI C:\Program Files (x86)\VMware\Infrastructure\vSphere PowerCLI> _
```

Profile001 is now listed as one of the image profiles available

How it works...

The PowerCLI session will have a list of Image Profiles available from the added Offline Bundle. During the process of creating a new Image profile, you verify whether a Software Depot is already added to the PowerCLI session using the `$DefaultSoftwareDepots` command. If there are no Software Depots added then the command will silently exit to the PowerCLI prompt. If there are Software Depots added then it would list the depots added showing the path to its XML file. This is referred to as a **depot URL**.

The process of adding the Software Depot is pretty straightforward. First you need to make sure that you have downloaded the needed Offline Bundles to the server where you have PowerCLI installed. In this case it was downloaded and saved to the `C:\AutoDeploy-VIBs` folder. Once the Offline Bundle is downloaded and saved to an accessible location, you can then issue the command `Add-EsxSoftwareDepot` to add the Offline Bundle as a depot to the PowerCLI session.

Once the software has been added, you can then list all the Image Profiles available from the Offline Bundle. Then the chosen Image Profile is cloned to form a new Image Profile, which can then be customized by adding/removing VIBs. It can then be published as an Offline Bundle or an ISO.

See also

For instructions on how to export an Image Profile read the recipe *Exporting an Image Profile as an ISO or Offline Bundle*.

Removing an Image Profile

With vSphere Image Builder 5.1, we now have a cmdlet `Remove-EsxImageProfile` to remove an Image Profile. However, it is important to know that you can't remove an Image Profile from a read-only Software Depot. For example, the predefined Image Profiles available in the ESXi Offline Bundle cannot be removed. The `Remove-EsxImageProfile` cmdlet can only be used to remove/delete the Image Profiles created by the user.

How to do it...

The following procedure will guide you through the steps required to remove/delete Image Profiles:

1. Issue the command `Get-EsxImageProfile` to list all the available Image Profiles.

```
PowerCLI C:\Program Files (x86)\VMware\Infrastructure\vSphere PowerCLI>
    Get-EsxImageProfile

Name                          Vendor         Last Modified    Acceptance Level
----                          ------         -------------    ----------------
ESXi-5.1.0-799733-no-tools    VMware, Inc.   8/2/2012 3:0...  PartnerSupported
Profile001                    VMware         3/24/2013 4:...  PartnerSupported
ESXi-5.1.0-799733-standard    VMware, Inc.   8/2/2012 3:0...  PartnerSupported


PowerCLI C:\Program Files (x86)\VMware\Infrastructure\vSphere PowerCLI> _
```

2. Identify the Image Profile to be deleted. In this example, we will delete the Image Profile `Profile001`.

3. Issue the `Remove-EsxImageProfile` command to delete the Image Profile.

   Remove-EsxImageProfile -ImageProfile "Profile001"

```
PowerCLI C:\Program Files (x86)\VMware\Infrastructure\vSphere PowerCLI>
    Remove-EsxImageProfile -ImageProfile "Profile001"
PowerCLI C:\Program Files (x86)\VMware\Infrastructure\v    here PowerCLI> _
```

Command to remove/delete the Image Profile

Adding a VIB (software package) to an Image Profile

When there is a need to patch an Auto Deployed ESXi server with a newer device driver version, you will have to modify an Image Profile in use so you can add an updated driver to it. Once the driver VIBs have been added to the Image Profile, it can then be used to re-deploy the same ESXi servers.

To add VIBs to an ESXi Image Profile, the Image Profile should meet the following requirements:

- The Image Profile should not be set to 'read-only'.
- The Image Profile should not be assigned to hosts. This is because the Image Profiles assigned to hosts are 'locked', hence not allowing you to add VIBs to them.
- The VIBs shouldn't conflict with any of the existing VIBs in the profile. In case it does, it will not allow the addition of the VIB to the profile and a message indicating the same will be displayed at the PowerCLI console.
- Install VIBs from only one OEM vendor at a time.

 Image Builder will perform a validation when VMware VIBs are added. It does not perform any validation when Partner VIBs are added.

How to do it...

The following procedure will guide you through the steps required to add VIBs to an Image Profile.

It is a four-step process:

1. Verifying whether the Image Profile is read-only. If the Image Profile is read-only then it has to be cloned first before the VIBs can be added.
2. Adding the driver's Offline Bundle to the Image Builder.
3. Checking the availability of the needed software package (VIB).
4. Adding the needed VIB to the Image Profile.
5. Verifying whether the VIB has been added to the Image Profile.

Verifying whether the Image Profile is read-only

An Image Profile cannot be in read-only mode if it has to be modified. If a profile is in read-only mode then it will have to be cloned so that the `ReadOnly` attribute is set to `False` on the newly formed Image Profile.

To verify whether the Image Profile is read-only, display the details of the Image Profile by using the `format-list` cmdlet. Let's view the properties on the predefined Image Profile `ESXi-5.1.0-799733-standard` from the ESXi 5.1 Offline Bundle, by issuing the following commands:

`$profiles = GetEsxImageProfile`

`$profiles[2] | Format-List`

Note that it shows that the `ReadOnly` attribute/property of the Image Profile is set to `True`. This is generally the case with all the default/predefined Image Profiles in an Offline Bundle.

In the previous recipe, we had cloned the Image Profile `ESXi-5.1.0-799733-standard` to form `Profile001`. So the `ReadOnly` attribute on `Profile001` should be `False`. To verify, let's issue the following command:

`$profiles[1] | Format-List`

As expected, the `ReadOnly` property for the Image Profile `Profile001` is set to `False`. The profile can now be modified to add VIBs.

Adding the driver's Offline Bundle to the PowerCLI

To add driver VIBs to an Image Profile, you need to procure the driver's Offline Bundle and present that to the PowerCLI session using the `Add-ESXSoftwareDepot` command.

In this example, we will be adding the Offline Bundle containing the network function driver for the `Emulex OneConnect OCe10102 10GbE` adapter. The driver's Offline Bundle has been downloaded and saved to the `C:\AutoDeploy-VIBS\DriverVIBS` folder.

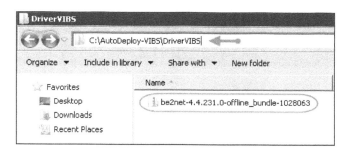

To add this Offline Bundle to the Software Depot, issue the following command:

```
Add-EsxSoftwareDepot -DepotUrl C:\AutoDeploy-VIBS\DriverVIBS\be2net-
4.4.231.0-ofline_bundle-1028063.zip
```

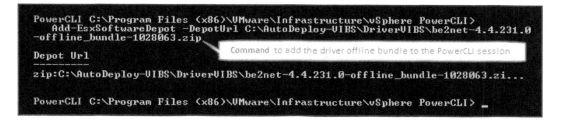

Checking the availability of the needed software package (VIB)

To verify whether the Offline Bundle has been successfully added and the VIB is available for use, issue the following command:

```
Get-EsxSoftwarePackage -Vendor "Emulex"
```

> [It is important to be aware of the package dependencies and conflicts.]

Package dependencies and conflicts information can be obtained by fetching more detailed information about the package, using the following command:

```
Get-EsxSoftwarePackage -Name net-be2net -Vendor "Emulex" | Format-List
```

Note the name, dependency, and conflicts information and source URL.

Adding the VIB to the Image Profile

Now that we know the name of the software package, issue the following command to add it to the Image Profile Profile001.

```
Add-EsxSoftwarePackage -ImageProfile Profile001 -SoftwarePackage net-
be2net
```

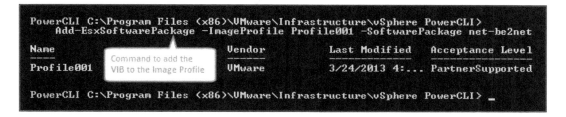

Verifying whether the VIB has been added to the Image Profile

To verify whether the software package has been added to the Image Profile, issue the following command:

```
Get-EsxImageProfile "Profile001" | Select -ExpandProperty viblist | where
{ $_.Name -like "net-be2net"}
```

Exporting an Image Profile as an ISO or Offline Bundle

The VMware PowerCLI session will not retain the Image Profile details upon its exit. If you need to preserve a customized profile that you created, you will have to export it as an Offline Bundle (ZIP or ISO). When you start a new VMware PowerCLI session, you could just add the Offline Bundle back to the Software Depot.

In this recipe we will learn how to export an Image Profile to an ISO or an Offline Bundle (ZIP archive).

How to do it...

The following procedures will guide you to export an Image profile to an ISO or a ZIP archive.

1. To export an existing Image Profile to an ISO, issue the following command:

   ```
   Export-EsxImageProfile -ImageProfile "Profile001" -ExportToIso
   -FilePath C:\AutoDeploy-VIBS\Exported\Profile001.iso
   ```

2. To export an existing Image Profile to an Offline Bundle, issue the following command:

   ```
   Export-EsxImageProfile -ImageProfile "Profile001" -ExportToBundle

   -FilePath C:\AutoDeploy-VIBS\Exported\Profile001.zip
   ```

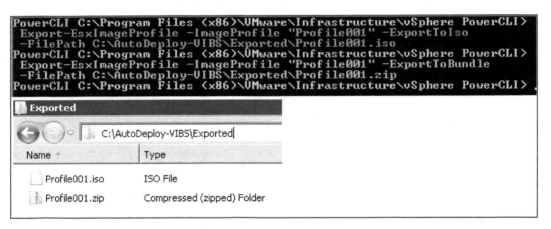

Creating an Image Profile from scratch

When creating an image from scratch, you would have to identify the software packages you need to be part of the image. This means that, unlike customizing an existing image, you will create a new one with only what you need, so that you don't have to go through the process of removing software packages from an Image Profile.

[It is important to pay careful attention to dependencies and acceptance levels when you create an Image Profile from scratch.]

How to do it...

The following procedure will guide you through the steps required to create an Image Profile from scratch:

1. Use the `Add-EsxSoftwareDepot` cmdlet to add all the needed Offline Bundles to the vSphere PowerCLI session.

   Add-EsxSoftwareDepot C:\AutoDeploy-VIBS\ESXi500-201111001.zip

```
PowerCLI C:\Program Files (x86)\VMware\Infrastructure\vSphere PowerCLI>
  Add-EsxSoftwareDepot C:\AutoDeploy-VIBS\VMware-ESXi-5.1.0-799733-depot.zip

Depot Url
--------
zip:C:\AutoDeploy-VIBS\VMware-ESXi-5.1.0-799733-depot.zip?index.xml

PowerCLI C:\Program Files (x86)\VMware\Infrastructure\vSphere PowerCLI>
```

2. Issue the command `Get-EsxSoftwareDepot` cmdlet to verify the Offline bundles have been added successfully.

```
PowerCLI C:\Program Files (x86)\VMware\Infrastructure\vSphere PowerCLI>
  Get-EsxSoftwareDepot

Depot Url
--------
zip:C:\AutoDeploy-VIBS\VMware-ESXi-5.1.0-799733-depot.zip?index.xml
file://custom/depot/index.xml
zip:C:\AutoDeploy-VIBS\DriverVIBS\be2net-4.4.231.0-offline_bundle-1028063.zi...

PowerCLI C:\Program Files (x86)\VMware\Infrastructure\vSphere PowerCLI>
```

Image Profile has been successfully added

3. Assign the output of the `Get-EsxSoftwareDepot` command to a user defined variable.

   $softdepot = Get-EsxSoftwareDepot

```
PowerCLI C:\Program Files (x86)\VMware\Infrastructure\vSphere PowerCLI>
  $softdepot = Get-EsxSoftwareDepot
PowerCLI C:\Program Files (x86)\VMware\Infrastructure\vSphere PowerCLI>
```

4. Use the `Get-EsxSoftwarePackage` cmdlet to list the needed software packages from the correct depot. Filter the results as needed and assign it to a variable. In this example, let's list all the packages released after `8/1/2012` (mm/dd/yyyy) by issuing the following command:

```
Get-EsxSoftwarePackage -SoftwareDepot $softdepot[0] -CreatedAfter
8/1/2012
```

5. Assign this output to a user-defined variable.

```
$afterAUG2012 = Get-EsxSoftwarePackage -CreatedAfter 8/1/2012
-SoftwareDepot $softdepot[0]
```

```
PowerCLI C:\Program Files (x86)\VMware\Infrastructure\vSphere PowerCLI>
$afterAUG2012 = Get-EsxSoftwarePackage -CreatedAfter 8/1/2012
-SoftwareDepot $softdepot[0]
PowerCLI C:\Program Files (x86)\VMware\Infrastructure\vSphere PowerCLI>
```

6. Use the `New-EsxImageProfile` cmdlet to create a new Image Profile by supplying a `Name`, a `Vendor`, and an `Acceptance Level`.

```
New-EsxImageProfile -NewProfile -Name "PostAUG2012PKG" -Vendor
"Abhilash" -SoftwarePackage $afterAUG2012 -AcceptanceLevel
CommunitySupported
```

```
PowerCLI C:\Program Files (x86)\VMware\Infrastructure\vSphere PowerCLI>
New-EsxImageProfile -NewProfile -Name "PostAUG2012PKG" -Vendor "Abhilash" -Sof
twarePackage $afterAUG2012 -AcceptanceLevel CommunitySupported

Name                     Vendor          Last Modified     Acceptance Level

PostAUG2012PKG           Abhilash        3/26/2013 1:...   CommunitySupp...

PowerCLI C:\Program Files (x86)\VMware\Infrastructure\vSphere PowerCLI> _
```

7. Export the Image Profile to an ISO or Offline Bundle.

```
Export-EsxImageProfile -ImageProfile "PostAUG2012PKG"
-ExportToBundle

-FilePath C:\AutoDeploy-VIBS\Exported\ PostAUG2012PKG.zip.
```

There's more...

When executing most of the PowerCLI commands, instead of specifying the parameters on the command line, you can also use the PowerShell's prompting mechanism to specify parameters.

See also

For information regarding the structure of an Image Profile, read the section *Structure of ImageProfile, SoftwarePackage, and ImageProfileDiff Objects* in the *vSphere Installation and Setup Guide for vSphere 5.1* at page 147, which can be found at:

```
http://pubs.vmware.com/vsphere-51/topic/com.vmware.ICbase/PDF/
vsphere-esxi-vcenter-server-511-installation-setup-guide.pdf
```

Applying an Image Profile to the host

The whole purpose of creating an Image Profile is to assign it to a host and apply it. This is particularly useful when performing upgrades or driver updates on Auto Deployed ESX Servers.

How to do it...

The following procedure will guide you through the steps required to assign and apply an Image Profile to an ESX Server.

1. Use the cmdlet `Connect-VIServer` to add the vCenter Server to the PowerCLI session.

```
Connect-VIServer -Server vcenter51 -User Administrator -Password
pass123
```

2. Use the `Get-VMHost` cmdlet to fetch a list of ESX Servers in `Maintenance` mode.

```
Get-VMHost -State Maintenance
```

```
PowerCLI C:\Program Files (x86)\VMware\Infrastructure\vSphere PowerCLI>
  ➜ Get-VMHost -State Maintenance

WARNING: 3 columns do not fit into the display and were removed.

Name                     ConnectionState  PowerState  NumCpu  CpuUsageMhz  CpuTotalMhz
192.168.193.21           Maintenance      PoweredOn   2       52           6414
vm02-esx51.vdescr...     Maintenance      PoweredOn   2       65           6414
vm01-esx51.vdescr...     Maintenance      PoweredOn   2       55           6414

PowerCLI C:\Program Files (x86)\VMware\Infrastructure\vSphere PowerCLI> _
```

We have found three servers in "Maintenance

3. Save the output of the `Get-VMHost` command to a user-defined variable.

```
$esxhost = Get-VMHost -State Maintenance
```

4. Use the `Apply-EsxImageProfile` cmdlet to apply the Image Profile to the ESX Servers.

```
Apply-ESXImageProfile -ImageProfile "Profile001" -Entities $esxhost
```

5. Check whether the ESX Server is compliant with the created profile.

```
Test-DeployRuleSetCompliance -VMHost $esxhost
```

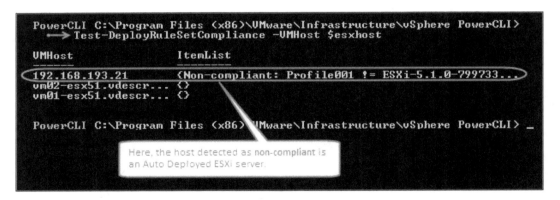

```
PowerCLI C:\Program Files (x86)\VMware\Infrastructure\vSphere PowerCLI>
  ➜ Test-DeployRuleSetCompliance -VMHost $esxhost

VMHost                   ItemList
192.168.193.21           {Non-compliant: Profile001 != ESXi-5.1.0-799733...}
vm02-esx51.vdescr...     {}
vm01-esx51.vdescr...     {}

PowerCLI C:\Program Files (x86)\VMware\Infrastructure\vSphere PowerCLI> _
```

Here, the host detected as non-compliant is an Auto Deployed ESXi server.

6. Assign the compliance test output to a user-defined variable and then use that to do the repair (remediate) operation.

```
$compliance_result = Test-DeployRuleSetCompliance -VMHost $esxhost
```

7. Use the cmdlet `Repair-DeployRuleSetCompliance` to remediate the ESXi server.

```
Repair-DeployRuleSetCompliance $compliance_result[0]
```

How it works...

Applying an Image Profile to an ESXi host is a method to update software changes, such as a driver update. The hosts need to be in 'maintenance mode' for this to be done. Although the host is checked for compliance and remediated, the software change (for example, the inclusion of a newer device driver version) is not immediately seen by the ESXi host. The ESXi host will start using the updated image only during its next reboot.

5
Creating and Managing VMFS Datastores

In this chapter we will cover the following:

- ▶ Viewing the LUNs presented to an ESXi host
- ▶ Viewing the datastores seen by the ESXi hosts
- ▶ Viewing the multipathing information of a LUN
- ▶ Creating a VMFS datastore
- ▶ Expanding/growing a VMFS datastore
- ▶ Extending a VMFS datastore
- ▶ Unmounting a VMFS datastore
- ▶ Mounting a VMFS datastore
- ▶ Deleting a VMFS datastore
- ▶ Upgrading VMFS-3 to VMFS-5
- ▶ Mounting VMFS on a snapshot LUN
- ▶ Resignaturing VMFS on a snapshot LUN
- ▶ Masking paths to a LUN
- ▶ Unmasking paths to a LUN
- ▶ Creating a datastore cluster
- ▶ Enabling Storage DRS

Introduction

To make the best use of your vSphere environment, your ESXi hosts need access to shared storage. The shared storage is generally presented to an ESXi host from a storage array (FC/iSCSI/NAS) and the storage entities are presented in the form of a LUN.

In this chapter, we learn how to create and manage VMFS datastores.

Datastore is the vSphere term for a volume presented to an ESXi. The volume can be a VMFS volume on a LUN or an NFS mount.

A LUN presented from an FC/iSCSI/DAS array can be formatted using the VMware's proprietary filesystem called VMFS. The following is a diagram from the *VMware vSphere®* *VMFS* technical whitepaper available at `http://www.vmware.com/files/pdf/vmfs-best-practices-wp.pdf`:

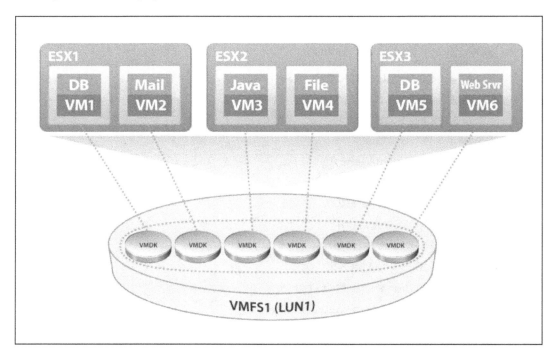

The current version of VMFS is Version 5. Unlike the traditional filesystems supported by the Windows/Linux operating system, VMFS will let more than one host have simultaneous read/write access to the volume. To make sure that a VM or its files are not simultaneously accessed by more than one ESXi host, VMFS uses an on-disk locking mechanism called **distributed locking**.

VMFS-5 supports:

▶ A maximum volume size of 64 TB

▶ A uniform block size of 1 MB

▶ Smaller sub-blocks of size 8 KB

To place a lock on a VMFS volume, vSphere will either have to using a SCSI-2 reservation or, if the array supports VAAI, it can then use **ATS** (**Atomic Test and Set**) primitive.

The VMware KnowledgeBase article on *vSphere 5.x FAQ for VMFS-5* available at `http://kb.vmware.com/kb/2003813` should be a good read.

A **NFS volume**, unlike a VMFS volume, is not formed by formatting a RAW LUN with the VMFS filesystems. NFS volumes are just mounts created to access the shared folders on an NFS server. The filesystems on these volumes are dependent on the type of NFS server.

vSphere API for Array Integration (**VAAI**) is a set of primitives that enable an ESXi host to offload certain operations to the storage array. For more information regarding VAAI refer the VMware KnowledgeBase article available at `http://kb.vmware.com/kb/1021976`.

Viewing the LUNs presented to an ESXi host

During the initial phase of adding shared storage to an ESXi host, LUN devices are presented to the servers. It is essential to make sure that the LUNs presented using the storage/fabric management software are visible to the ESXi host. Once available, it can then be used to create datastores as needed.

How to do it...

In this section, we will learn how to view the LUN information on ESXi hosts using the vSphere Web Client user interface.

All the LUNs presented to the ESXi host can be viewed in the following three ways:

▶ Using the vSphere Web Client to View the LUNs

▶ Using the ESXi Console to view the LUN information.

▶ Using the vSphere Client

 We will not be discussing the vSphere Client method for any of the tasks in this chapter or the book unless it is necessary.

Using the vSphere Web Client to view LUNs

The following procedure will help you view the LUN information using the vSphere Web Client:

1. Use the vSphere Web Client to connect to the vCenter Server.

2. Navigate to **Home | Hosts and Clusters | Cluster | Hosts**.

3. Click on **ESXi Host** to view its page.

4. Go to the **Manage** tab and then click on **Storage**. This will show you all the LUNs seen by that ESXi host:

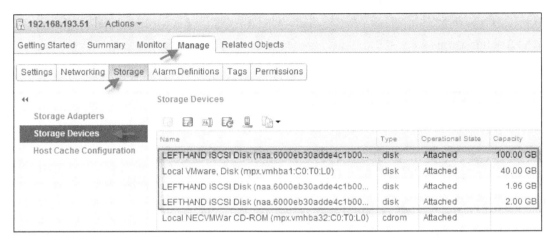

Using the ESXi Console to view the LUN information

The following procedure will help you view the LUN information using the ESXi CLI:

1. Connect to the ESXi Console using the console access methods such as **ILO** (for HP) or **DRAC** (for Dell). You could also SSH to the ESXi host using tools such as putty or SecureCRT.

   The download page for putty is available at `http://www.chiark.greenend.org.uk/~sgtatham/putty/download.html`.

   The download page for secure CRT is available at `http://www.vandyke.com/download/securecrt/download.html`.

   For SSH to work, SSH should be enabled. For instructions on how to enable SSH on the ESXi host, refer to the VMware KnowledgeBase article available at `http://kb.vmware.com/kb/2004746`.

2. At the ESXi console, login as `root`.

3. Issue to the following command:

```
esxcfg-scsidevs -u
```

The command will list all the devices seen by the ESXi host, with their NAA and VML IDs:

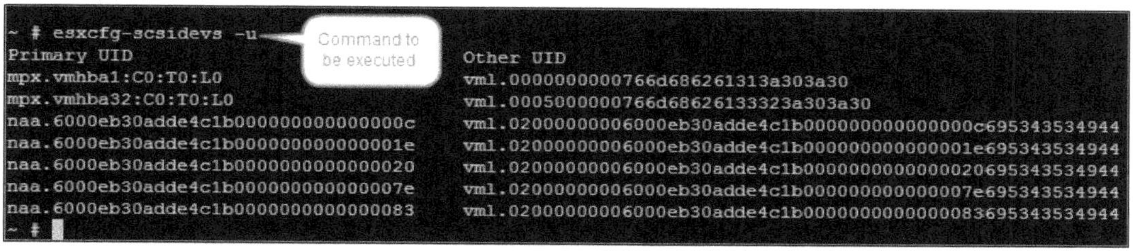

Viewing the datastores seen by the ESXi host

LUNs formatted with the VMFS or NFS mounts are generally referred to as datastores. All the datastores seen by an ESXi host can be viewed separately at the vCenter Web Client GUI or using a CLI command.

How to do it...

In this section we will learn both the GUI and CLI methods to list the datastores seen by an ESXi host.

Using the vSphere Web Client to view LUNs

The following steps will help you view the datastores from the vSphere Web Client GUI:

1. Use the vSphere Web Client to connect to the vCenter host.

2. Navigate to **Home** | **Hosts and Clusters**. Click on the cluster first and then on the host of your choice.

3. Click on the particular ESXi host to view its page.

4. Click on the **Related Objects** tab and then the **Datastores** sub tab to view all the datastores:

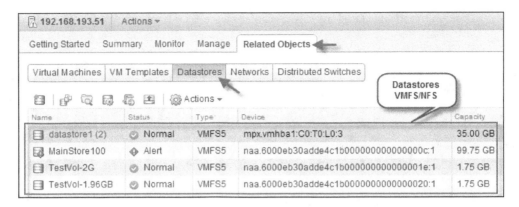

Using the ESXi Console to view the datastores

The following steps will help you list the datastores seen by the ESXi host:

1. Connect to the ESXi Console using the ILO (for HP), DRAC (for Dell), or SSH to the ESXi sever using tools such as putty or SecureCRT.

2. At the ESXi console, login as `root`.

3. Issue the following command to list the datastores:

   ```
   esxcli storage filesystem list
   ```

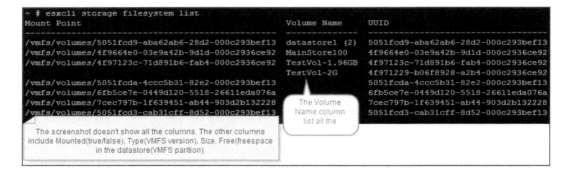

Viewing the multipathing information of a LUN

SAN storage presented to the ESXi hosts should be highly available. This can be achieved by configuring multiple connectivity paths between the ESXi hosts and the SAN storage. Once configured correctly, these paths can then be used to either failover or load balance I/O.

A path to a LUN includes the **HBA (Host Bus Adapter)**/initiator, the fabric/network switches, and the storage controllers at the array. The availability of a path will be affected if any of these hardware components along the path stop functioning.

Storage multipathing on ESXi hosts is achieved with the help of a framework of APIs called **PSA (Pluggable Storage Architecture)**. These APIs can be used by the storage vendors to write their own **Multipathing Plugins (MPP)**. At the time of writing this book, there were three third-party MPP available:

- ▶ EMC PowerPath

  `http://www.emc.com/storage/powerpath/powerpath.htm`

- ▶ Dell EqualLogic MEM for iSCSI Multipathing

  `http://www.dellstorage.com/WorkArea/DownloadAsset.aspx?id=3064`

- ▶ Veritas Dynamic Multipathing for VMware

  `http://www.symantec.com/dynamic-multi-pathing-for-vmware`

The default multipathing plugin on an ESXi host is called **Native Multipathing Plugin (NMP)**. The NMP adds support for all the supported storage arrays in the VMware compatibility list.

The NMP has two sub plugins called the **Storage Array Type Plugin (SATP)** and **Path Selection Plugin (PSP)**. VMware does include the SATP and PSP associations for all tested and supported storage arrays, in the form of claim rules.

SATP detects the path state and handles path failover whereas the PSP determines which available physical path should be used for sending the I/O.

How to do it...

Information regarding the multipathing for a LUN can be viewed either from the vSphere Web Client GUI or using ESXi CLI.

Using the vSphere Web Client GUI

The following steps will help you view the multipathing information using the vSphere Web Client:

1. Use the vSphere Web Client to connect to the vCenter Server.

2. Navigate to **Home | Storage**:

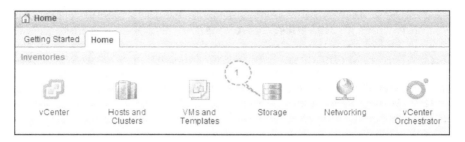

3. From the inventory list, click on the datastore whose multipathing needs to be verified:

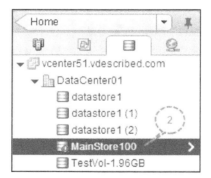

4. Navigate to **Manage | Settings | Connectivity and Multipathing** to view all the ESXi severs to which the datastore is accessible:

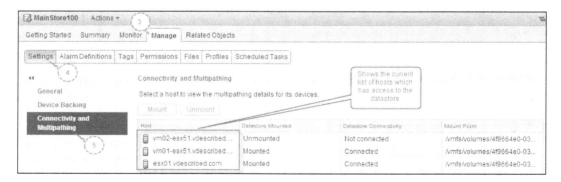

5. Highlight the host for which you would like to verify the details and click on **Edit Multipathing**:

6. Once you have clicked on the **Edit Multipathing** option, it should bring up a separate window showing the mutipathing details of the LUN on that host:

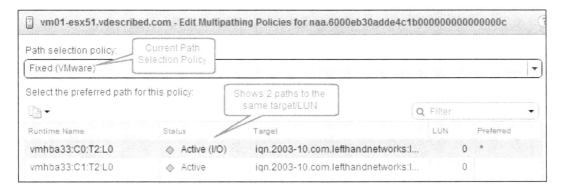

Using the esxcfg-mpath

1. Connect to the ESXi Console using the console access methods such as ILO (for HP) or DRAC (for Dell). You could also SSH to the ESXi host using tools such as putty or SecureCRT.

2. Login as `root` to perform the task.

3. Issue the `esxcfg-mpath -L -d <NAA ID of the LUN>` command to view the multipathing information, for example:

   esxcfg-mpath -L -d naa.6001438005dec70f0000900001000000

```
~ # esxcfg-mpath -L -d naa.6001438005dec70f0000900001000000
vmhba4:C0:T0:L1 state:active naa.6001438005dec70f0000900001000000 vmhba4 0 0 1 NMP active san
 fc.2000b499baaa8af3:1000b499baaa8af3 fc.50001fe1501add40:50001fe1501add48
vmhba3:C0:T1:L1 state:active naa.6001438005dec70f0000900001000000 vmhba3 0 1 1 NMP active san
 fc.2000b499baaa8aef:1000b499baaa8aef fc.50001fe1501add40:50001fe1501add4d
vmhba3:C0:T0:L1 state:active naa.6001438005dec70f0000900001000000 vmhba3 0 0 1 NMP active san
 fc.2000b499baaa8aef:1000b499baaa8aef fc.50001fe1501add40:50001fe1501add49
vmhba4:C0:T3:L1 state:active naa.6001438005dec70f0000900001000000 vmhba4 0 3 1 NMP active san
 fc.2000b499baaa8af3:1000b499baaa8af3 fc.50001fe1501add40:50001fe1501add4a
vmhba4:C0:T2:L1 state:active naa.6001438005dec70f0000900001000000 vmhba4 0 2 1 NMP active san
 fc.2000b499baaa8af3:1000b499baaa8af3 fc.50001fe1501add40:50001fe1501add4e
vmhba4:C0:T1:L1 state:active naa.6001438005dec70f0000900001000000 vmhba4 0 1 1 NMP active san
 fc.2000b499baaa8af3:1000b499baaa8af3 fc.50001fe1501add40:50001fe1501add4c
~ #
```

Creating a VMFS datastore

Once we have presented LUNs to an ESXi host for it to be used as a storage container for virtual machine data, it needs to be formatted using VMFS. Creating a VMFS datastore is the process of formatting a LUN and creating a VMFS partition on it. This section of the chapter discusses both the methods involved in creating a new VMFS datastore.

How to do it...

We can create a VMFS datastore using the following two methods:

- Using the **New Datastore** wizard

- Using `vmkfstools -C`

Make sure you have the NAA ID, LUN ID and the Size of the LUN that you have presented to the ESXi host. This is to make sure that you don't end up using an unintended LUN. Do a rescan on the HBAs for the ESXi to detect the presented LUN.

Using the New Datastore wizard

The following steps will help you create a VMFS volume on a LUN identified using the **New Datastore** wizard of the vSphere Web Client GUI:

1. Use the vSphere Web Client to connect to the vCenter Server.
2. Navigate to **Home | Storage**.
3. With the **Datacenter** object selected, navigate to **Related Objects | Datastores**:

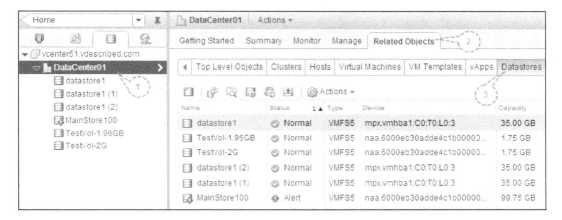

4. Click on the **New Datastore** icon:

5. In the **New Datastore** wizard, supply a **Datastore Name** and click on **Next**:

6. Select **VMFS** as the filesystem type and click on **Next**:

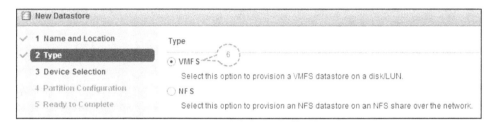

7. Select a host from the list to which the LUN was presented. This will show all the RAW LUNs seen by the selected ESXi host:

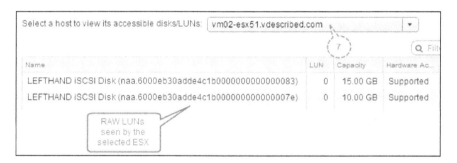

8. Identify and select the RAW LUN you intend to create the VMFS volume on and click on **Next**:

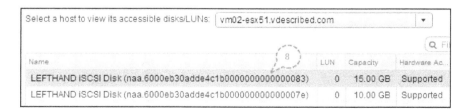

9. Choose the VMFS version and click on **Next**:

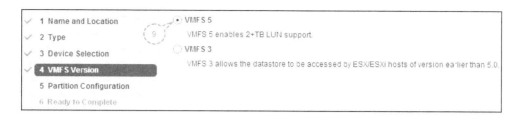

 We have chosen **VMFS 5** since the LUN is presented only to
ESXi hosts version 5 and above.

10. In the partition configuration screen, select **Use all available Partitions** and
click on **Next**.

The datastore size slider can be used to adjust the size of the VMFS partition that will
be created on the LUN. In this example, we have slid the size to 10 GB:

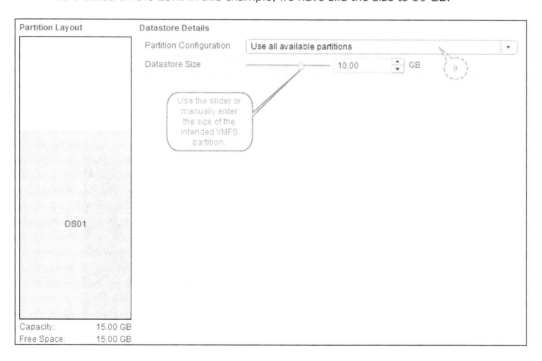

11. In the **Ready to Complete** screen, review the information and click on **Finish**:

Using vmkfstools

Keep the NAA ID, LUN ID, and the size of the LUN handy. This is to make sure that you don't end up using an unintended LUN.

For this example, the NAA ID of the LUN is `naa.6000eb30adde4c1b0000000000000083`.

1. Fetch the details of the device corresponding to the NAA ID, using the following command, and make a note of the Devfs path

   Syntax:

   ```
   esxcli storage core device list -d <NAA ID of the device>
   ```

   Command to be executed:

   ```
   esxcli storage core device list -d naa.6006048cea95042c3e14f1524e7
   0e300
   ```

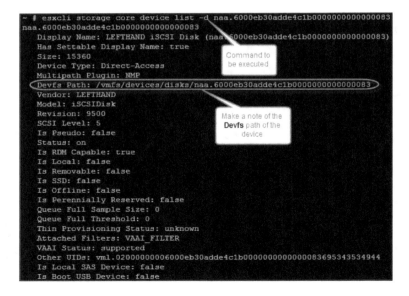

DevFs is nothing but the "console device" path of the LUN.

2. Verify the partition table of the device, using the following command:

Syntax:

```
partedUtil getptbl "Devfs Path of the device"
```

Command to be executed:

```
partedUtil getptbl /vmfs/devices/disks/ naa.6000eb30adde4c
1b0000000000000083
```

From the output, we can see that this is a blank LUN with a CHS value of 394[cylinders], 255[heads], 63[sectors per track], and 6340608 sectors.

3. Get the GUID value for VMFS by issuing the following command:

```
partedUtil  showGuids
```

```
~ # partedUtil showGuids
 Partition Type        GUID
 vmfs                  AA31E02A400F11DB9590000C2911D1B8
 vmkDiagnostic         9D27538040AD11DBBF97000C2911D1B8
 vsan                  381CFCCC728811E092EE000C2911D0B2
 VMware Reserved       9198EFFC31C011DB8F78000C2911D1B8
 Basic Data            EBD0A0A2B9E5443387C068B6B72699C7
 Linux Swap            0657FD6DA4AB43C484E50933C84B4F4F
 Linux Lvm             E6D6D379F50744C2A23C238F2A3DF928
 Linux Raid            A19D880F05FC4D3BA006743F0F84911E
 Efi System            C12A7328F81F11D2BA4B00A0C93EC93B
 Microsoft Reserved    E3C9E3160B5C4DB8817DF92DF00215AE
 Unused Entry          00000000000000000000000000000000
~ #
```

4. Create a new partition on the device using the following command:

Syntax:

```
partedUtil setptbl "Devfs path of the device" DiskLabel "partNum
startSector endSector type/guid attribute"
```

Syntax with the `type`/`guid` attributes values:

```
partedUtil setptbl "Devfs path of the device" DiskLabel "partNum
startSector endSector AA31E02A400F11DB9590000C2911D1B8 0"
```

From step 2, we know that the number of sectors available is `31457280`. But since the start sector is set to `128`, the end sector value will be `31457280` minus `128` which is `31457152`.

Hence the command to be executed is:

```
partedUtil setptbl "/vmfs/devices/disks/ naa.6000eb30adde4c
1b0000000000000083" gpt "1 128 31457152 AA31E02A400F11DB9590000C29
11D1B8 0"
```

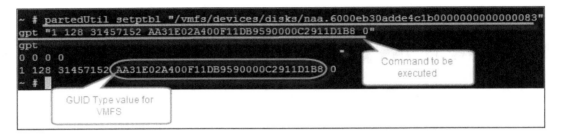

5. Create VMFS volume on the device partition, using the following command:

    Syntax:

    ```
    vmkfstools --createfs vmfs5 --blocksize 1M --setfsname datastore
    name  Devfs path of the device:Partition Number
    ```

    ```
    vmkfstools -C --createfs [vmfs3|vmfs5]
                  -b --blocksize #[mMkK]
                  -S --setfsname fsName
          -Z --spanfs span-partition
          -G --growfs grown-partition
       deviceName

          -P --queryfs -h --humanreadable
          -T --upgradevmfs
       vmfsPath
    ```

Command to be executed:

```
vmkfstools --createfs vmfs5 --blocksize 1M --setfsname NewDS /
vmfs/devices/disks/ naa.6000eb30adde4c1b0000000000000083:1
```

```
~ # vmkfstools --createfs  vmfs5 --blocksize 1M --setfsname DS01 /vmfs/devices
/disks/naa.6000eb30adde4c1b0000000000000083:1
create fs deviceName:'/vmfs/devices/disks/naa.6000eb30adde4c1b0000000000000083
:1', fsShortName:'vmfs5', fsName:'DS01'
deviceFullPath:/dev/disks/naa.6000eb30adde4c1b0000000000000083:1 deviceFile:na
a.6000eb30adde4c1b0000000000000083:1
Checking if remote hosts are using this device as a valid file system. This ma
y take a few seconds...
Creating vmfs5 file system on "naa.6000eb30adde4c1b0000000000000083:1" with bl
ockSize 1048576 and volume label "DS01".
Successfully created new volume: 5080368b-6ec44f54-5d45-000c293bef13
~ #
```

> Command to be executed

> Indicates successful creation of the filesystem

There's more...

`AA31E02A400F11DB9590000C2911D1B8` is the GUID type value for a VMFS partition. The decimal type is `251` and the hexadecimal type is `0xFB`.

The start sector value for a VMFS partition can also set to `2048`. I have used `128` for demonstration purposes only. In fact, when you create a datastore using the **Add Storage** wizard, it sets the start sector to `2048` by default. The default start sector for VMFS-3 was `128` and it works with VMFS-5 as well.

Expanding/growing a VMFS datastore

It is likely that you run out of free space on a VMFS volume over time, as you end up deploying more and more VMs on it. Fortunately, accommodating additional free space on a VMFS volume is possible. But this requires that the LUN either has free space left on it or has been expanded.

In this section, we will learn how to increase the size of a VMFS volume on a LUN that has been expanded or already has RAW free space on it.

How to do it...

We can expand a VMFS datastore by using the following two methods:

- Using the **Increase Datastore Capacity** wizard
- Using `vmkfstools`

Before attempting to grow the VMFS datastore, issue a rescan on the HBAs to make sure that the ESXi sees the increased size of the LUN.

Make a note of the NAA ID, LUN number, and size of the LUN backing the VMFS datastore that you are trying to expand/grow.

Using the Increase Datastore Capacity wizard

We will go through the following process to expand an existing VMFS datastore:

1. Use the vSphere Web Client to connect to the vCenter Server.

2. Navigate to **Home | Storage**.

3. With the **Datacenter** object selected, navigate to **Related Objects | Datastores**:

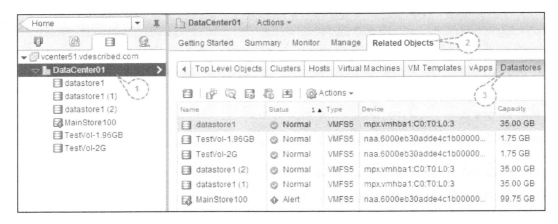

4. Right-click on the datastore you intend to expand and click on **Increase Datastore Capacity...**:

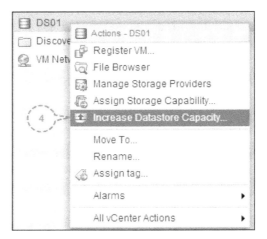

5. Select the LUN backing the datastore and click on **Next**:

6. Use the **Partition Configuration** drop-down menu to select the free space left in **DS01** to expand the datastore:

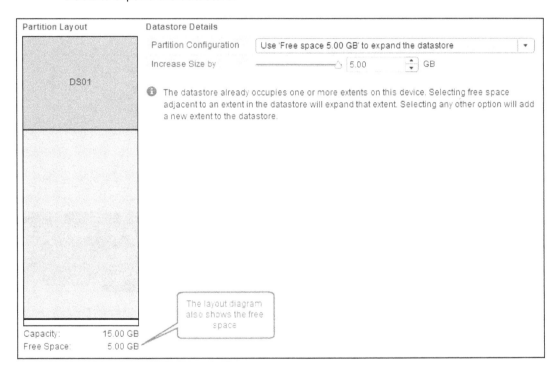

7. On the **Ready to Complete** screen review the information and click on **Finish** to expand the datastore:

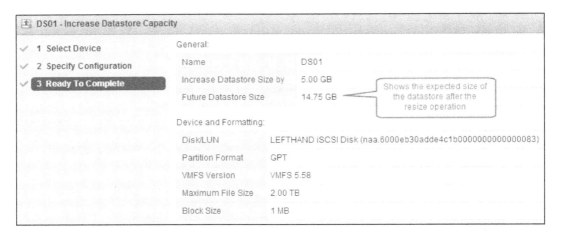

Using vmkfstools

The following steps will help you expand/grow the VMFS volume:

1. Identify the datastore you want to expand, using the following command, and make a note of the corresponding NAA ID.

   Command to be executed:

   ```
   esxcli storage vmfs extent list
   ```

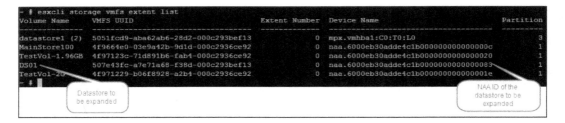

The NAA ID corresponding to the DS01 datastore in this example is naa.6000eb30a dde4c1b0000000000000083.

2. Verify whether ESXi sees the new size of the LUN backing the datastore, by issuing the following command:

```
esxcli storage core device list -d naa.6000eb30adde4c
1b0000000000000083
```

3. Get the current partition table information using the following:

Syntax:

```
partedUtil getptbl "Devfs Path of the device"
```

Command to the issued:

```
partedUtil getptbl /vmfs/devices/disks/ naa.6000eb30adde4c
1b0000000000000083
```

4. To calculate the new last sector value, moving the last sector value closer to the total sector value is necessary to use the additional space. The formula to calculate the last sector value is as follows:

Total number of Sectors minus Start sector value = Last Sector Value

So the last sector value to be used is:

(31457280 – 2048) = 31455232

5. Resize the VMFS partition, by issuing the following:

Syntax:

```
partedUtil resize "Devfs Path" PartitionNumber NewStartingSector
NewEndingSector
```

Command to be executed:

```
partedUtil resize /vmfs/devices/disks/ naa.6000eb30adde4c
1b0000000000000083 1 2048 31455232
```

```
~ # partedUtil resize /vmfs/devices/disks/naa.6000eb30adde4c1b0000000000000083 1 2048 31455232
~ # partedUtil getptbl /vmfs/devices/disks/naa.6000eb30adde4c1b0000000000000083
gpt
1958 255 63 31457280
1 2048 31455232 AA31E02A400F11DB9590000C2911D1B8 vmfs 0
~ #
```

> Resize command with the new END SECTOR Value "31455232"

> Partition table now shows the new END SECTOR Value "31455232"

6. Issue the following command to grow the VMFS partition:

Syntax:

```
vmkfstools --growsfs <Devfs Path: Partition Number> <Same Devfs
Path: Partition Number>
```

Command to be executed:

```
vmkfstools --growfs /vmfs/devices/disks/ naa.6000eb30adde4c
1b0000000000000083:1 /vmfs/devices/disks/ naa.6000eb30adde4c
1b0000000000000083:1
```

```
~ # vmkfstools --growfs /vmfs/devices/disks/naa.6000eb30adde4c1b0000000000000083:1
/vmfs/devices/disks/naa.6000eb30adde4c1b0000000000000083:1
~ #
```

> Note that the source and the destinaltion devFS value is the same since we are growing volume on the same LUN and NOT extending onto a different LUN.

Once the command is executed successfully, it will take you back to the root prompt. There is no on-screen output for this command.

How it works...

Expanding a VMFS datastore refers to the act of increasing its size within its own extent. This is possible only if there is free space available immediately after the extent. The maximum size of a LUN is 64 TB and hence the maximum size of a VMFS volume is also 64 TB.

The virtual machines hosted on this VMFS datastore can continue to be in the powered-on state while this task is being accomplished.

Extending a VMFS datastore

The *Expanding/growing a VMFS datastore* recipe discusses the method involved in increasing the size of a datastore on the same LUN backing the VMFS volume, which is only possible if the LUN has unused free space on it.

You can run into a situation wherein there is no unused space on the LUN backing the VMFS volume, but your datastore ran out of space. Fortunately, vSphere supports spanning of the VMFS volume onto a new LUN. This process of spanning a VMFS volume on to another LUN is called "extending a VMFS datastore". In this chapter, we will learn two methods that can be used to extend a datastore onto a new RAW LUN.

Getting ready

To get started with this recipe, we need to:

- Present a new blank LUN to the ESXi host
- Issue a re-scan on the HBAs
- Make a note of the following:
    - The NAA ID, LUN number, and size of the new blank LUN
    - The NAA ID, LUN number, and size of the new blank LUN backing the datastore you are intending to extend

How to do it...

We can extend the size of a VMFS datastore by using the following two tools:

- The **Increase Datastore Capacity** wizard
- The `vmkfstools`

Using the Increase Datastore Capacity wizard

The following steps will guide you through the process of extending a VMFS datastore using the vSphere Web Client.

1. Use the vSphere Web Client to connect to the vCenter Server.
2. Navigate to **Home** | **Storage**.

3. With the **Datacenter** object selected, navigate to **Related Objects | Datastores**:

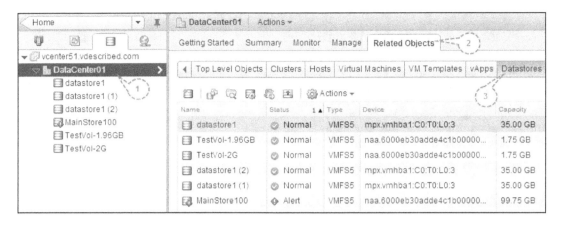

4. Right-click on the datastore you intend to expand and click on **Increase Datastore Capacity...**:

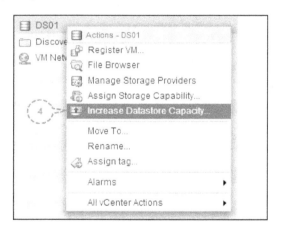

5. Select the RAW LUN that is available to extend the datastore onto it:

6. Select **Use all available partitions** from the partition configuration dropdown box, select a suitable size for use, and click on **Next**:

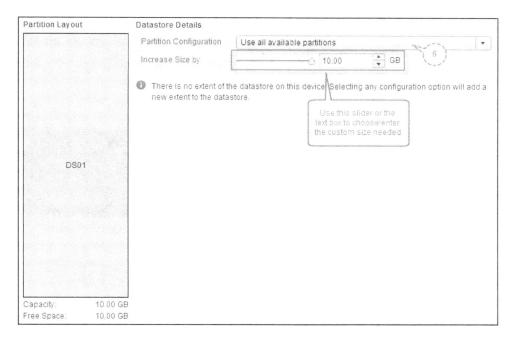

7. Review the details in the **Ready to Complete** screen and click on **Finish**:

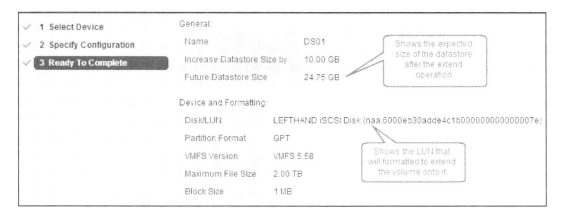

Using vmkfstools

In this section, we will learn how to use the CLI to extend the VMFS volume. To demonstrate, we have presented a 5 GB blank LUN to the ESXi hosts.

The following are steps that you should be following, to extend a VMFS volume using CLI:

1. Identify the datastore you want to expand, using the following command, and make a note of the corresponding NAA ID:

   ```
   esxcli storage vmfs extent list
   ```

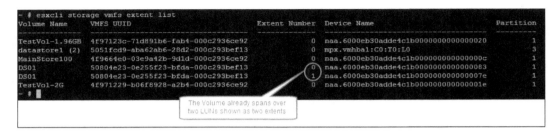

2. Verify the list of extents used currently by the volume using the following command:

   ```
   Vmkfstools -P /vmfs/volumes/DS01
   ```

3. Get the Devfs/console device path of the VMFS datastore and the LUN that will be used as an extent for the datastore.

   Syntax:

   ```
   esxcli storage core device list -d <NAA ID of the device>
   ```

   From step 2, we know that the NAA ID of DS01 is naa.6000eb30adde4c 1b0000000000000083.

   Command to be executed:

   ```
   esxcli storage core device list -d naa.6000eb30adde4c
   1b0000000000000083
   ```

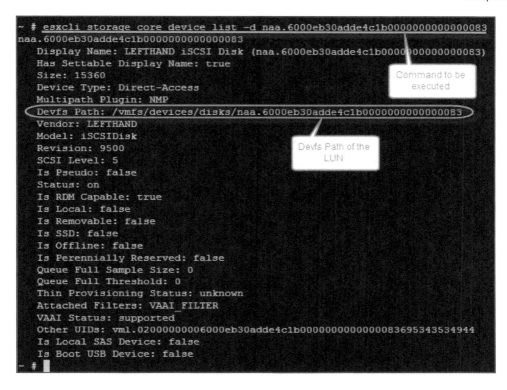

4. If you don't have the NAA ID of the new blank LUN handy, we can look up the LUN info using the size:

```
esxcfg-scsidevs -l | grep "Size: 5" -B 3 -A 3
```

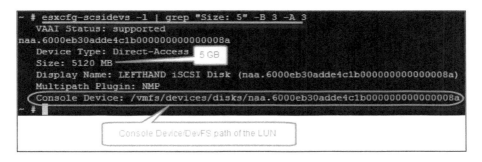

5. Get the partition table information of the first extent (LUN) backing the datastore `DS01` and the new 5 GB blank LUN.

   Commands to be executed:

   ```
   partedUtil getptbl /vmfs/devices/disks/naa.6000eb30adde4c
   1b0000000000000083
   ```

   ```
   partedUtil getptbl /vmfs/devices/disks/naa.6000eb30adde4c1b0000000
   00000008a
   ```

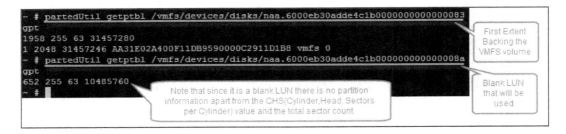

6. Create a partition of the type VMFS on the new extent-LUN (blank LUN being used to add an extent to the datastore `DS01`). To find the end sector value use the following formula:

   Total number of Sectors minus Start sector value = Last Sector Value

   10485760 (total sectors) - 2048(start sector) = 10483712 (end sector value)

   Command to be executed:

   ```
   partedUtil setptbl " /vmfs/devices/disks/naa.6000eb30adde4c1b00000
   0000000008a" gpt "1 2048 10483712 AA31E02A400F11DB9590000C2911D1B8
   0"
   ```

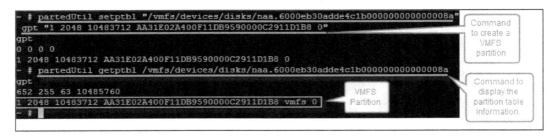

7. Extend the VMFS volume on to the new partition on the extent-LUN by issuing the following:

   Syntax:

   ```
   vmkfstools --spanfs <partition on the extent-LUN> <partition on
   the VMFS volume LUN>
   ```

Here the partitions are specified by using the following format:

`<Devfs Path>:< Partition Number>`

Command to be executed:

vmkfstools --spanfs /vmfs/devices/disks/naa.6006048c00e2cfeec4f4df
7b671fd574:1 /vmfs/devices/disks/naa.6006048c99a9f599493c52669bb2
ea63:1

Enter *0* for `_yes` when prompted to confirm the action:

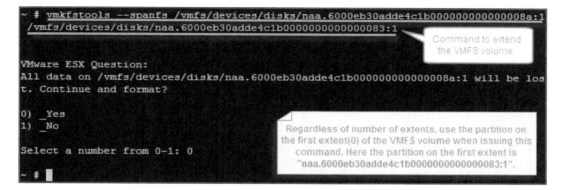

> Regardless of the number of extents, use the partition on the first extent (0) of the VMFS volume when issuing this command. Here the partition on the first extent is `naa.6000eb30adde4c1b0000000000000083:1`. And the first argument to the command is the partition on the LUN onto which VMFS will be extended.

8. Issue the command `vmkfstools -P` to check if the volume now spans to more than one extent. In this case, it should span across to three extents in all:

How it works...

Unlike expanding/growing a VMFS volume, extending a volume will make the volume span across multiple LUNs; it is done by adding extents to the VMFS volume.

Here, an extent refers to the primary partition on the extent-LUN. A VMFS datastore can span across a maximum of 32 LUN extents.

The size of the extent can now be greater than 2 TB, the limit being the maximum VMFS volume size of 64 TB.

[The VMs running on the volume can still remain powered-on while this task is being accomplished.]

There's more...

The first extent on the VMFS volume contains the metadata for the entire set of extents. If the LUN with the first extent is lost, then you would end up losing data on all the other dependent extents.

Unmounting a VMFS datastore

It is recommended to unmount a VMFS datastore before the LUN that is backing it is un-presented from an ESXi host.

It is advised that you take care of the following before you proceed with the unmount operation:

▶   All the VMs should be migrated off to a different datastore

▶   The datastore should be removed from a datastore cluster

▶   The datastore should remain unmanaged by **SDRS (Storage DRS)**

▶   **SIOC (Storage I/O Control)** should be disabled for the datastore

▶   The datastore should not be in use as a vSphere HA Heartbeat datastore.

How to do it...

A VMFS volume can be unmounted from the vSphere Web Client GUI or by using esxcli at the ESXi console.

Using the vSphere Web Client GUI to unmount

vSphere Web Client can be used to unmount a datastore. It is particularly useful when you have to unmount the datastore from multiple ESXi hosts.

The following steps will guide you through the process of unmounting a VMFS datastore using the vSphere Web Client:

1. Use the vSphere Web Client to connect to the vCenter Server.
2. Navigate to **Home** | **Storage**.
3. With the **Datacenter** object selected, navigate to **Related Objects** | **Datastores**:

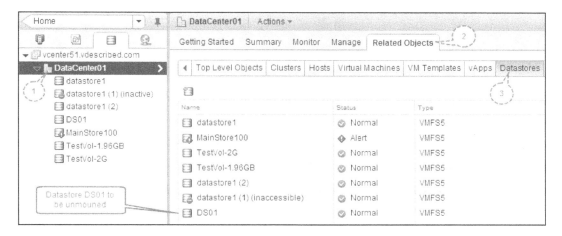

4. Right-click on the datastore you wish to unmount and navigate to **All vCenter Actions** | **Unmount Datastore**:

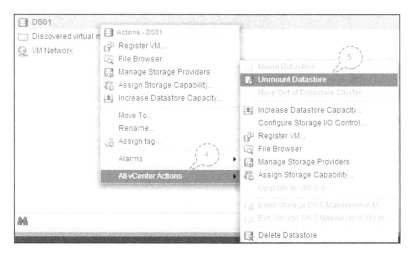

5. Select the ESXi host that you wish to unmount the volume from and click on **OK**:

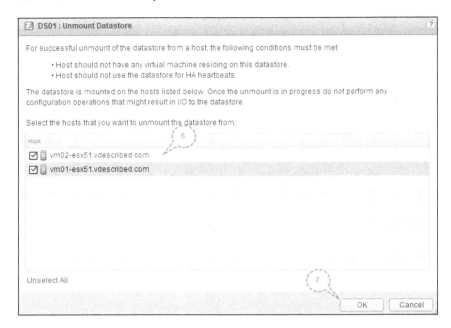

6. Verify the **Recent Tasks** pane to make sure that the volume unmount operation has completed successfully on the selected ESXi hosts:

Using esxcli to unmount

vSphere esxcli can be used to unmount the VMFS datastore. But keep in mind that in this way it is done at a per host level. If you need to unmount the datastore this way on more than one ESXi host, then you will have to SSH/console into each of those ESXi hosts and issue the unmount command.

In this section, we will learn how to unmount a VMFS datastore using the CLI. The following procedure will guide you through the steps required to unmount a VMFS volumes using the CLI:

1. View all the volumes available using the following command:

```
esxcli storage filesystem list
```

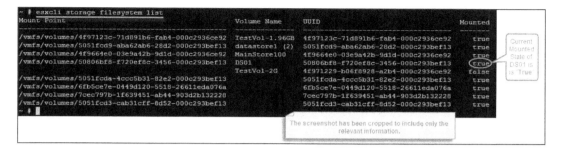

2. Unmount the datastore by issuing the following:

Syntax:

```
esxcli storage filesystem unmount --volume-label <name of the datastore>
```

Command to be executed:

```
esxcli storage filesystem unmount --volume-label DS01
```

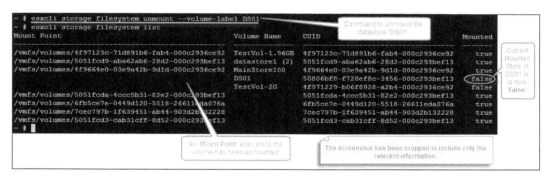

 In the previous screenshot, we have executed a second command to list the volumes.

Mounting a VMFS datastore

In this recipe you will see how a previously unmounted VMFS datastore can be mounted back to the ESXi host.

How to do it...

The mount operation can be performed from the vSphere Web Client GUI or using the CLI.

Using the vSphere Web Client UI to mount

The following procedure will guide you through the steps required to mount a VMFS volume using the vSphere Web Client:

1. Use the vSphere Web Client to connect to the vCenter Server.

2. Navigate to **Home** | **Storage**.

3. With the **Datacenter** object selected, navigate to **Related Objects** | **Datastores** and find the datastore in the **unmounted** state:

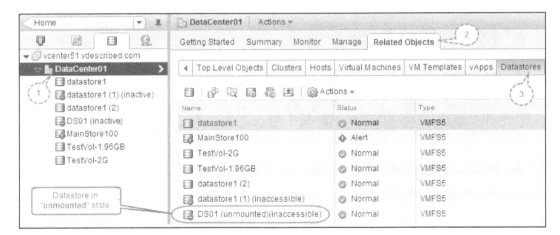

4. Right-click on the unmounted datastore and navigate to **All vCenter Actions** | **Mount Datastore**:

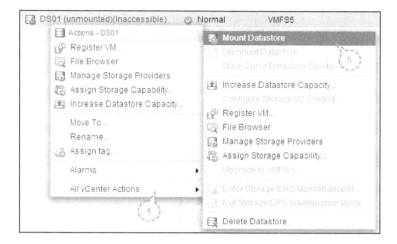

5. Select the ESXi host to which the volume should be mounted and click on **OK** to initiate the mount operation:

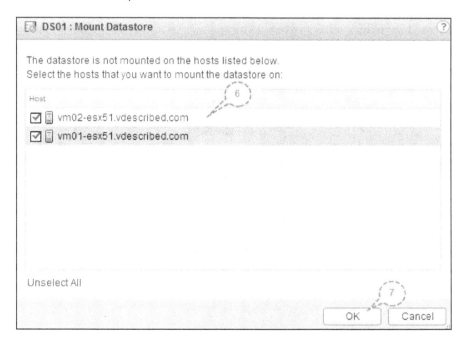

6. Verify the **Recent Tasks** pane to make sure that the mount operations have been successfully completed on all the ESXi hosts that were selected:

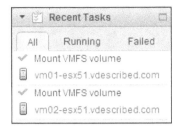

Using esxcli to mount an unmounted volume

vSphere esxcli can also be used to mount an unmounted volume but the CLI operation can only be performed on a per-host basis. If a volume needs to be mounted in this way to multiple hosts then you will have to SSH/console into each of those hosts and issue the mount command.

The following procedure will help you mount an unmounted VMFS datastore:

1. View all the volumes available on the host, which should also list the volumes in the unmounted state, using the following command:

   ```
   esxcli storage filesystem list
   ```

2. Issue the following to mount the volume:

   Syntax:

   ```
   esxcli storage filesystem mount --volume-label <name of the
   datastore>
   ```

Command to be executed:

```
esxcli storage filesystem mount --volume-label DS01
```

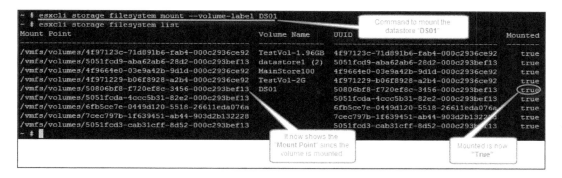

Deleting a VMFS datastore

Unlike the unmount operations, the delete operation will destroy all the data on the datastore. Once done, you cannot revert this operation. Hence, make sure to move all the virtual machine data currently on the datastore to another datastore.

How to do it...

The following procedure will guide you to delete a datastore from the vSphere Web Client:

1. Use the vSphere Web Client to connect to the vCenter Server.

2. Navigate to **Home | Storage**.

3. With the **Datacenter** object selected, navigate to **Related Objects | Datastores** operation and identify the VMFS datastore to be deleted:

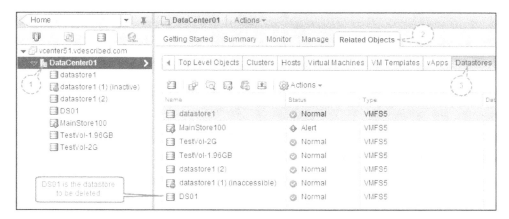

4. Right-click on the datastore to be deleted and navigate to **All vCenter Actions** | **Delete Datastore**:

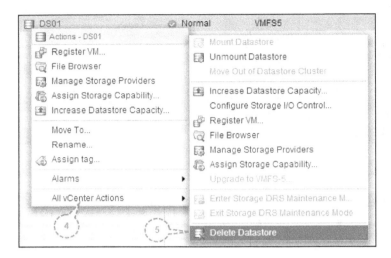

5. Click on **Yes** in the **Confirm Delete Datastore** dialog box:

6. Verify the **Recent Tasks** pane, which should show a **Remove datastore** completed successfully:

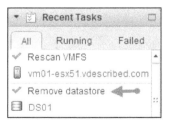

Upgrading VMFS-3 to VMFS-5

There are several enhancements added to VMFS Version 5. Knowing these enhancements will definitely motivate you to upgrade to this version. Nevertheless, the upgrade process is non-disruptive.

Although this is an in-place upgrade, you should take the following precautions before you do the upgrade:

 ▸ Backup the virtual machines on the volume or migrate them off to a different datastore

 ▸ Make sure that there are no ESX 3.*x* or ESX 4.*x* servers in the environmert accessing the same datastore.

The *VMware® vSphere® VMFS-5 Upgrade Considerations* whitepaper explains more about VMFS-5 enhancement and the upgrade considerations, available at `http://www.vmware.com/files/pdf/techpaper/VMFS-5_Upgrade_Considerations.pdf`.

How to do it...

VMFS upgrade can be done in the following two ways:

 ▸ By using the vSphere Web Client GUI
 ▸ By using vmkfstools

Upgrading the VMFS using vSphere Web Client GUI

The following procedure will guide you through the steps required to upgrade a VMFS datastore:

1. Use the vSphere Web Client to connect to the vCenter Server.
2. Navigate to **Home** | **Storage**.

3. With the **Datacenter** object selected, navigate to **Related Objects | Datastores** and identify the VMFS datastore to be upgraded:

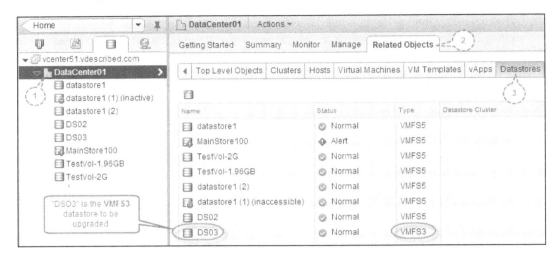

4. Right-click on the VMFS-3 datastore and navigate to **All vCenter Actions | Upgrade to VMFS-5...**:

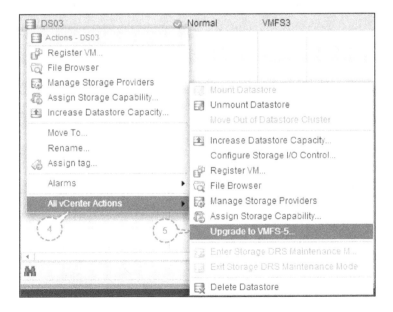

5. Select the datastore from the list and click on OK:

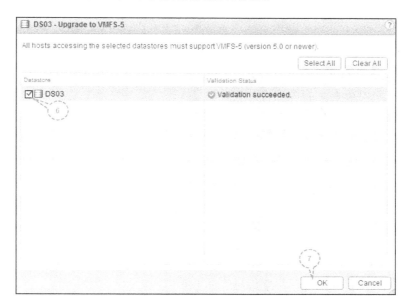

6. Verify the **Recent Tasks** pane to make sure that the **Upgrade VMFS** tasks have been successfully completed:

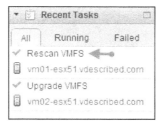

Upgrading using vmkfstools

A VMFS-3 volume can also be upgraded from the ESXi CLI. The tool used for this purpose is `vmkfstools`. The following procedure will guide you through the usage of commands to accomplish VMFS-3 to VMFS-5 upgrade:

1. Identify the VMFS-3 volume to be upgraded by issuing the following command:

    ```
    esxcli storage filesystem list
    ```

2. Query the filesystem details for reference using the following command (this step is not mandatory):

    ```
    vmkfstools -Ph -v10 /vmfs/volumes/DS03
    ```

3. Issue the following command to perform the upgrade:

```
vmkfstools --upgradevmfs /vmfs/volumes/DS03/
```

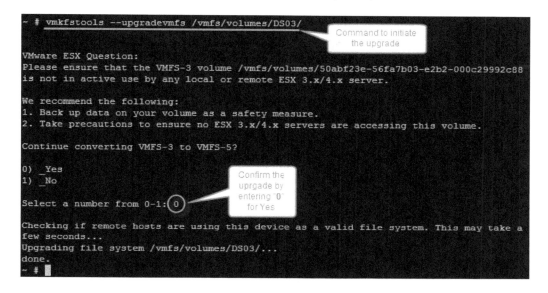

4. Verify that the upgrade is complete by querying the filesystem again:

```
vmkfstools -Ph -v10 /vmfs/volumes/DS03
```

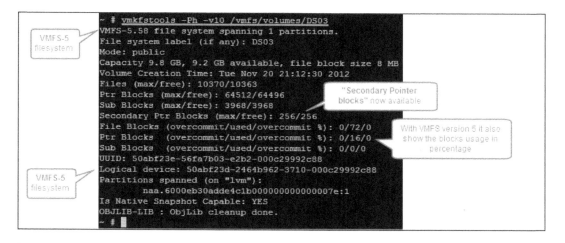

How it works...

The upgrade process—regardless of the method—is in-place. The VMFS-5 data structures are appended to the existing VMFS-3 data structures, making the process seamless.

However, a few things don't change even after an upgrade from VMFS3 to VMFS5:

- ▶ The uniform 1 MB block size is not implemented during the upgrade. The upgrade will retain the VMFS-3's block size value.
- ▶ The sub-block size will also remain unchanged at 64 KB.
- ▶ VMFS-3's limit on the maximum number of files per datastore will be retained.
- ▶ The MBR partition type will be retained until the volume grows beyond 2 TB.
- ▶ The VMFS partitions start sector value is also retained at 128.

 To fully utilize VMFS-5's features, you can create a new VMFS-5 volume, migrate the VMs from the VMFS-3 volume to the VMFS-5 volume, and then destroy the VMFS-3 volume.

Mounting VMFS on a snapshot LUN

Some environments maintain copies of the production LUNs as a backup, by replicating them. These replicas are exact copies of the LUNs that are already presented to the ESXi hosts. If, for any reason, a replicated LUN is presented to an ESXi host, then the host will not mount the VMFS volume on the LUN. This is a precaution to prevent data corruption.

 You can however force-mount such a volume. But you need to make sure that the original LUN is unpresented.

How to do it...

The act of mounting a snapshot volume can be done in two ways:

- ▶ Using the vSphere Web Client's **New Datastore** wizard
- ▶ Using esxcli

Using the New Datastore wizard

The following procedure will guide you through the steps required to mount a VMFS volume on a replica LUN or a LUN detected as snapshot:

1. Use the vSphere Web Client to connect to the vCenter Server.
2. Navigate to **Home | Storage**.
3. With the **Datacenter** object selected, navigate to **Related Objects | Datastores** and click on the **New Datastore** icon:

4. In the **New Datastore** wizard, there is no need to supply a new name, since it will not be used. Leave it at its default and click on **Next**:

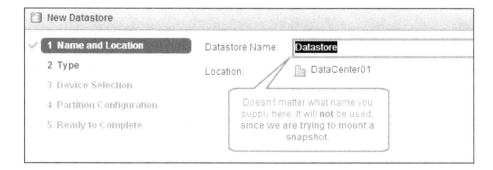

5. Select the filesystem type as **VMFS** and click on **Next**:

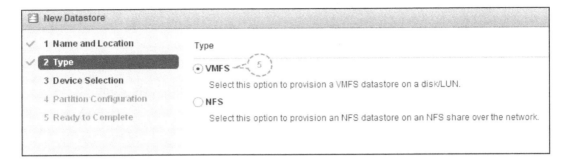

6. Select an ESXi host from the list to populate the LUN devices seen by it, select the LUN marked as **Snapshot Volume**, and click on **Next**:

7. Select the option **Keep existing signature** and click on **Next**:

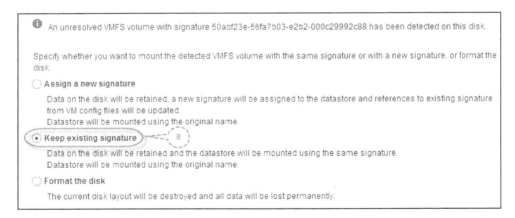

8. Review the **Ready to Complete** screen and click on **Finish** to mount the volume:

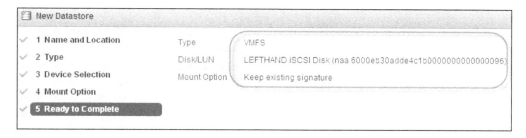

9. Verify in the task pane that the task **Resolved VMFS volumes** has completed successfully:

Using ESXi CLI

A volume on a snapshot LUN can also be mounted using the ESXi CLI commands.

The following procedure will guide you through the steps required to mount such a volume:

1. List all the volumes detected as snapshots by the ESXi host using the following command:

   ```
   esxcli storage vmfs snapshot list
   ```

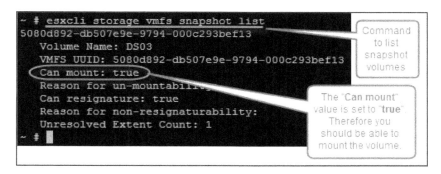

2. Issue the following command to mount the snapshot volume:

Syntax:

```
esxcli storage vmfs snapshot mount -n -l "Volume_Label"
```

Command to be executed:

```
esxcli storage vmfs snapshot mount -n -l "DS03"
```

 The -n option in the previous command will do a non-persistent mount of the volume. This means that you will not find the LUN mounted after a host reboot. Issuing the command without the -n switch will do a persistent mount of the volume, which means the LUN will remain mounted, even after a reboot.

How it works...

Every VMFS volume when created gets assigned a UUID that is unique. When a LUN is replicated, it would still have the same UUID, because the UUID is stored in the VMFS's superblock. When an ESXi host detects that a different LUN has the same UUID, it marks the volume on that LUN as a snapshot and by default will not mount it. The decision to mount the VMFS is left to the administrator.

If an administrator chooses to mount the snapshot volume to an ESXi host which already has the original volume presented to it, then he will have to unpresent the original volume and then mount the snapshot volume.

Resignaturing VMFS on a snapshot LUN

Resignaturing is done when you know that the LUN that has been detected as a snapshot is indeed a snapshot and you intend to use it going forward. For example, if the LUN is not presented at a DR site, and if you do not want to retain the same UUID, then you can choose to resignature the VMFS volume.

How to do it...

Resignaturing can be done in two ways:

▶ Using the vSphere Web Client's **New Datastore** wizard
▶ Using esxcli

Using the New Datastore wizard

Much like mounting a VMFS volume on a snapshot LUN, as discussed in the previous section, you can follow the same new storage wizard to resignature the snapshot LUN.

The following procedure will guide you through the steps required to mount a VMFS volume on a replica of a LUN or a LUN detected as snapshot:

1. Use the vSphere Web Client to connect to the vCenter Server.

2. Navigate to **Home | Storage**.

3. With the **Datacenter** object selected, navigate to **Related Objects | Datastores** and click on the **New Datastore** icon.

4. In the **New Datastore** wizard, there is no need to supply a new name, since it will not be used. Leave it at its default name and click on **Next**.

5. Select the filesystem type as **VMFS** and click on **Next**.

6. Select an ESXi host from the list to populate the LUN devices seen by it, select the LUN marked as **Snapshot Volume**, and click on **Next**.

 For screenshots until step 6, refer to the previous recipe, *Mounting VMFS on a snapshot LUN*. Screenshots were not included in this section because they are exactly the same.

7. Select the option **Assign a new signature** and on click on **Next**:

ⓘ An unresolved VMFS volume with signature 5080d892-db507e9e-9794-000c293bef13 has been detected on this disk.

Specify whether you want to mount the detected VMFS volume with the same signature or with a new signature, or format the disk.

⦿ Assign a new signature ---(8)

    Data on the disk will be retained, a new signature will be assigned to the datastore and references to existing signature from VM config files will be updated.
    Datastore will be mounted using the original name.

○ Keep existing signature

    Data on the disk will be retained and the datastore will be mounted using the same signature.
    Datastore will be mounted using the original name.

○ Format the disk

    The current disk layout will be destroyed and all data will be lost permanently.

---

8. Review the **Ready to Complete** screen and click on **Finish**:

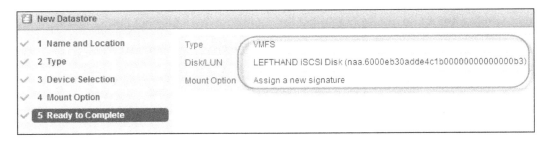

9. Verify the **Recent Tasks** pane to make sure that the task **Resignature unresolved VMFS volume** has completed successfully:

Using ESXi CLI

The VMFS volume can also be resignatured using CLI commands. The following procedure will guide you through the commands to be executed to resignature a snapshot volume:

1. List all the VMFS volumes detected as snapshots, using the following command:

```
esxcli storage vmfs snapshot list
```

```
~ # esxcli storage vmfs snapshot list
50ac2480-34aab91d-fb4b-000c29992c88
   Volume Name: DS-15G
   VMFS UUID: 50ac2480-34aab91d-fb4b-000c29992c88
   Can mount: true
   Reason for un-mountability:
   Can resignature: true
   Reason for non-resignaturability:
   Unresolved Extent Count: 1
~ #
```

2. Issue the following command to resignature the volume:

Syntax:

```
esxcli storage vmfs snapshot resignature -l <volume_Label>
```

Command to be executed:

```
esxcli storage vmfs snapshot resignature -l "DS-15G"
```

How it works...

You would choose to resignature the volume if you are conscious of the fact that you are not presenting the LUN to a DR site.

The resignature operation will update the VMFS super block with a new UUID. The datastore aliases are prepended with `snap-`:

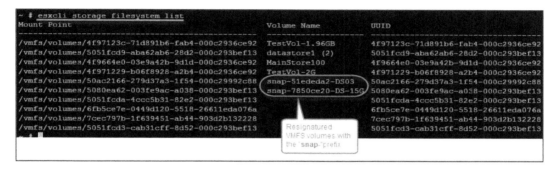

The following screenshot shows the vSphere Web Client GUI listing the resignatured volumes, prepended with the text `snap-`:

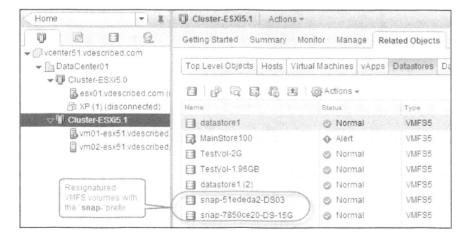

You will have to power-off the running VM, rename the datastores as needed, and then re-register the VMs, since the inventory registrations use the absolute path (with the UUID) to the VMX file.

Masking paths to a LUN

You can remove access to a LUN by masking all of its paths to the ESXi host. This is done at the ESXi host, by using the MASK_PATH PSA plugin to claim the paths to the intended LUN.

In this recipe we will learn how to create a claim rule to mask paths to a chosen LUN.

How to do it...

The following procedure will help you mask paths to a LUN:

1. Get the NAA ID of the LUN that needs to be masked by issuing the following command. The command will list all the NAA IDs seen by the ESXi:

   ```
   esxcfg-scsidevs -u
   ```

2. Get the multipathing information of the LUN by issuing the following command:

   Syntax:

   ```
   esxscfg-mpath -l -d <naa-id of the LUN>
   ```

   Command to be executed:

   ```
   esxcfg-mapth -l -d naa.6000eb30adde4c1b0000000000000112
   ```

```
~ # esxcfg-mpath -l -d naa.6000eb30adde4c1b0000000000000112
iqn.1998-01.com.vmware:localhost-6ec490dc-00023d000002,iqn.2003-10.com.lefthandnetwo
   Runtime Name: vmhba33:C1:T2:L0
   Device: naa.6000eb30adde4c1b0000000000000112
   Device Display Name: LEFTHAND iSCSI Disk (naa.6000eb30adde4c1b0000000000000112)
   Adapter: vmhba33 Channel: 1 Target: 2 LUN: 0
   Adapter Identifier: iqn.1998-01.com.vmware:localhost-6ec490dc
   Target Identifier: 00023d000002,iqn.2003-10.com.lefthandnetworks:labmainstroage:2
   Plugin: NMP
   State: active
   Transport: iscsi
   Adapter Transport Details: iqn.1998-01.com.vmware:localhost-6ec490dc
   Target Transport Details: IQN=iqn.2003-10.com.lefthandnetworks:labmainstroage:274

iqn.1998-01.com.vmware:localhost-6ec490dc-00023d000001,iqn.2003-10.com.lefthandnetwo
   Runtime Name: vmhba33:C0:T2:L0
   Device: naa.6000eb30adde4c1b0000000000000112
   Device Display Name: LEFTHAND iSCSI Disk (naa.6000eb30adde4c1b0000000000000112)
   Adapter: vmhba33 Channel: 0 Target: 2 LUN: 0
   Adapter Identifier: iqn.1998-01.com.vmware:localhost-6ec490dc
   Target Identifier: 00023d000001,iqn.2003-10.com.lefthandnetworks:labmainstroage:2
   Plugin: NMP
   State: active
   Transport: iscsi
   Adapter Transport Details: iqn.1998-01.com.vmware:localhost-6ec490dc
   Target Transport Details: IQN=iqn.2003-10.com.lefthandnetworks:labmainstroage:274
```

3. Create a claim rule for each of the paths to the LUN by issuing the following command:

    Syntax:

    ```
    esxcli storage core claimrule add -r <rule number> -t location -A
    <hba> -C <channel number> -L <LUN Number> -P MASK_PATH
    ```

    Command to be executed:

    ```
    esxcli storage core claimrule add -r 120 -t location -A vmhba33 -C
    1 -L 0 -P MASK_PATH
    ```

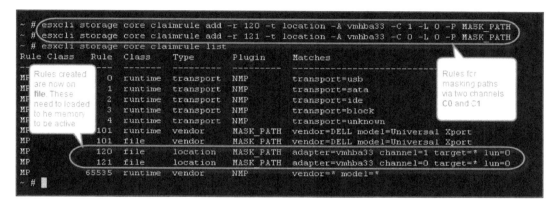

4. Load the rules on the file into the memory by issuing the following command:

    ```
    esxcli storage core claimrule load
    ```

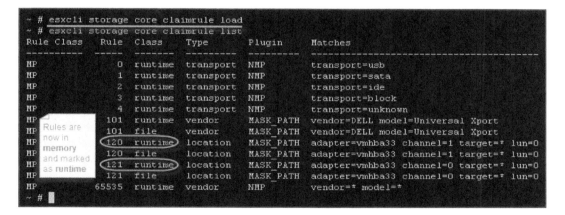

5. Reclaim the paths for MASK_PATH from NMP by issuing the following command.

Syntax:

```
esxcli storage core claiming reclaim -d <NAA ID of the LUN>
```

Command to be executed:

```
esxcli storage core claiming reclaim -d naa.6000eb30adde4c
1b0000000000000112
```

```
~ # esxcli storage core claiming reclaim -d naa.6000eb30adde4c1b0000000000000112
~ # esxcfg-mpath -l -d naa.6000eb30adde4c1b0000000000000112
Unknown device naa.6000eb30adde4c1b0000000000000112
~ #
```

esxcfg-mpath -l is now unable to find the device. Paths have been sucessfully masked

Command to reclaim the paths from NMP to MASK_PATH

Unmasking paths to a LUN

It is possible to unmask paths to a LUN. This is done by deleting the claim rules that are using the MASK_PATH and unclaiming the paths from the plugin. Understanding how the paths to a LUN are masked will be a good starting point for this task. Refer to the recipe *Masking paths to a LUN* before you begin.

How to do it...

The following procedure will help you mask paths to a LUN:

1. Identify the claim rules corresponding to the LUN and remove them.

Syntax:

```
esxcli storage claimrule remove -r <rule ID>
```

We know that the rule IDs are `120` and `121` from the recipe *Masking paths to a LUN*.

Commands to be executed:

```
esxcli storage core claimrule remove -r 120
esxcli storage core claimrule remove -r 121
```

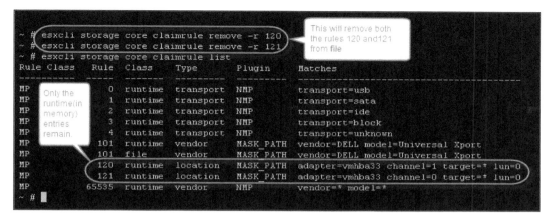

2. Now that the rules are deleted from file, reload the claim rules to the memory to remove the runtime entries. Issue the following command to load the rules in the memory:

    ```
    esxcli storage core claimrule load
    ```

    The run time entries for 120 and 121 will be removed from memory because they don't have a corresponding file entry.

3. Unclaim all the paths for the LUN from the MASK_PATH plugin by issuing the following command:

    Syntax:

    ```
    esxcli storage core claiming unclaim -t location -A <HBA> -C
    <Channel> -L <LUN ID> -P MASK_PATH
    ```

    Commands to be executed:

    ```
    esxcli storage core claiming unclaim -t location -A vmhba33 -C 0
    -L 0 -P MASK_PATH
    esxcli storage core claiming unclaim -t location -A vmhba33 -C 1
    -L 0 -P MASK_PATH
    ```

4. Issue a rescan on the HBAs.

    Syntax:

    ```
    esxcfg-rescan <HBA>
    ```

    Command to be executed:

    ```
    esxcfg-rescan vmhba33
    ```

5. Verify the LUN visibility by listing all the paths corresponding to it.

   Syntax:

   ```
   esxscfg-mpath -l -d <naa-id of the LUN>
   ```

   Command to be executed:

   ```
   esxcfg-mapth -l -d naa.6000eb30adde4c1b0000000000000112
   ```

Creating a datastore cluster

Datastores presented to the ESXi servers can be grouped together into a single I/O and capacity pool called the **datastore cluster**. The main purpose of creating a datastore cluster is to leverage Storage DRS's functionality to load-balance datastore space utilization and I/O capacity.

For datastores to be in a datastore cluster, they should meet the following requirements:

▸ The datastores in a datastore cluster should only be accessible to ESXi hosts from a single datacenter

▸ A datastore cluster cannot contain both VMFS and NFS volumes

In this recipe we will learn how to create a datastore cluster.

How to do it

The following procedure will guide you through the steps required to create a datastore cluster:

1. Use the vSphere Web Client to connect to the vCenter Server.

2. Navigate to **Home** | **Storage**:

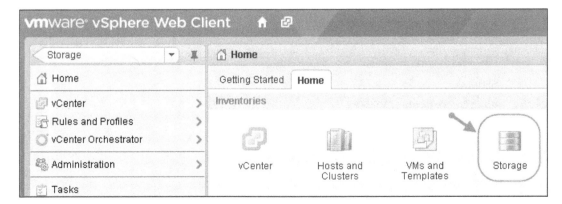

3. Right-click on the datacenter in which you intend to create the datastore cluster and click on **New Datastore Cluster...** to bring up the **New Datastore Cluster** wizard:

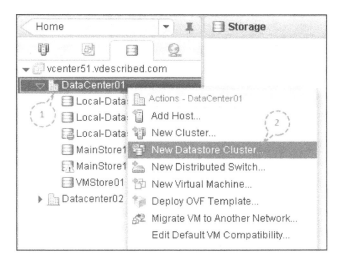

4. In the **New Datastore Cluster** wizard, specify a datastore cluster name. By default, the wizard will enable SDRS on the new datastore cluster. You will notice that the checkbox **Turn ON Storage DRS** is preselected. Since we are not enabling Storage DRS now, uncheck the box **Turn ON Storage DRS** and click on **Next** to continue:

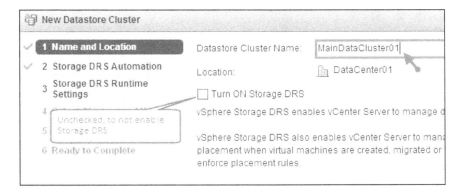

5. The next screen will prompt you to select **Storage DRS Automation** levels. Since we have chosen not to enable Storage DRS, we do not have to modify any of these settings. Click on **Next** to continue.

6. The next screen will prompt you to select **Storage DRS Runtime Settings**. Since we have chosen not to enable Storage DRS, do not modify any of the runtime settings. Click on **Next** to continue.

7. On the next screen select the ESXi host cluster or individual hosts and click on **Next** to continue:

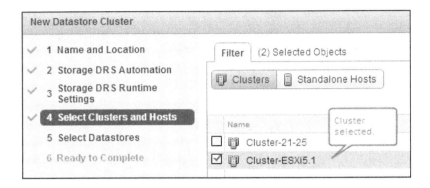

8. The next screen will by default list only the datastores connected to all the selected ESXi hosts. In this case we had selected a cluster, so datastores connected to all the ESXi hosts in the cluster will be listed for selection. Select the datastores and click on **Next** to continue:

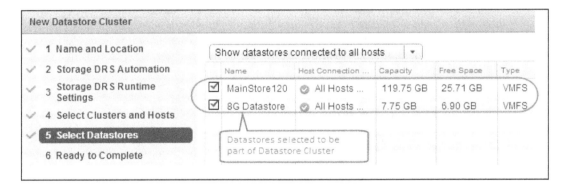

9. In the **Ready to Complete** screen, review the configuration and click on **Finish** to create the datastore cluster.

10. The **Recent Tasks** pane should show a **Move datastores into a datastore cluster** task completed successfully:

How it works...

A datastore cluster created without enabling Storage DRS is just a container for the selected datastores. Although Storage DRS is not enabled, the statistics will be collected but there will be no load balancing.

The **New Datastore Cluster** wizard will by default list only those datastores that are connected to all the selected ESXi hosts. This is because, SDRS wouldn't be able to migrate the VM storage on to datastores inaccessible to the ESXi hosts.

When you choose datastores to be part of a datastore cluster, it is a best practice to choose similar datastores. The similarities include, RAID level, VAAI, storage protocols (FC, iSCSI, NFS), storage type (SSDs, SATA, and so on). It is also considered a best practice to choose datastores of the same size.

Enabling Storage DRS

Storage DRS is a mechanism to balance space utilization and I/O load on datastores in a datastore cluster by migrating (Storage vMotion) the VMs. Storage DRS can only be enabled on a datastore cluster. To learn how to create a datastore cluster read the recipe *Creating a datastore cluster*.

It also influences the initial placement of the VMs on the datastores. For Storage DRS's I/O load balancing to work, all the hosts accessing the datastores should be of ESXi Version 5.0 or above. Also, the cluster cannot contain replicated and non-replicated datastores.

In this recipe we will learn how to enable Storage DRS.

How to do it...

The following procedure will guide you through the steps required to enable SDRS on a datastore cluster:

1. Use the vSphere Web Client to connect to the vCenter Server.

2. Navigate to **Home | Storage**.

3. Select the datastore cluster from the left pane; navigate to the **Manage** tab and then to the **Settings** sub tab:

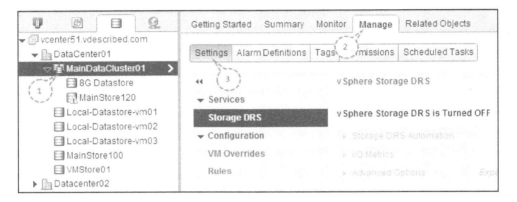

4. Click on **Storage DRS** and click on **Edit...** to bring up the **Edit Storage DRS Settings** window:

5. In the **Edit Storage DRS Settings** windows, select the checkbox **Turn ON vSphere Storage DRS**:

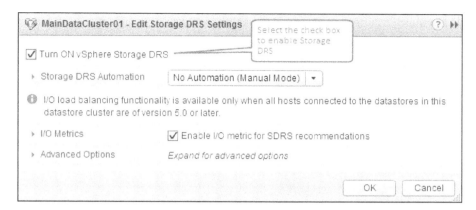

6. Click on **Storage DRS Automation** to expand the automation settings and choose an automation level and the space utilization threshold. By default the automation level is set to **No Automation (Manual Mode)**. You can also select **Fully Automated**. The space utilization threshold is set to **80%** by default. Do not change the slider position unless it is necessary:

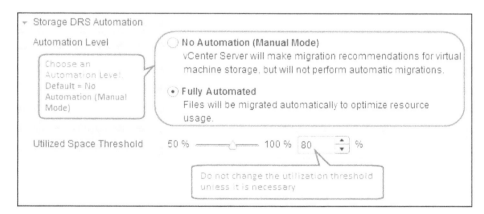

7. Click on **I/O Metrics** to expand the I/O metrics settings. Choose to enable/disable I/O load balancing for Storage DRS, selecting/deselecting the checkbox **Enable I/O metric for SDRS recommendations**. It is enabled by default. Also select **I/O Latency Threshold**. The default value is **15** ms (milliseconds):

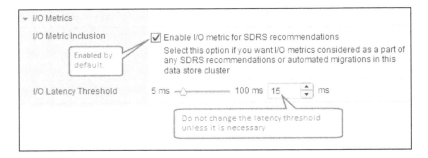

8. Click on **Advanced Options** to expand the window to display the advanced options.

9. Select to enable/disable the Default VM affinity rule, by selecting/deselecting the check box **Keep VMDKs together by default**.

10. Select the periodicity of the cluster imbalance check. It is **8** hours by default. Do not change this unless it is necessary.

11. Select **I/O Imbalance Threshold**. Leave the slider at its default position, unless a change is necessary.

12. Select **Minimum Space Utilization Difference**. The default is **5%**. Do not change this value unless it is necessary.

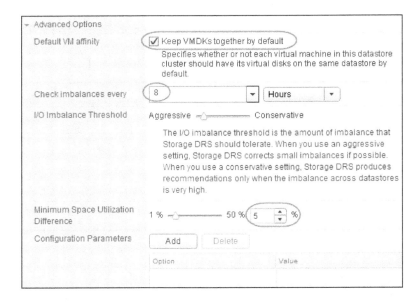

13. Click on **OK** to confirm the settings and enable Storage DRS.

14. The **Recent Tasks** pane should show a **Configure Storage DRS** task complete successfully.

How it works...

Once Storage DRS is enabled on a datastore cluster, it generates Storage vMotion recommendations based on the space usage and the latency threshold.

▸ The default value for **Space Utilization Threshold** is **80%**

▸ The default value for **I/O Latency** is **15** milliseconds

Load balancing based on the space utilization cannot be disabled but load balancing based on I/O load can be disabled.

Initial placement

When you deploy a VM onto a datastore cluster with SDRS enabled, SDRS will provide placement recommendations based on the space utilization and the I/O load on the datastores. This reduces the complexity in decision making when you have a large number of datastores in the environment; of course, they should be part of a datastore cluster for this to work. SDRS provides placement recommendations and chooses one of recommended datastores. However, the user can opt to select another recommended datastore. Although I/O load balancing can be disabled, the SDRS will still have access to the I/O statistics of the datastores. If SDRS finds more than one datastore suitable for placing the virtual machine, then it will choose the datastore with the lowest I/O load.

Balancing space utilization

With Storage DRS not enabled, it is quite possible that over time, when you deploy more and more virtual machines, you end up saturating the free space on a set of datastores, while leaving a few other datastores underutilized. This could eventually cause "out of space" conditions, affecting the running VMs. But with Storage DRS enabled in a datastore cluster, the space utilization on the datastores and the growth rate of the VMDKs (if thin provisioned) are monitored. The default threshold for space utilization is 80%. Storage DRS will start generating Storage vMotion recommendations when the threshold is exceeded.

Balancing I/O load

The I/O load on a datastore is measured based on the current I/O latency as seen by the virtual machines running on them. The default threshold for the latency is 15 milliseconds (15000 microseconds). If I/O load balancing is enabled, then the I/O latency statistics are evaluated every 8 hours. SDRS uses 16 hours' data to generate Storage vMotion recommendations. The migrations based on I/O load imbalance, occur only once during a day.

There's more...

There is much more that you need to know about SDRS. Refer to *Chapter 11, Creating a Datastore Cluster*, (page 107) and *Chapter 12, Using Datastore Clusters to Manage Storage Resources*, (page 115) in the *vSphere Resource Management guide* available at `http://pubs.vmware.com/vsphere-51/topic/com.vmware.ICbase/PDF/vsphere-esxi-vcenter-server-51-resource-management-guide.pdf`.

6

Managing iSCSI and NFS Storage

In this chapter, we will cover the following:

- ▶ Adding the software iSCSI adapter
- ▶ Creating a new VMkernel interface for iSCSI or NFS
- ▶ Preparing the vSphere network for iSCSI multipathing
- ▶ Binding VMkernel interfaces to the software iSCSI adapter
- ▶ Adding an iSCSI target server to the software iSCSI adapter
- ▶ Creating an NFS datastore

Introduction

iSCSI and NAS are storage solutions that can leverage the existing TCP/IP network infrastructure. Before we start learning how to configure them, let's delve into some iSCSI fundamentals. They are listed as follows:

- ▶ **iSCSI initiator**: An iSCSI initiator can be either a software iSCSI adapter or a hardware iSCSI adapter. The hardware iSCSI adapter can further be dependent or independent. The initiator or HBA resides on the ESXi server.

- ▶ **iSCSI target**: An iSCSI target is a term used to refer to either a network interface on the array or the LUN itself. Some arrays, such as Dell EqualLogic and HP LeftHand Networks, present each LUN as a target to the iSCSI initiator.

▶ **iSCSI session**: An iSCSI session is established between an iSCSI initiator and an iSCSI target. Each session can have one or more connections to the target. With software iSCSI configured, a session is established between each bound VMkernel interface (vmk) and an iSCSI target. For example, if there are two vmk interfaces bound to the iSCSI initiator, then the initiator will establish two separate sessions for each target it sees.

▶ **iSCSI connection**: Each iSCSI session can have multiple connections to the target portal.

▶ **iSCSI portal**: An iSCSI portal at the target is a combination of the target server's IP and the default listening port 3260. An iSCSI portal at the initiator is the IP address of the initiator/VMkernel interface.

▶ **CHAP: Challenge-Handshake Authentication Protocol** is used by iSCSI to make sure that the initiator and target trust each other.

▶ **Dynamic Discovery**: Dynamic Discovery is one of the common methods of target discovery implementation. This is particularly useful when the iSCSI server has made a larger number of LUNs/targets available via its interface.

▶ **Static discovery**: Static discovery is primarily used in scenarios where the iSCSI array has presented fewer targets/LUNs. It is also used to provide restrictive access to the initiator; that is, it can be used to configure the initiator in such a manner that it only sees specified targets.

For more information regarding the iSCSI implementation read the *Using ESXi with iSCSI SAN* section in the *VMware vSphere 5.1 Documentation Centre* available at `http://pubs.vmware.com/vsphere-51/index.jsp`.

Adding the software iSCSI adapter

The software iSCSI adapter is not created by default. It has to be manually created and enabled. In this recipe, we will learn how to enable the software iSCSI adapter. There can only be one software iSCSI adapter per ESXi server.

How to do it...

The following procedure will help you to create and enable the software iSCSI adapter:

1. Connect to vCenter using the vSphere Web Client and, at the inventory **Home**, click on **Hosts and Clusters**:

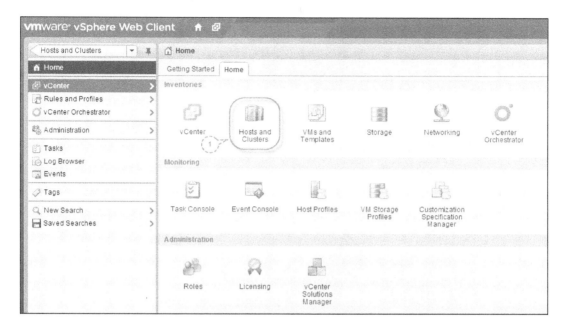

2. Highlight an ESX server and navigate to **Manage | Storage | Storage Adapters**:

3. Click on the **+** icon and select **Software iSCSI adapter:**

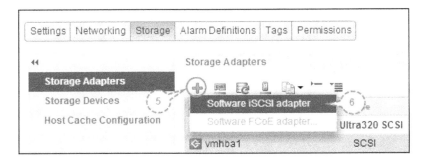

4. Click on **OK** to confirm the addition of a software iSCSI adapter:

5. You should see the following two tasks complete in the **Recent Tasks** pane:

   ❏ **Open firewall ports**

   ❏ **Change Software Internet SCSI Status**

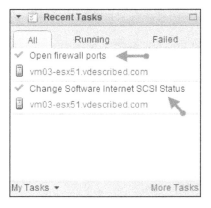

6. Once done, the software iSCSI adapter will be listed under **Storage Adapters**:

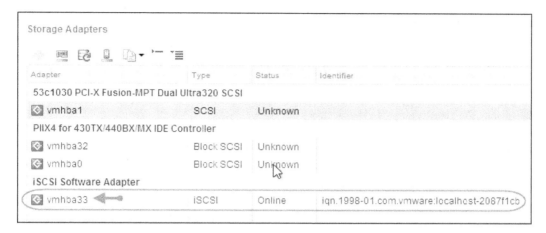

7. The iSCSI adapter is **Enabled** by default when it is created:

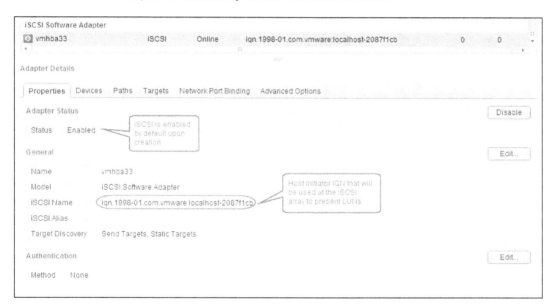

How it works...

During the creation of the software iSCSI adapter, all it does is enable the software iSCSI plugin and open all outgoing connections for the TCP port 3260 in the ESXi server's firewall.

The following is a screenshot from the **Security Profile** page showing the firewall configuration for the software iSCSI client:

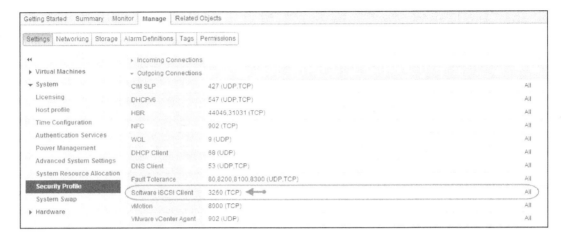

Creating a new VMkernel interface for iSCSI or NFS

The software iSCSI adapter will use VMkernel's network stack for establishing sessions with the iSCSI targets.

By default it will use the management network's VMkernel interface vmk0.

It is recommended to create a different VMkernel interface for iSCSI or NFS. This would become essential when the management network is in a different subnet. The software iSCSI adapter requires a VMkernel interface in the same subnet to which the iSCSI array is connected.

In this section, we will learn how to create a new VMkernel interface for iSCSI or NFS.

How to do it...

The following procedure will help you to set up a new VMkernel adapter:

1. With the ESX server selected from the inventory, navigate to **Manage** | **Networking** | **Virtual switches** and click on the **Add Networking** icon:

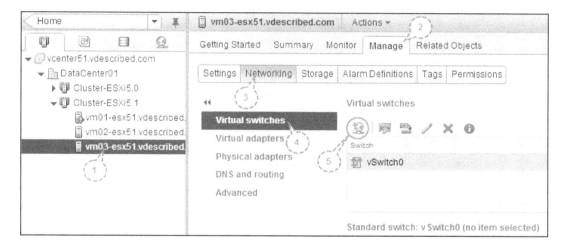

2. Select the **VMkernel Network Adapter** connection type and click on **Next**:

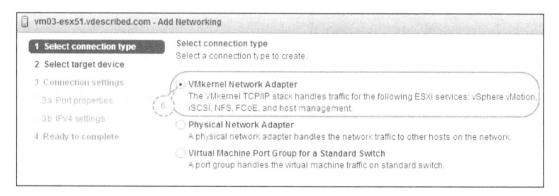

3. Select the option to create a **New standard switch** and click on **Next**:

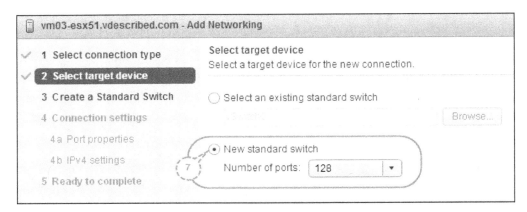

4. Assign unused physical adapters (vmnic) to the vSwitch. Click on the **+** sign to bring up the **Add Physical Adapters to the Switch** window:

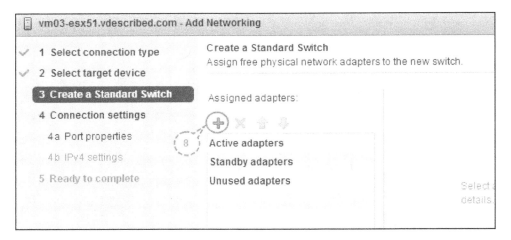

5. Select the vmnic to be added (keeping *CTRL* pressed, left-click on each vmnic for multiple selection) and click on OK:

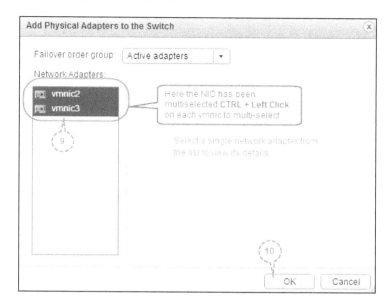

6. Click on **Next** to continue:

7. Supply a value in the **Network Label** field for the VMkernel port group and click on **Next** to continue:

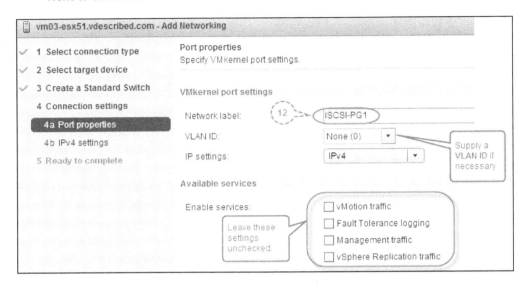

8. Specify a static IP configuration and click on **Next** to continue:

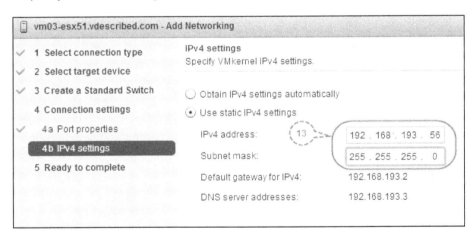

9. Review the **Ready to complete** screen and click on **Finish**:

10. There should now be a new vSwitch, in this case **vSwitch1**, showing in the port group with the new VMkernel interface (**vmk1**):

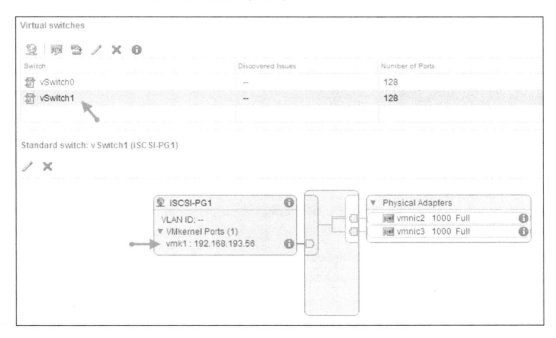

There's more

Enabling Jumbo Frames can significantly increase the iSCSI throughput. We will not discuss the procedure to enable Jumbo Frames in this recipe, because it has been well documented in the VMware KnowledgeBase article 1007654 available at `http://kb.vmware.com/kb/1007654`.

For Jumbo Frames to work on all the TCP/IP network components between the source and the destination, the components should also have support for Jumbo Frames enabled.

Preparing the vSphere network for iSCSI multipathing

iSCSI multipathing can be achieved by having two VMkernel interfaces configured with an active adapter each, but no standby adapters.

Once done, these VMkernel (vmk) interfaces should be bound to the software iSCSI adapter. This type of multipathing is needed when you use a single portal storage array such as the HP LeftHand and Dell EqualLogic.

 In the *vSphere Storage* guide, it is mentioned that a virtual machine I/O might be delayed for up to 60 seconds while path failover takes place. These delays allow the SAN to stabilize its configuration after topology changes. In general, the I/O delays might be longer on active-passive arrays and shorter on active-active arrays.

How to do it...

The following procedure will guide you through the steps required to create and configure port groups to aid in iSCSI multipathing:

1. Create an additional VMkernel interface using the **Add Networking** wizard. You could follow the same instructions from the *Creating a new VMkernel interface for iSCSI or NFS* recipe, which is an obvious exception of using the same vSwitch, a new port group, and a different static IP configuration, similar to the one shown in the following table:

Port Group Name	IP address	Subnet Mask
iSCSI-PG2	192.168.193.57	255.255.255.0

2. Once done, you should see two port groups connected to the same vSwitch:

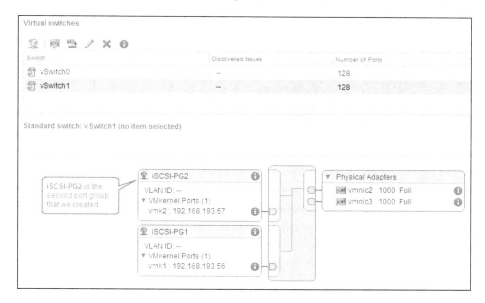

3. Select the port group, by clicking on its name that is a hyperlink, and click on the pencil icon to bring up the **Edit Settings** window, so that the failover order can be modified, in such a manner that a port group uses only one active vmnic and no standby vmnic.

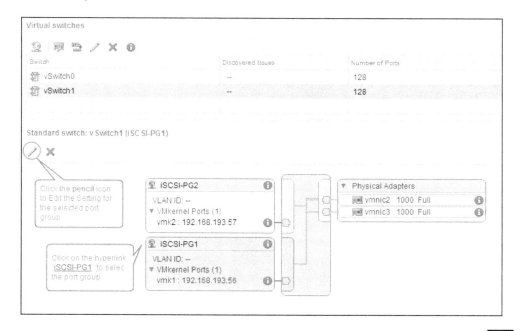

4. On the **Edit Settings** windows, go to **Teaming and failover** and select the checkbox **Override** under the **Failover order** section:

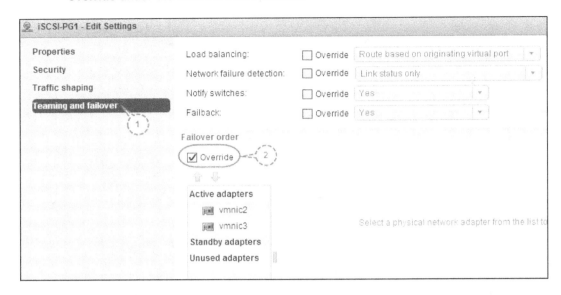

5. Select one of the adapters (vmnic), move it to the **Unused adapters** section, and click on **OK**:

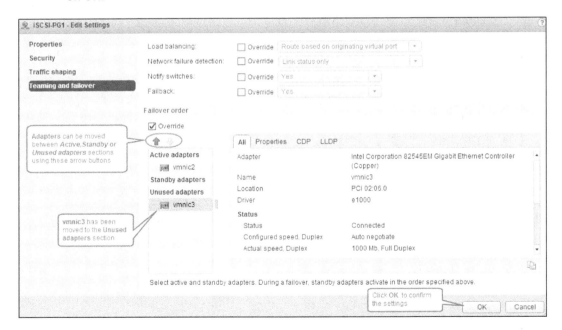

6. Follow the same procedure on the second port groups as well. Once done, the vmnic allocation to the iSCSI port groups should look like the one in the following diagram:

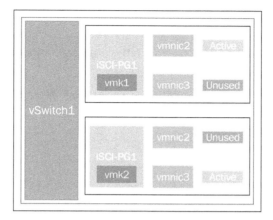

Now the VMkernel interfaces should be bound to the software iSCSI adapter. This is discussed in the next section.

There's more...

Dell EqualLogic have its own **Multipathing Extension Module** (**MEM**).

The following is the URL for the *Installation and Configuration Guide* for EqualLogic's MEM:

`http://www.dellstorage.com/WorkArea/DownloadAsset.aspx?id=3064`

Binding VMkernel interfaces to the software iSCSI adapter

Binding is the final stage of configuration to be done at the ESXi server to enable iSCSI multipathing. It refers to the process of associating existing VMkernel (vmk) interfaces to the software iSCSI adapter, thereby letting NMP manage multiple paths to the iSCSI targets.

 Keep in mind that the iSCSI initiator and the iSCSI target should be in the same subnet. iSCSI port binding does not support routing.

The VMkernel interfaces should be first prepared with only one active and no standby adapters. This is discussed in detail in the *Preparing the vSphere network for iSCSI multipathing* recipe.

Once the VMkernel interfaces have been prepared, you could use the instructions in this recipe to bind the interfaces to the software iSCSI adapter.

How to do it...

The following instructions will guide you through the process of binding the VMkernel interfaces to the software iSCSI adapter:

1. On the ESXi server, navigate to **Manage | Storage | Storage Adapters** and select the iSCSI software adapter of your choice:

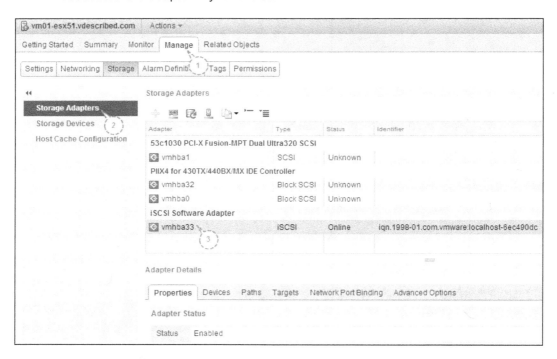

2. Navigate to the **Network Port Binding** tab for the iSCSI software adapter and click on the green **+** icon to bring up the **Bind vmhba3x with VMkernel Adapter** window:

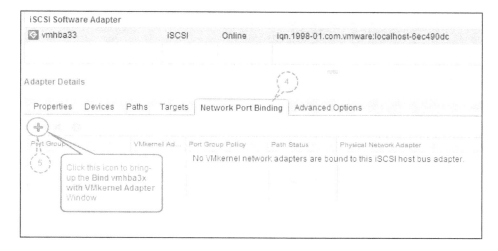

3. On the **Bind vmhba3X with VMkernel Adapter** window, select the port group associated with the VMkernel interfaces and click on **OK** to bind them:

4. Once the adapters are bound, you will see them listed under the **Network Port Binding** tab:

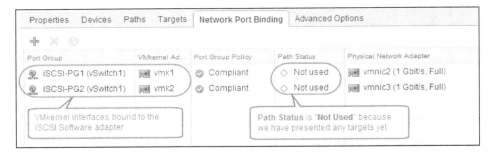

Adding an iSCSI target server to the software iSCSI adapter

For the ESXi server to be able to see iSCSI targets/LUNs, the iSCSI adapter needs to be configured with the details of the iSCSI target server. The target server is nothing but an iSCSI array. Here the term target can refer to the network interfaces on the iSCSI array or individual LUNs. The definition changes depending on the type of array being used. For example, a Dell EqualLogic array will present its LUNs as targets.

In this recipe of the chapter, we will learn how to provide the iSCSI array details to the iSCSI software adapter.

How to do it...

The following procedure will guide you through the steps required to add an iSCSI target server:

1. On the ESXi server, navigate to **Manage** | **Storage** | **Storage Adapters** and select the iSCSI software adapter of your choice.

2. With the adapter selected, go to the **Targets** tab and then under **Dynamic Discovery** click on **Add** to bring up the **Add Send Target Server** window:

3. In the **Add Send Target Server** window, supply the IP address/FQDN of the iSCSI server and click on **OK**:

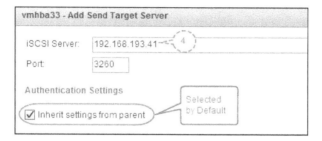

4. The **Recent Tasks** pane should show the following two tasks completed successfully:

   ❑ **Add Internet SCSI send targets**
   ❑ **Update Internet SCSI authentication properties**

5. Issue a rescan on the software iSCSI adapter to find presented LUN devices.

6. Once the rescan is complete, the **Devices** tab should show all the detected LUNs:

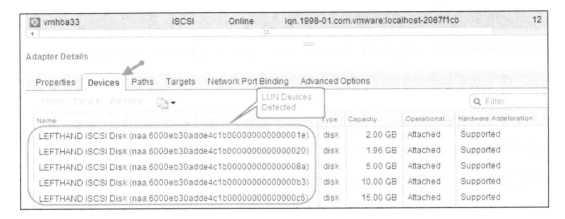

How it works...

Once the iSCSI target information has been added to the iSCSI software initiator, it will appear as an iSCSI server entry under the **Dynamic Discovery** tab.

A "SEND TARGETS" command is sent from each vmk interface to the target portal; in response, the array will send a list of all available targets presented to the initiator. The target list received from the array will appear in the **Static Discovery** tab:

Since we have two VMkernel interfaces bound to the iSCSI software initiator, we will have two sessions for each LUN seen by the initiator, as depicted in the following diagram:

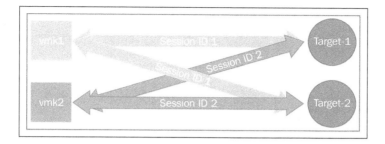

The following screenshot shows the session from each vmk interface to a LUN on a LeftHand iSCSI. Keep in mind that LeftHand is a single portal storage.

```
~ # esxcli iscsi session list | grep vmhba33 -A 3
vmhba33,iqn.2003-10.com.lefthandnetworks:labmainstroage:198:15gb-vol-ss-1,00023d000001
    Adapter: vmhba33
    Target: iqn.2003-10.com.lefthandnetworks:labmainstroage:198:15gb-vol-ss-1
    ISID: 00023d000001              Session from vmk1 to "15gb-vol-ss-1"
    TargetPortalGroupTag: 1

--
vmhba33,iqn.2003-10.com.lefthandnetworks:labmainstroage:198:15gb-vol-ss-1,00023d000002
    Adapter: vmhba33
    Target: iqn.2003-10.com.lefthandnetworks:labmainstroage:198:15gb-vol-ss-1
    ISID: 00023d000002              Session from vmk2 to "15gb-vol-ss-1"
    TargetPortalGroupTag: 1

--
vmhba33,iqn.2003-10.com.lefthandnetworks:labmainstroage:179:10gb-vol-ss-2,00023d000001
    Adapter: vmhba33
    Target: iqn.2003-10.com.lefthandnetworks:labmainstroage:179:10gb-vol-ss-2
    ISID: 00023d000001              Session from vmk1 to "10gb-vol-ss-2"
    TargetPortalGroupTag: 1

--
vmhba33,iqn.2003-10.com.lefthandnetworks:labmainstroage:179:10gb-vol-ss-2,00023d000002
    Adapter: vmhba33
    Target: iqn.2003-10.com.lefthandnetworks:labmainstroage:179:10gb-vol-ss-2
    ISID: 00023d000002              Session from vmk2 to "10gb-vol-ss-2"
    TargetPortalGroupTag: 1

--
```

Now if you review the multipathing information for a LUN, you should see two paths:

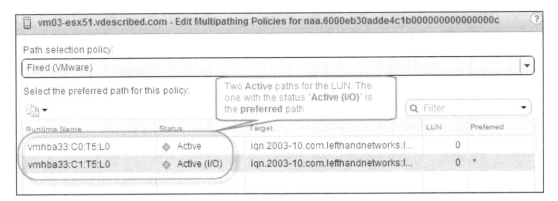

You might have noticed that one of the paths has been marked as **Active (I/O)**. This is the path to the storage controller that can issue the commands to the LUN. Such a controller is referred to as a **managing controller**. The path to a managing controller will be tagged as the optimized path to the LUN.

Creating an NFS datastore

An NFS datastore is also a supported storage for hosting virtual machines. Although there are environments that run virtual machines on NFS datastores, they are commonly used to store ISOs, templates, and so on. In this section of the chapter we will learn how to mount an NFS share as a datastore.

Getting ready

Prepare a VMkernel interface for NFS. Read the *Creating a new VMkernel interface for iSCSI or NFS* recipe for instructions.

How to do it...

The following procedure will guide you through the steps required to mount an NFS share as a datastore to the ESXi server.

1. With the ESXi server selected, navigate to **Related Objects | Datastores** and click on the new datastore icon to start the **New Datastore** wizard:

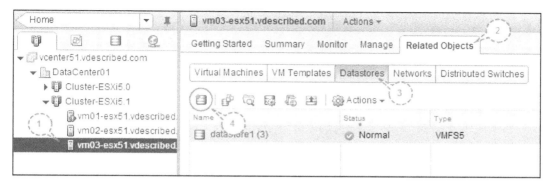

2. In the **New Datastore** wizard, specify a name for the datastore and click on **Next**:

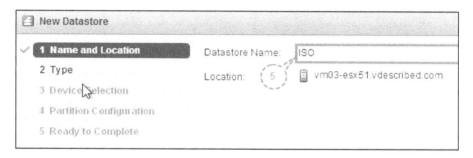

3. Select **NFS** as the filesystem type and click on **Next**:

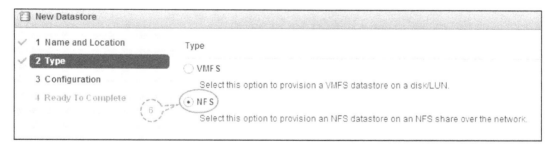

4. Specify the NFS server name and the absolute path to the folder share created at the NFS server:

5. Review the **Ready to Complete** screen and click on **Finish**:

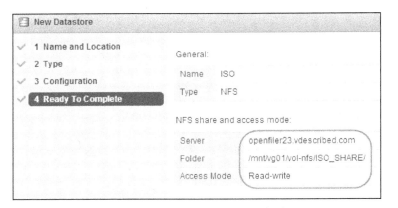

6. The **Recent Tasks** pane should show a **Create NAS datastore** task completed successfully:

How it works...

By default you can only create 8 NFS mounts per ESXi server. Although, this limit can be increased up to 256, by using the advanced setting **NFS.MaxVolumes**, increasing this limit, would require an increase in the minimum amount of VMkernel TCP/IP heap memory. The minimum heap memory value can be specified using the advanced setting **Net.TcpipHeapSize**.

You can also set the maximum amount of heap size, using the advanced setting **Net.TcpipHeapMax**.

For more information regarding these parameters refer to VMware KnowledgeBase article 2239 `http://kb.vmware.com/kb/2239`.

There is no limit on the size of an NFS datastore. If there is any such limit then it is imposed by the NFS server and not by the ESXi server.

7
Profile-driven Storage and Storage I/O Control

In this chapter we will cover the following:

- ▶ Adding a storage provider
- ▶ Creating user-defined storage capabilities
- ▶ Mapping user-defined storage capabilities to datastores
- ▶ Creating and using a VM storage profile
- ▶ Assigning storage profiles to a virtual machine and checking compliance
- ▶ Enabling Storage I/O Control (SIOC)
- ▶ Modifying disk shares on a VM

Introduction

In this chapter, we will learn how to use storage profiles to ensure that the VMs are placed in appropriate datastores and how to use Storage I/O Control to manage queue bandwidth between VMs.

Before we begin with the configuration tasks, it will be beneficial to understand the concepts.

Profile-driven storage

Profile-driven storage will allow an administrator to group datastores under profiles based on the datastore's capability. The capabilities can be related to the capacity, performance, and redundancy characteristics. The capabilities can either be learned via **VASA (vSphere Storage API for Storage Awareness)** if the storage array supports the API, or they can be user defined. Once the profiles are defined, the virtual machine disks can be associated to these profiles. This will allow vSphere to make VM placement decisions.

Storage I/O Control (SIOC)

SIOC is used to throttle the VMkernel device queue depth of a LUN, based on the shares set on the virtual machine disks contending for I/O bandwidth. SIOC can only be enabled on datastores (FC/ISCSI/NFS) and not on RDMs. It cannot be enabled on datastores with multiple extents.

Adding a storage provider

If you have a VASA capable array, then you can add a VASA provider to the vCenter Server so that it can generate array capabilities for each LUN/datastore. A capability generated by the provider is called a **system storage capability**.

To check whether the array used in your environment is VASA capable, use the *VMware Compatibility Guide* available at `http://www.vmware.com/resources/compatibility/search.php?deviceCategory=vasa`.

The P4000 VSA used in the lab for this book, is VASA capable. In this recipe we will learn how to add a storage provider corresponding to the array to the vCenter Server.

Getting ready

Since we are using a HP P4000 VSA, you will need a storage provider server configured with HP Insight Control for Storage installed. Since the installation instructions are beyond the scope of this book, we assume that the insight control for storage is installed and configured correctly. For storage provider-specific instructions, refer the vendor documentation.

How to do it...

The following instructions explain how to add a storage provider to the vCenter Server:

1. From the inventory **Home**, navigate to **Storage** to bring up the storage view:

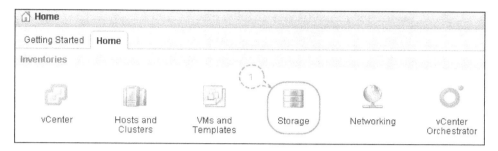

2. In the vCenter Server, navigate to **Manage | Storage Providers**, and click on the green **+** icon to bring up the **Register Storage Provider** window:

3. At the **Register Storage Provider** window, specify a name for the provider, the provider URL, the login credentials, and click on **OK**. Check the *VASA Provider* documentation for the provider URL syntax:

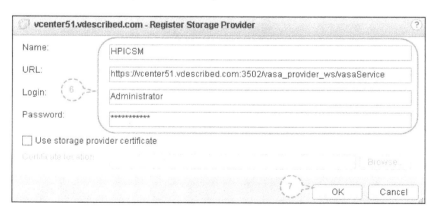

As per the *vSphere 5.1* documentation, vendor providers can run anywhere, except on the vCenter Server. The URL in the previous screenshot says **vCenter51**, because I had installed the provider on the same machine, which is not supported.

4. Click on **Yes** to trust the certificate from the host.

5. The storage provider should now be listed as **Online**:

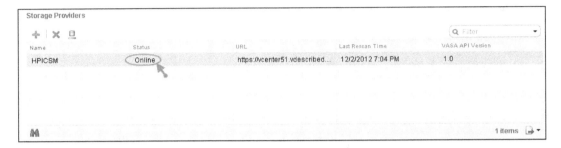

How it works...

Once the storage provider is added, the **Manage Storage Capabilities** window will now show all the storage capabilities that can be detected by the provider. A provider can detect capabilities from different array models of the same vendor.

To bring up the **Manage Storage Capabilities** window, navigate to the vSphere Web Client inventory **Home**, then to **VM Storage Profiles**, and then click on the wrench icon:

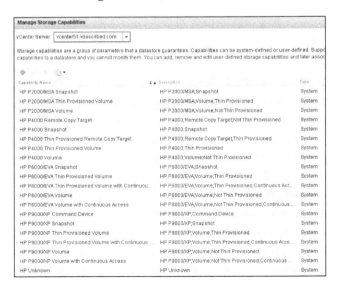

The datastores corresponding to the LUNs on the array will show the VASA-propagated system storage capabilities. None of the capabilities have to be manually assigned. VASA will auto-propagate the capability of the underlying LUN to its corresponding datastore.

For example, the following is a screenshot showing the system-generated capability of one of the datastores:

There's more...

For more information on using storage providers, read the *Using Storage Vendor Providers* section in the *vSphere Storage* guide, which is available at `http://pubs.vmware.com/ vsphere-51/topic/com.vmware.ICbase/PDF/vsphere-esxi-vcenter-server- 51-storage-guide.pdf`.

Creating user-defined storage capabilities

If the array backing the LUNs is not VASA capable, then the vSphere administrator can create user-defined storage capabilities. This allows the administrator to manually check the storage properties of the LUN and create a capability matching the same.

How to do it...

The following procedure explains how to create user-defined storage capabilities:

1. From the inventory **Home,** click on **VM Storage Profiles**, which should take you to the storage profiles administration page:

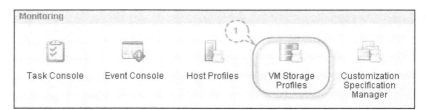

2. On the **VM Storage Profiles** screen, click on the icon with a wrench on it to bring up the **Manage Storage Capabilities** window:

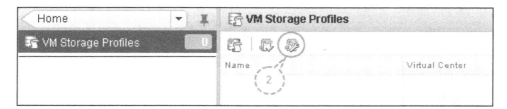

3. In the **Manage Storage Capabilities** window, click on the green **+** icon to bring up the **Create Storage Capability** window:

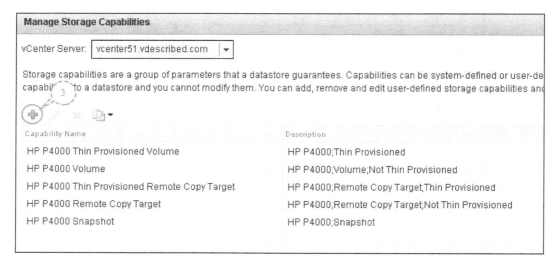

4. In the **Create Storage Capacity** window, supply a name and description for the capability:

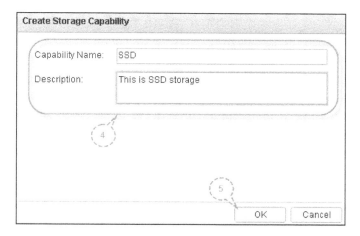

5. The newly-created user-defined storage capability will be listed along with the provider's list of capabilities:

 Unlike the system storage capabilities, the user-defined storage capabilities should be manually mapped to the datastores.

Mapping user-defined storage capabilities to datastores

The user-defined storage capabilities that we create are not automatically mapped to the datastores. The reason for this is that these were not learned using VASA.

A vSphere administrator should map the user-defined capabilities to appropriate datastores, based on the information collected by verifying the LUN properties at the storage array.

> The storage capabilities can only be assigned on a per-datastore basis. They cannot even be assigned at a datastore cluster level.

In this recipe we will learn how to associate/assign a user-defined storage capability to a datastore.

How to do it...

The following procedure explains how to map the user-defined storage capabilities to the datastores:

1. From the inventory **Home**, click on **Storage**:

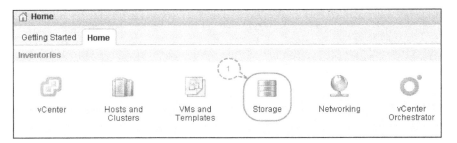

2. Select a datastore from the inventory and navigate to **Manage | Profiles**, and click on **Assign Storage Capability...**:

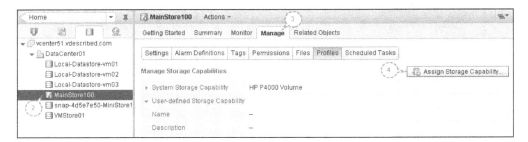

3. In the **Assign User-Defined Storage Capability** window, select the appropriate capability, and click on **OK**:

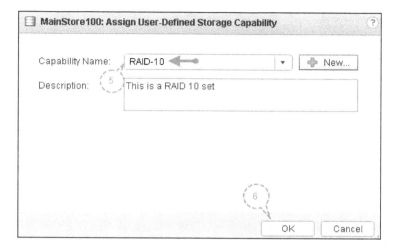

4. The **Profiles** section for the datastore should now show the **User-defined Storage Capability** assigned to it:

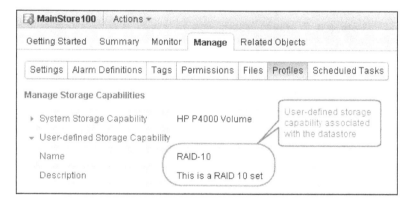

Creating a VM storage profile and enabling it

VM storage profiles are a way of categorizing storage based on the type/capability of the storage. For example, LUNs thin provisioned, wherein **Thin Provisioned Volume**, being a capability, can be categorized so that VMs running applications that do not demand first-write performance can be placed on these datastores. The first-write performance could be impacted on a thin provisioned volume because the volume should be increased in size before the data is first written to it.

In this recipe we will learn how to create a VM storage profile by using the System Storage Profiles and User-defined Storage Profiles.

How to do it...

The following procedure explains how to create VM storage profiles. For the sake of demonstration we will create two VM storage profiles, one for a system storage profile: and the other for the user-defined storage profile.

1. From the inventory **Home**, click on **VM Storage Profiles**, which should take you to the storage profiles administration page.

2. On the **VM Storage Profiles** screen, click on the create new storage profile icon.

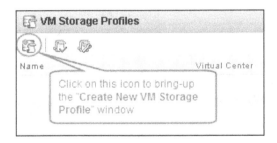

3. In the **Create New VM Storage Profile** wizard, filter all the user-defined storage capabilities and pick one of them, supply a name to it, and click on **OK**:

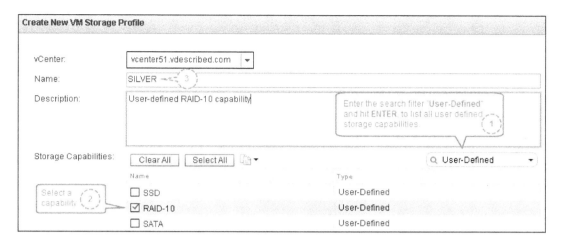

4. Start the **Create New VM Storage Profile** wizard again, and specify all the system storage capabilities associated with **P4000**:

5. You should now see two profiles listed:

6. Click on the icon with a tick mark to bring up the **Enable VM Storage Profiles** window:

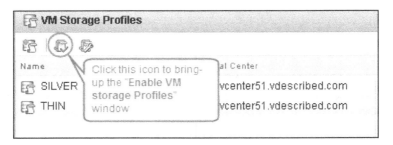

7. In the **Enable VM Storage Profiles** window, select the cluster listed, and click on **Enable** and then **Close**:

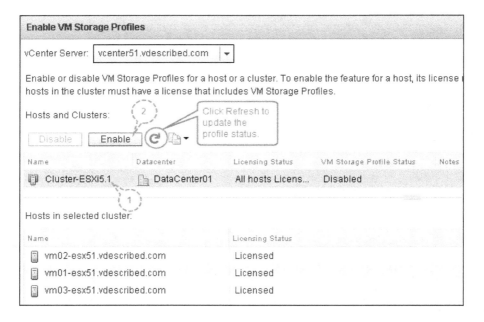

Assigning storage profiles to virtual machine disks and checking compliance

The whole idea behind profile-driven storage is to segregate and tie VM disks (VMDK) on to appropriate storage backing. Before you proceed with assigning the storage profiles to VMs, follow the instructions in the *Creating a VM storage profile and enabling it* recipe.

How to do it...

The following procedure explains how to assign VM storage profiles to VMs:

1. From the inventory **Home**, go to **VMs and Templates**:

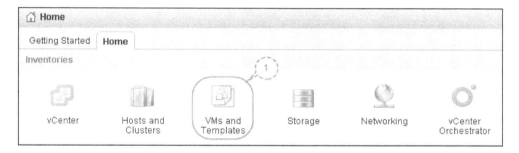

2. Select the required VM, navigate to **Manage | Profiles**, and click on **Manage Storage Profiles**:

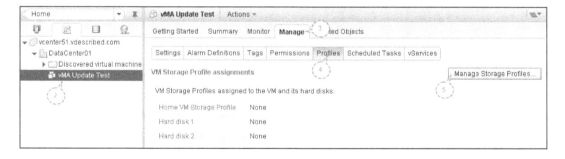

3. In the **Manage Storage Profiles** window, select a profile for the virtual machine configuration files, and then either propagate that to all the disks associated with the VM or assign different profiles to each of the virtual disks:

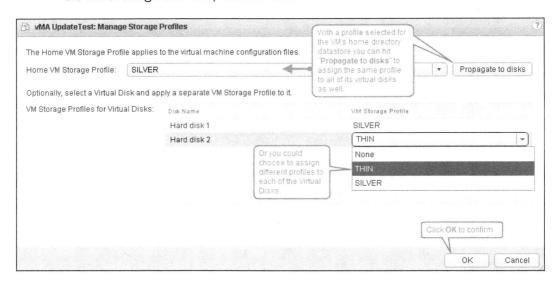

4. After the profiles are assigned, the profile assignment summary will show profiles attached to both the virtual disks and the VM's configuration files:

5. Next, navigate to the **Summary** tab of the VM, and the **VM Storage Profiles** section will show the profile compliance status:

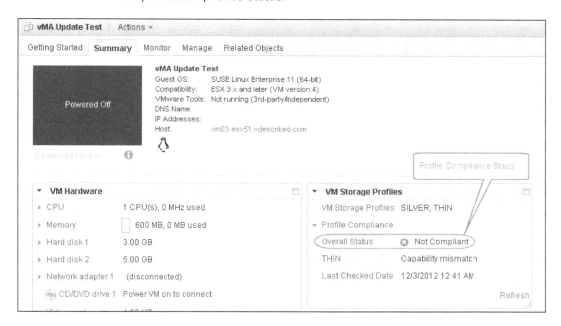

 [Migrate the VM's storage to a profile-compliant datastore.]

Enabling Storage I/O Control (SIOC)

As with sharing computing resources amongst the running virtual machines, you can share the I/O bandwidth to a LUN amongst the virtual machines. Based on the shares set on the virtual disks residing on the SIOC-enabled datastores, SIOC will throttle the VMkernel LUN queue depth during contention. In this recipe we will learn how to enable SIOC on a datastore.

How to do it...

SIOC has to be enabled on each datastore. The following procedure explains how to achieve the same:

1. From the inventory **Home**, click on **Storage**.

2. Select a datastore from the inventory and navigate to **Manage | Settings**, and edit the datastore capabilities:

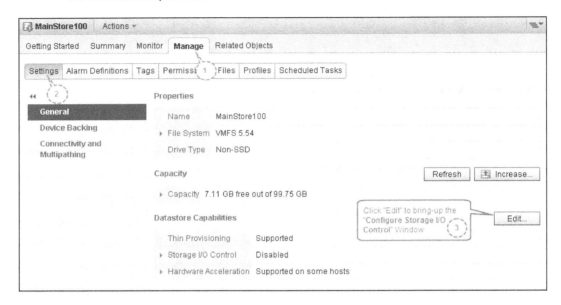

3. In the **Configure Storage I/O Control** window, select the **Enable Storage I/O Control** checkbox. Unless you want to modify the **Congestion Threshold** criteria and its value, you can leave the **Percentage of peak throughput** value at its default of **90%**. You can also set the **Congestion Threshold** to be the latency. By default the latency threshold value is 30 ms.

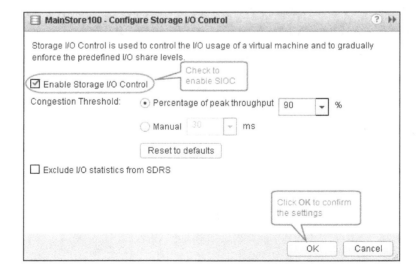

How it works...

Once Storage IO Control has been enabled, the datastore will be monitored for bandwidth congestion. If congestion is detected, it checks the peak throughput or latency values against the value configured when SIOC was enabled.

Based on the level of congestion, the VMkernel device queue depth is throttled accordingly.

 The vSphere 5.1 SIOC is enabled by default, but only in the **Stats Only** mode. While in this mode, the SIOC will not throttle the queue depth but only collect I/O statistics.

For more information on SIOC read the *vSphere 5.1 Resource Management* guide available at `http://pubs.vmware.com/vsphere-51/topic/com.vmware.ICbase/PDF/vsphere-esxi-vcenter-server-51-resource-management-guide.pdf`.

Modifying disk shares on a VM

Setting custom disk shares is particularly useful when you want to make sure that a VM receives a larger chunk of the disk bandwidth during contention. By default, the disk share is set to **Normal (1000)**. The other presets available to set custom shares are **Low (500)** and **High (2000)**.

In this recipe, we will learn how to set custom disk shares.

How to do it...

The following procedure explains how to set customize disk share values on a VM:

1. Go to **Edit Settings** for the VM that you are concerned with.

2. Expand the hard disk entry, select a planned shares value, and click on **OK** to confirm your settings. You can also set a **Limit - IOPs** value if necessary:

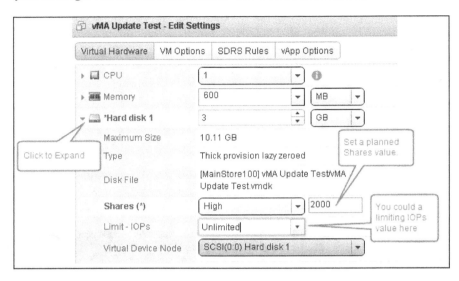

SIOC will take into account the custom share value when throttling the VMkernel device queue.

How it works...

Disk shares are applied at the virtual machine disk (VMDK) level. The shares will come into effect only when there is contention for the disk bandwidth. The shares are relative to the shares set for the other VMDKs on the same ESXi host.

SIOC will take into account the custom share value when throttling the VMkernel device queue.

8
Configuring the vSphere Network

In this chapter we will cover the following:

- ▶ Creating a vSphere Standard Switch
- ▶ Deleting a vSphere Standard Switch
- ▶ Creating a VMkernel interface on a vSphere Standard Switch
- ▶ Deleting a port group
- ▶ Adding an uplink to a vSphere Standard Switch
- ▶ Creating a vSphere Distributed Switch
- ▶ Creating a distributed port group
- ▶ Adding hosts to a vSphere Distributed Switch
- ▶ Mapping a physical adapter (vmnic) to a dvUplink
- ▶ Migrating a virtual machine network from a vSphere Standard Switch to a vSphere Distributed Switch
- ▶ Migrating management and VMkernel interfaces between vSphere Standard and Distributed Switches
- ▶ Creating a VMkernel interface on a vSphere Distributed Switch
- ▶ Exporting the vSphere Distributed Switch configuration
- ▶ Restoring the vSphere Distributed Switch configuration
- ▶ Importing a vSphere Distributed Switch into the datacenter from a backup
- ▶ Enabling port mirroring on a DSwitch
- ▶ Enabling NetFlow on a DSwitch
- ▶ Configuring private VLANs (PVLANs) on a DSwitch

Introduction

Networking is the backbone of any infrastructure, be it virtual or physical. In this chapter, we will learn how to create and configure the basic switching constructs of vSphere networking.

Before we start learning how to create these constructs, it is important to have a brief understanding of them.

> ▶ **vSphere Standard Switch** (**vSS**): It is a software switching construct local to each ESXi server that provides a network infrastructure for the virtual machines running on that server. Unlike a physical switch, the vSphere Standard Switch is not a managed switch. It doesn't learn MAC addresses and build a CAM table like a physical switch, but it does know the MAC addresses of the virtual machine vNICs connected to it.

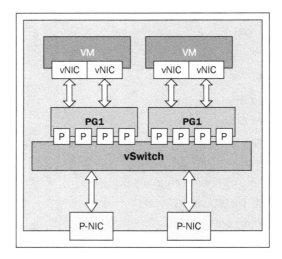

The vSwitch has logical ports to which a virtual machine's virtual NIC connects.

 The logical ports themselves cannot be chosen during the configuration; it is always a port group "label" that a virtual machine's vNIC would be configured to use.

- **vSphere Distributed Switch (vDS)**: It is a software switching construct that spans across multiple ESXi severs. It is not locally managed at the ESXi host. It requires VMware vCenter Server for configuration and management. vSphere Distributed Switch is only available with vSphere Enterprise Plus License. It has a control plane which resides at the vCenter Server and a data plane which resides on an ESXi host that is connected to the vDS.

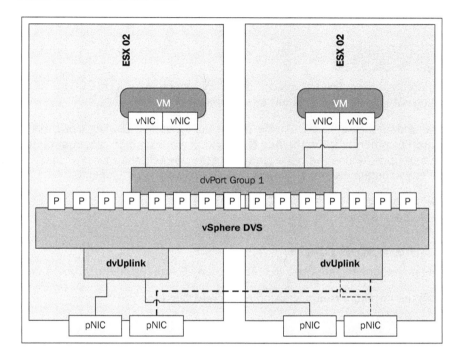

- **Port group or dvPortGroup**: It is a way to group a set of virtual ports on a vSS/vDS under a common configuration umbrella.

- **VMkernel port**: It is a virtual adapter, which would act as network interface for VMkernel. There are many services that mandate the presence of this interface, including vMotion, iSCSI, and management.

- **dvUplink**: With DSwitch, you can no longer apply teaming, load balancing, or failover policies directly for physical NICs. Instead, we now have an additional layer of abstraction called a dvUplink which can be mapped to a physical NIC. The dvUplink count dictates the number of physical NICs from each host that can participate in the network configuration.

For more information on the new networking features introduced with vSphere 5.1, read the technical whitepaper, *What's New in VMware vSphere 5.1 – Networking*, available at `http://www.vmware.com/files/pdf/techpaper/Whats-New-VMware-vSphere-51-Network-Technical-Whitepaper.pdf`.

Creating a vSphere Standard Switch

vSwitches operate at the VMkernel layer. Unlike most of the physical switches in a modern environment, a vSwitch is not a managed switch. However, it does know the MAC addresses of the virtual machine adapters mapped to it.

By default, a vSwitch—vSwitch0—is created during the ESXi installation.

How to do it...

To manually create a new vSwitch, you can use the vSphere Web Client GUI, the vSphere Windows Client GUI, or the `esxcfg-vswitch` command.

There is one fundamental difference in the process of creating a vSwitch using the **esxcfg-vswitch** command. Unlike the **Add Networking** wizard, which requires you to create a port group to proceed with the creating of the vSwitch, the `esxcfg-vswitch` command lets you create a vSwitch with no port groups and with no uplinks.

When a vSwitch is created it will have 128 ports by default. The number of ports per vSwitch is configurable up to a maximum of 4096 ports.

Using vSphere Web Client

The following procedure explains how to create a new vSwitch using the vSphere Web Client:

1. From the inventory **Home**, click on **Hosts and Clusters**:

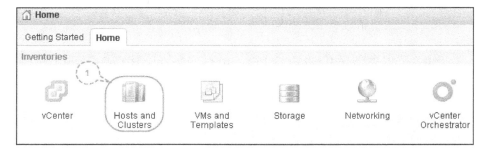

2. Select the ESXi host from the inventory and navigate to **Manage | Networking | Virtual switches**, and click on the add host networking icon to bring up the **Add Networking** wizard:

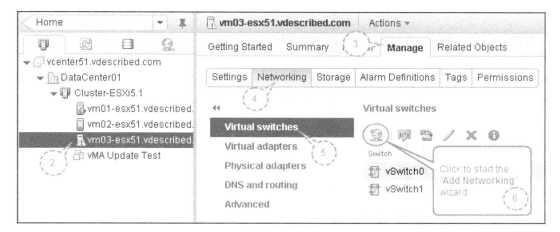

3. In the **Add Networking** wizard, select the required connection type, and click on **Next**. In the following screenshot, we have chosen a connection type of **Virtual Machine Port Group for a Standard Switch**:

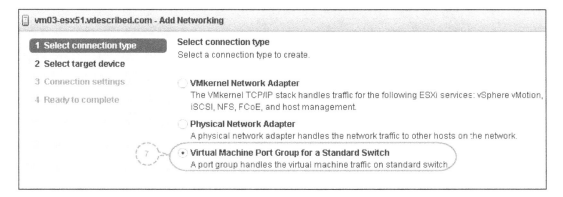

4. Select **New standard switch**, modify the value of **Number of ports** if needed, and click on **Next**:

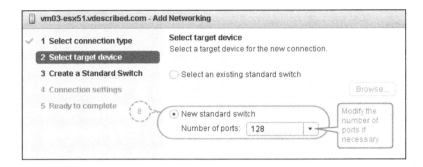

5. On the next screen, click on the green **+** icon to bring up the **Add Physical Adapters to the Switch** window, in order to assign physical adapters (vminc) to the vSwitch:

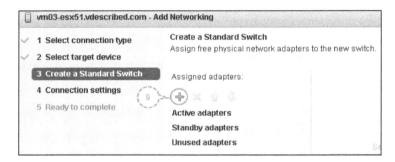

6. Select the vmnic (physical uplink) that is to be added, and click on **OK**:

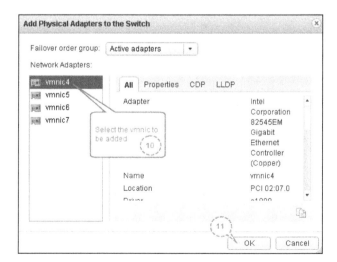

7. Review the assigned adapter/adapters, and click on **Next** to continue:

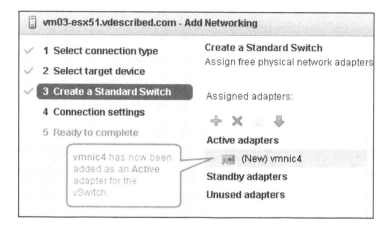

8. Supply a **Network Label** for the port group that will be created on the vSwitch, and click on **Next**:

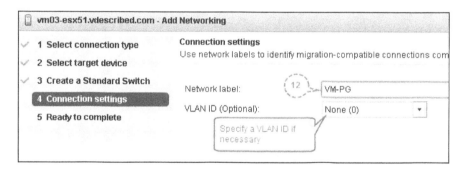

9. Review the **Ready to complete** screen, and click on **Finish**:

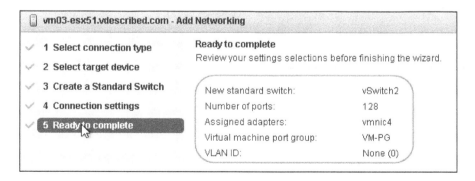

Using esxcfg-vswitch

The following procedure guides you through the commands that need to be executed in order to create a new vSphere Standard Switch:

1. SSH to the ESXi host as `root`, or use a direct console access method such as HP ILO or DRAC, and log in as `root`.

2. List all the available vmnic adapters by issuing the following command:

   ```
   esxcfg-nics -l
   ```

3. Issue the following command to create a new vSphere Standard Switch:

   ```
   esxcfg-vswitch -a vSwitch1
   ```

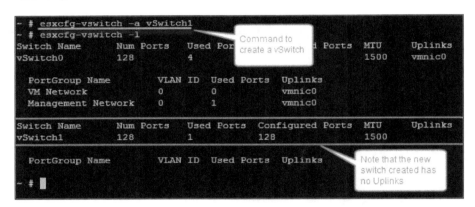

4. Add an uplink to the new vSwitch `vSwitch1` by issuing the following command:

   Syntax:

   ```
   esxcfg-vswitch -L <vmnic> vSwitch1
   ```

   Example:

   ```
   esxcfg-vswitch -L vmnic1
   esxcfg-vswitch -L vmnic4
   ```

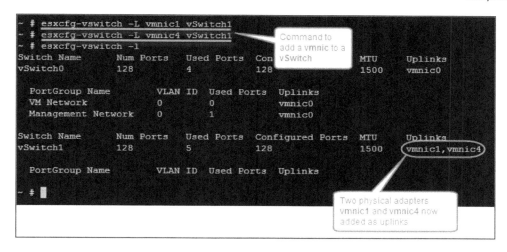

5. Create a Port Group on the new vSwitch by issuing the following command:

   Syntax:

   ```
   esxcfg-vswitch -A "NetworkLabel" vSwitch1
   ```

   Example:

   ```
   esxcfg-vswitch -A "Development" vSwitch1
   ```

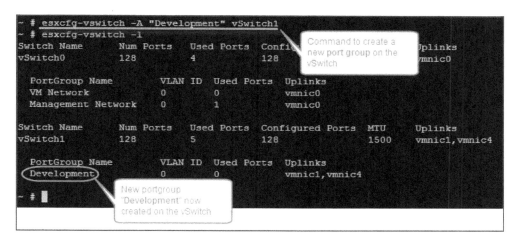

Deleting a vSphere Standard Switch

When you choose to delete a vSwitch in a production environment, make sure that the virtual machines have been reconfigured to use a port group on another vSwitch, which would provide them with network access.

How to do it...

A vSwitch can be deleted either from the vSphere Web Client GUI or by using the `esxcfg-vswitch` command.

Using the vSphere Web Client

The following procedure explains how to delete a vSwitch by using the vSphere Web Client:

1. Select the ESXi host from the inventory and navigate to **Manage | Networking | Virtual switches**.

2. Select the vSwitch to be deleted, and click on the delete (**X**) icon to remove the vSwitch from the ESXi host:

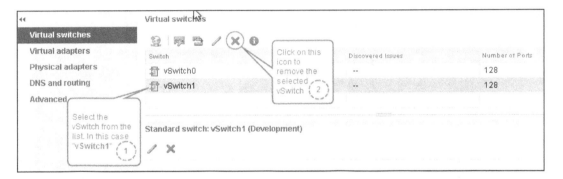

3. Click on **Yes** to confirm the removal:

4. You should see the **Update network configuration** and **Remove virtual switch** tasks completed successfully in the **Recent Tasks** pane:

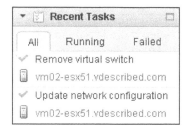

Using esxcfg-vswitch

The following procedure guides you through the commands required to delete a vSwitch:

1. SSH to the ESXi host as `root`, or use a direct console access method such as HP ILO or DRAC, and log in as `root`.

2. List all the vSwitches on the ESXi server by issuing the following command:

   `esxcfg-vswitch -l`

3. Identify the vSwitch that needs to be deleted, and issue the following command to delete the vSwitch:

   Syntax:

   `esxcfg-vswitch -d <name of the vSwitch>`

   Example:

   `esxcfg-vswitch -d vSwtich1`

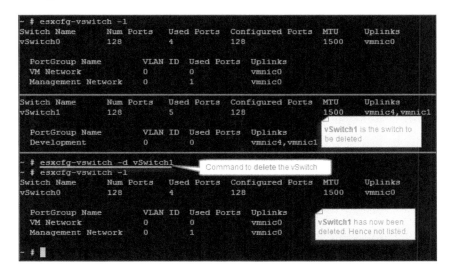

Creating a VMkernel interface on a vSphere Standard Switch

A VMkernel port group is created when there is a need to create a VMkernel network interface (VMK). It is used for iSCSI, NAS, and vMotion.

There can only be one VMkernel port per subnet. Although it doesn't stop you from creating multiple VMkernel ports per subnet, it will only use one of them. Usually, the VMkernel port that was first created is used. VMkernel traffic can be routed, although this is not recommended for vMotion, as it can cause latency issues. The VMkernel gateway IP address should also be in the same subnet.

 Only one VMkernel default gateway can be configured on an ESXi host.

How to do it...

The port group can be created either from the vSphere Web Client GUI or by using the `esxcfg-vswitch` and `esxcfg-vmknic` commands.

Using vSphere Web Client

The following procedure explains how to create a VMkernel port group by using a vSphere Web Client:

1. Select the ESXi host from the inventory and navigate to **Manage | Networking | Virtual switches**, select the vSwitch on which you would like to create the VMkernel port groups, and click on the add host networking icon to bring up the **Add Networking** wizard.

2. Select a connection type of **VMkernel Network Adapter**:

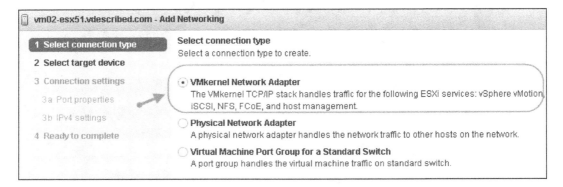

3. Select the vSphere Standard Switch on which you would like the new VMkernel port to be configured, and continue to the next step. Since we selected the vSwitch before starting the **Add Networking** wizard, the correct vSphere Standard Switch will be pre-selected in the wizard screen:

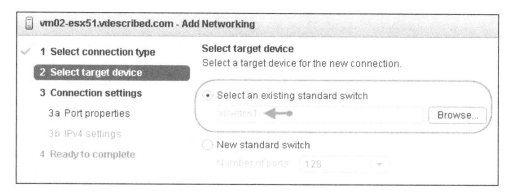

4. Supply a value for the **Network Label** field, an optional **VLAN ID**, and an appropriate function for the VMkernel port group. The functions available are **vMotion**, **Fault Tolerance logging**, **Management traffic**, and **vSphere Replication traffic**:

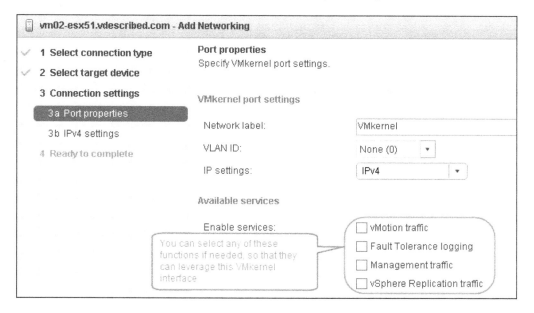

5. Supply an IP configuration for the VMkernel interface, and click on **Next:**

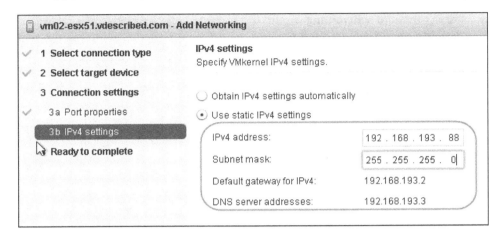

6. On the **Ready to complete** screen, verify the configuration, and click on **Finish** to create the VMkernel port group.

Using esxcfg-vswitch and esxcfg-vmknic

The following procedure guides you through the commands needed to create a VMkernel interface on an existing vSwitch:

1. SSH to the ESXi host as `root`, or use a direct console access method such as HP ILO or DRAC, and log in as `root`.

2. List all the vSwitches on the ESXi server by issuing the following command:

   ```
   esxcfg-vswitch -l
   ```

3. Create a new port group on an existing vSwitch by using the following command:

   Syntax:

   ```
   esxcfg-vswitch -A portgroup_name vSwitch_name
   ```

   Example:

   ```
   esxcfg-vswitch -A NewKer vSwitch1
   ```

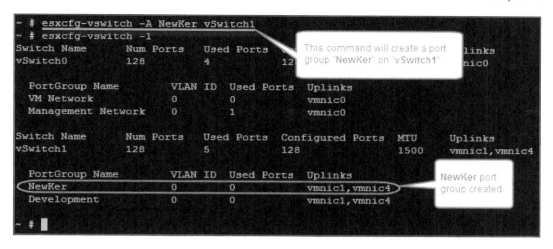

4. Issue either of the following commands in order to add a VMkernel interface to an existing port group:

```
esxcfg-vmknic -a -i DHCP -p NewKer
```

Or:

```
esxcfg-vmknic -a -i 192.168.193.88 -n 255.255.255.0 NewKer
```

There's more...

Although we can have only one VMkernel default gateway on an ESXi host, we can configure static routes to additional gateways. For instructions on how to configure static routes, refer the VMware KnowledgeBase article 2001426, available at http://kb.vmware.com/kb/2001426.

We could enable vMotion and FT functionalities on a selected VMkernel interface from the command line by using vim-cmd.

The corresponding commands are as follows:

```
vim-cmd hostsvc/vmotion/vnic_set vmk1
vim-cmd hostsvc/advopt/update FT.VMknic string vmk1
```

You need to refresh to apply the changes, by issuing the following command:

```
vim-cmd hostsvc/net/refresh
```

See also

You can refer to iSCSI and Jumbo Frames configuration on ESX/ESXi (VMware KnowledgeBase article 1007654) available at `http://kb.vmware.com/kb/1007654`.

Deleting a port group

Similar to deleting a vSwitch, when you choose to delete a port group make sure that the virtual machines have been reconfigured to use another port group which will provide them with network access.

How to do it...

A port group can be deleted by using either the vSphere Web Client GUI or the `esxcfg-vswitch` command.

Using vSphere Web Client

The following procedure explains how to delete a port group by using vSphere Web Client.

1. Select the ESXi host from the inventory, navigate to **Manage** | **Networking** | **Virtual switches**, and select the vSwitch from which would like to delete the port group.

2. Identify the port group from the switch diagram, click on the name of the port group, and click on the delete (**X**) icon to remove the port group:

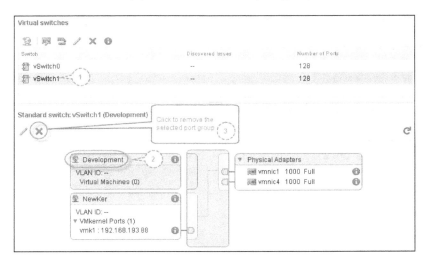

3. Click on **Yes** to confirm the removal of the device:

4. The **Recent Tasks** pane should show the **Remove Port Group** task completed successfully.

Using esxcfg-vswitch

The following procedure explains how to remove a port group from the ESXi Console:

1. SSH to the ESXi host as `root`, or use a direct console access method such as HP ILO or DRAC, and log in as `root`.

2. List all the vSwitches on the ESXi server by issuing the following command:

    `esxcfg-vswitch -l`

3. Identify the port group that needs to be deleted, and issue the following command to delete it:

    Syntax:

    `esxcfg-vswitch -D 'portgroup name' vSwitch1`

    Example:

    `esxcfg-vswitch -D 'Development' vSwitch1`

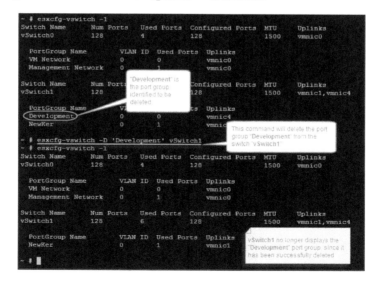

Adding an uplink to a vSphere Standard Switch

There can be situations where you would need to add additional uplinks (physical NICs) for a vSphere Standard Switch. Such an addition is generally done with the intention of enabling the use of teaming and load balancing features.

How to do it...

You can present the uplinks to the vSphere Standard Switch either by using the vSphere Web Client GUI or by using the `esxcfg-vswitch` command.

Using vSphere Web Client

The following procedure explains how to add an uplink to an existing vSwitch by using the vSphere Web Client:

1. Select the ESXi host from the inventory, navigate to **Manage | Networking | Virtual switches**, and select the vSwitch to which you want to add an uplink (vmnic).

2. With the vSwitch selected, click on the manage physical adapters icon:

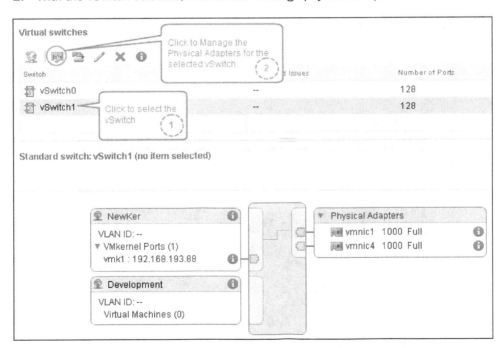

3. In the **Manage Physical Network Adapters for vSwitch** window, click on the green **+** icon to bring up the **Add Physical Adapters to the Switch** window:

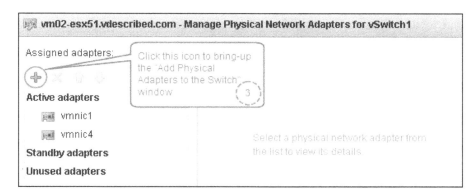

4. In the **Add Physical Adapters to the Switch** window, select the physical adapter (vmnic) to be added and click on **OK**:

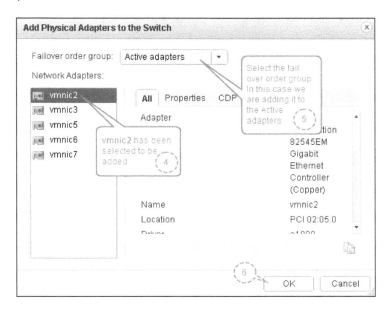

5. The **Manage Physical Network Adapters for vSwitch** window should now show the added vmnic. Click on **OK** to finish the configuration:

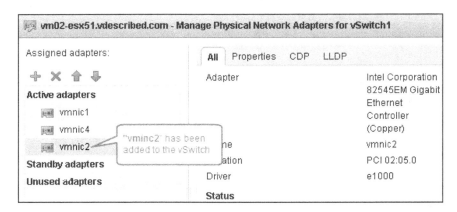

6. The network diagram for **vSwtich1**, will now show the added vmnic:

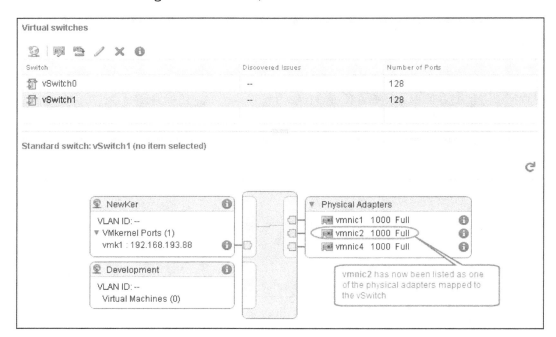

Using esxcfg-vswitch

The following procedure explains how to link a vmnic (physical NIC) to an existing vSphere Standard Switch by using the command line:

1. SSH to the ESXi host as `root`, or use a direct console access method such as HP ILO or DRAC, and log in as `root`.

2. List all the vSwitches on the ESXi server by issuing the following command:

   `esxcfg-vswitch -l`

3. Identify the vSwitch to which the uplinks need to be added, and issue the following commands to add the uplinks:

   `esxcfg-vswitch -L vmnic5 vSwitch1`

   `esxcfg-vswitch -L vmnic6 vSwitch1`

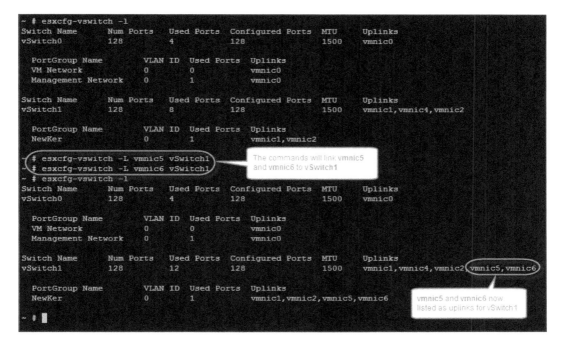

 To remove an uplink, you can issue the same command with the `-U` option. For example, you can use `esxcfg-vswitch -U vmnic5 vSwitch1`.

Creating a vSphere Distributed Switch

A vSphere Distributed Switch is a virtual switch that spans multiple ESXi hosts. Unlike a vSphere Standard Switch, which has to be locally configured on a per-ESXi basis, configuration of a vSphere Distributed Switch is done only once and the data plane is pushed to all of the ESXi hosts connected to it.

> A vSphere Distributed Switch cannot be created on an ESXi server. You need to be connected to the vCenter Server either by using the vSphere Client or by using the vSphere Web Client.

How to do it...

The following procedure explains how to create a new distributed vSwitch by using the vSphere Web Client:

1. From the inventory **Home**, click on **Networking**:

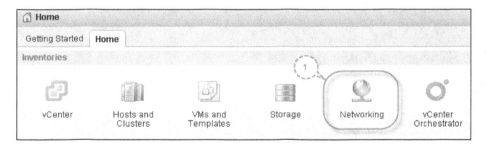

2. Select the datacenter, and navigate to **Related Objects | Distributed Switches** click on the new distributed switch icon:

3. Supply a name for the distributed switch, and click on **Next**:

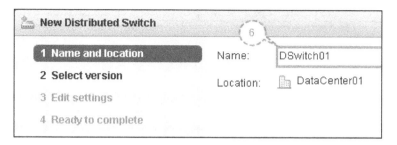

4. Select a distributed switch version, and click on **Next**:

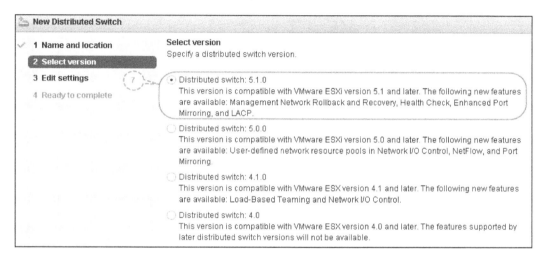

5. Select **Number of uplinks** planned, change the default port group name if necessary, and click on **Next**:

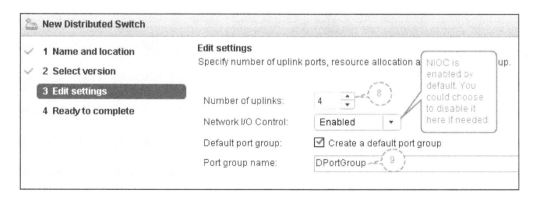

The wizard, by default, creates a dvPortGroup. You can choose not to create the dvPortGroup by deselecting the **Create a default port group** checkbox.

6. Review the **Ready to Complete** screen, and click on **Finish** to create the distributed switch:

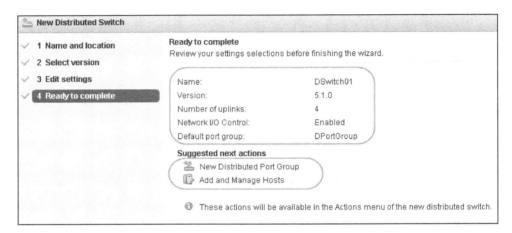

How it works...

A **vSphere Distributed Switch** (**vDS**) is created at the datacenter level and spans across multiple participating hosts. Therefore, it can only be created by using the vCenter Server.

A vDS will have a single control plane and multiple data planes. The control plane is at the vCenter Server and is used to create and manage the vDS. There will be a data plane created on each of the participating ESXi hosts. This means that all of the packet switching will happen at the ESXi hosts. A data plane is nothing but a hidden vSphere Standard Switch on the ESXi server. The use of a vDS reduces the administrative complexity of configuring vSphere Standard Switches on individual ESXi hosts in a large environment.

Four different versions of the vSphere Distributed Switches are available during its creation: 4.0, 4.1.0, 5.0.0, and 5.1.0. Choosing 5.1.0 will make the Distributed Switch incompatible with older versions of the ESXi hosts (if they are managed using the same vCenter Server).

A dvUplink is another layer of abstraction added to reduce the administrative complexity.

As you can see in this diagram, even though the vmnics used from both the ESXi hosts are different, they are logically mapped to **dvUplink1** and **dvUplink2**. This helps in setting the NIC teaming configuration without having to worry about the underlying vmnic number. On a vSphere Distributed Switch, the teaming is done by using the dvUplinks.

Every DSwitch with dvUplink/dvUplinks will have a dvUplinks port group. Every dvPortGroup created will increase the network count by 1.

Additional ports will always be consumed by the number of dvUplinks in the dvUplinks port group. This is true regardless of whether or not a dvUplink is backed by a vmnic from the participating ESXi servers.

Creating a distributed port group

A **distributed port group** (**DPortGroup**) can only be created from the vCenter Server. Every DPortGroup created has a default of eight available ports. Port allocation is elastic, which means that the port count will be automatically increased/decreased as needed.

How to do it...

The following procedure explains how to create a distributed port group:

1. Right-click on the DSwitch on which you want to create a dvPortGroup, and click on the menu item **New Distributed Port Group...**:

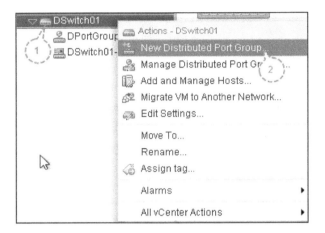

2. In the **New Distributed Port Group** wizard, supply a name for the distributed port group, and click on **Next**:

3. Configure the port settings (**Port binding**, **Port allocation**, **Number of ports**, **Network resource pool**, and **VLAN type**) as per your requirements, and click on **Next** to continue:

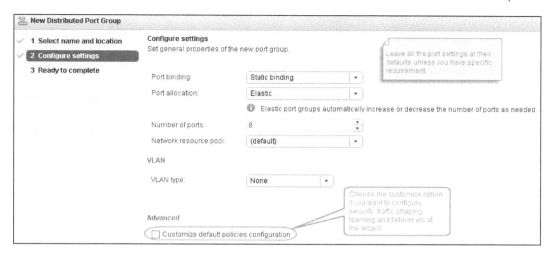

4. Review the **Ready to complete** screen, and click on **Finish** to create the distributed port group:

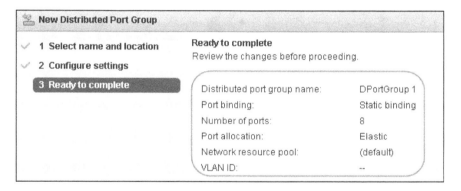

How it works...

Every distributed port group created will increase the network count by 1 on the dvSwitch and will also increase the number of available ports on the dvSwitch. The increase in the number of available ports (referred to as capacity of the DSwitch) depends on the number of ports allocated to the dvPortGroup.

The dvUplinks port group will also increase the network count by 1:

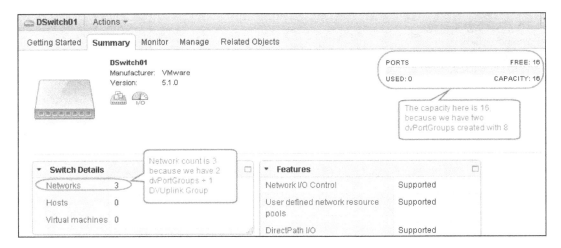

Adding hosts to a vSphere Distributed Switch

Once a DSwitch has been created, we now have to add the ESXi hosts to the DSwitch, so that its physical NIC can be mapped.

How to do it...

The following procedure explains how to attach ESXi hosts to the DSwitch:

1. Right-click on the DSwitch to which you want to add the hosts, and click on the **Add and Manage Hosts...** menu item:

2. In the **Add and Manage Hosts** wizard, select **Add hosts**, and click on **Next**:

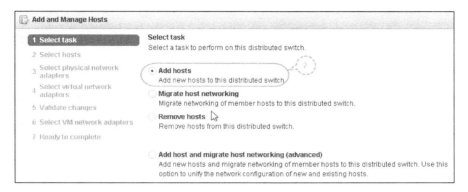

3. Click on the green **+** icon to bring up the selected new host's window:

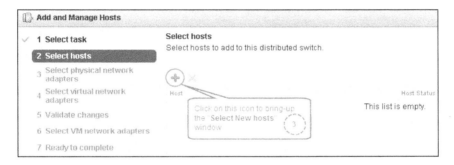

4. In the **Select new hosts** window, select the hosts which you want to add to the DSwitch, and click on **OK**:

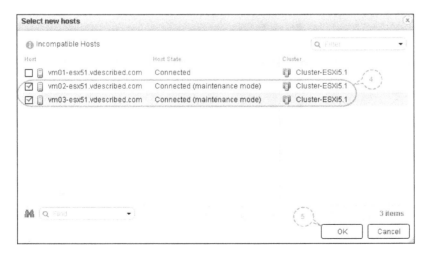

5. The **Select hosts** wizard should now show the added hosts. Click on **Next** to continue:

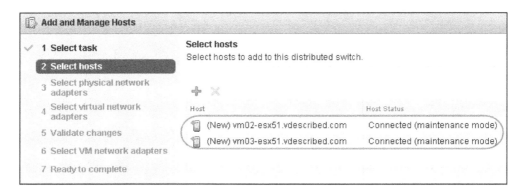

6. Select the unused physical adapters (vmnic), and click on **Next**:

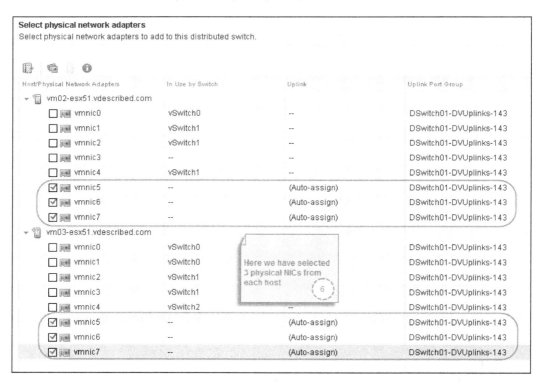

The physical NICs being selected will generally have their network backing configured correctly, so that the virtual machine will not lose connectivity when they are migrated to the DSwitch.

The number of physical adapters that you choose from each host cannot exceed the number of dvUplinks.

7. Select the VMkernel interfaces to be migrated, and click on the assign port group icon to map a destination dvPortGroup:

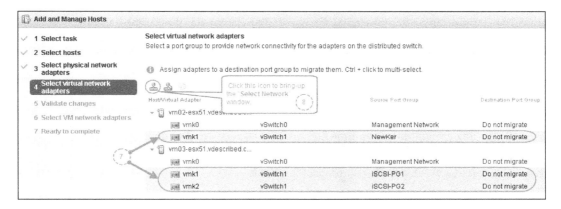

8. In the **Select Network** window, select the dvPortGroup (DPortGroup) to which the selected VMkernel adapters should be migrated, and click on **OK**:

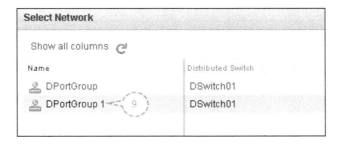

9. The **Destination Port Group** column in the **Select virtual network adapters** wizard should now show the selected dvPortGroup:

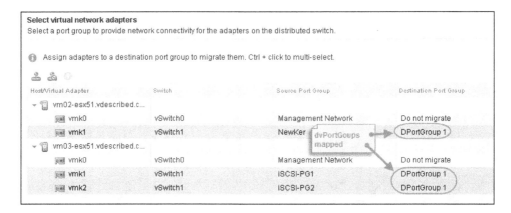

10. Review the **Validate Changes** screen, and click on **Next** to continue.

11. Choose to **Migrate the Virtual Machine Networking** and map a DPortGroup, as we did for the VMK adapters, and click on **Next**:

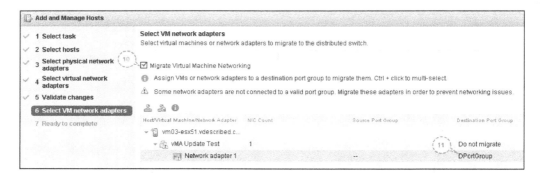

12. Review the **Ready to complete** screen, and click on **Finish**:

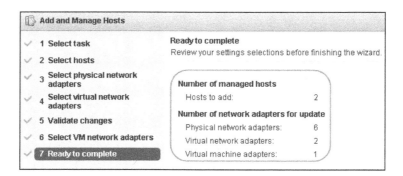

Mapping a physical adapter (vmnic) to a dvUplink

Mapping a physical adapter to an existing dvUplink has to be done per host. Keep in mind that the physical adapter count cannot exceed the dvUplink count.

How to do it...

A physical adapter (vmnic) can be connected to a DSwitch either by using the vSphere Web Client GUI or by using the ESXi CLI.

Using the vSphere Web Client

The following procedure explains how to add an uplink to a DSwitch by using vSphere Web Client:

1. Navigate to the **Host and Clusters** inventory, and select a host from the list.

2. With the host selected, navigate to **Manage | Networking | Virtual switches**, select the DSwitch from the list, and click on the icon for managing the physical adapters:

3. In the **Manage Physical Network Adapters for DSwitch** window, click on the green **+** icon to bring up the **Assign Physical Adapter to the Switch** window:

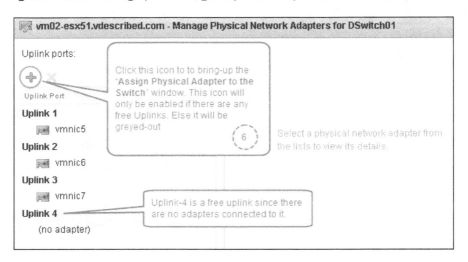

4. In the **Assign Physical Adapter to the Switch** window, select the available vmnic, and click on **OK**:

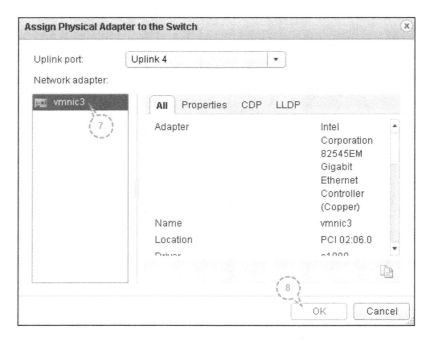

5. The **Manage Physical Network Adapters for DSwitch** window should now list the selected vmnic against one of the uplink ports.

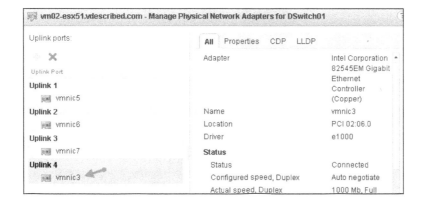

 To remove/unlink a physical adapter, highlight the uplink and click on the red (**X**).

Using esxcfg-vswitch

The following procedure explains how to map a physical NIC to a DSwitch:

1. SSH to the ESXi host as `root`, or use a direct console access method such as HP ILO or DRAC, and log in as `root`.

2. List all the vSwitches on the ESXi server by issuing the following command, and identify the DSwitch to which the physical NICs needs to be mapped:

```
esxcfg-vswitch -l
```

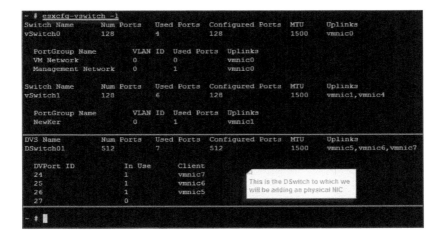

3. Use the following command to map a physical NIC (vmnic) to a DVPort ID:

Syntax:

```
esxcfg-vswitch -P <physical  NIC> -V <DVPort ID>  <dvSwitch>
```

Example:

```
esxcfg-vswitch -P vmnic3 -V 27 DSwitch01
```

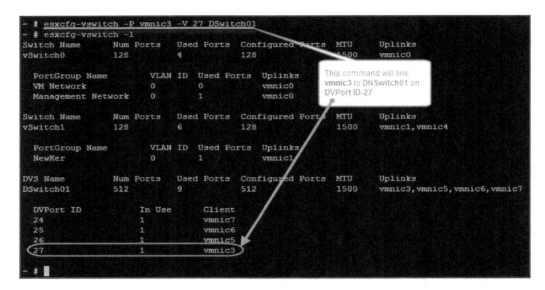

[To unmap, issue the same command, but replace -P with -Q. For example, `esxcfg-vswitch -Q vmnic5 -V 26 DSwitch01`.]

How it works...

As you have already seen in the previous sections, when you create a DSwitch, you choose the number of dvUplinks allowed. The number of dvUplinks dictates the maximum number of physical NICs that can be used from each of the ESXi servers.

Every dvUplink needs a port on the DSwitch; hence it gets a port ID, referred to as the DVPort ID.

Unlike using the vSphere Web Client GUI, where, you choose the dvUplink and then map a vmnic to it, the `esxcfg-vswitch` command requires you to specify the DVPort ID corresponding to the dvUplink. If you attempt to do this by using the port ID for another uplink, the `esxcfg-vswitch` command will fail with an error:

```
~ # esxcfg-vswitch -P vmnic4 -V 27 DSwitch01
Sysinfo error on operation returned status : Busy. Please see the VMkernel log for
detailed error information
~ #
```

Migrating virtual machine network from vSphere Standard Switch to vSphere Distributed Switch

You can migrate virtual machine networking to a DSwitch. But before you do that, make sure that the DSwitch has an uplink that supports the virtual machine's traffic. Refer to the *Mapping a physical adapter (vmnic) to a dvUplink* recipe for instructions on how to do this.

How to do it...

The following procedure explains how to migrate Virtual Machine networking to a DSwitch:

1. Right-click on the datacenter which has the DSwitch created, and click on the **Migrate VM to Another Network** menu item:

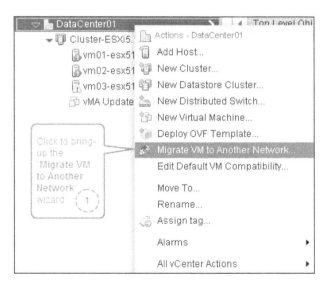

2. In the **Migrate Virtual Machine Networking** wizard, in the **Source network** section, click on **Browse...** to bring up the **Select Network** window:

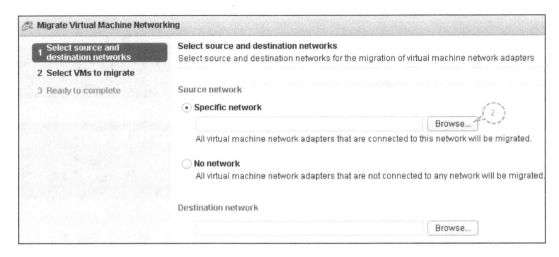

3. In the **Select Network** window, highlight the port group on the standard vSwitch to which the VMs are mapped, and click on **OK**:

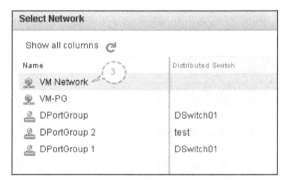

4. In the **Destination network** section, click on **Browse...** to bring up the **Select Network** window, and select the dvPortGroup.

5. With both source and destination networks selected, click on **Next** to continue:

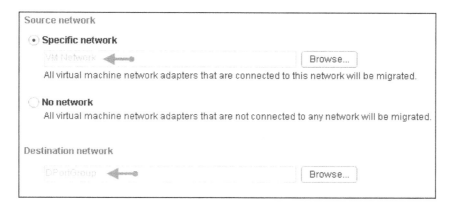

6. Select the virtual machines to be migrated and click on **Next**:

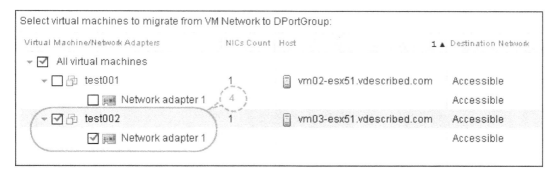

7. Review the **Ready to complete** screen, and click on **Finish**:

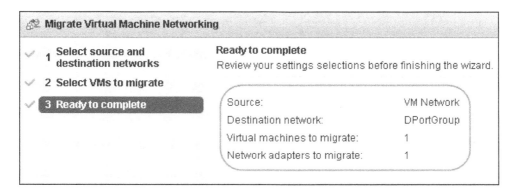

How it works...

When you migrate the virtual machine network from the vSphere Standard Switch to a vSphere Distributed Switch, it changes the network label (port group) mapping for the selected vNICs to match the dvPortGroup's name. As long as the destination dvPortGroup has uplinks that support virtual machine network traffic (for example, it is on the same VLAN), the network connectivity for the VMs will remain unaffected.

There's more...

When you try to migrate the virtual machine network, you also have the option to migrate virtual machines that are not configured for network access:

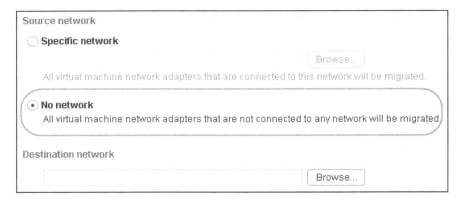

Migrating management and VMkernel interfaces between vSphere Standard and Distributed Switches

The VMkernel interfaces are still managed at the host level. When you plan to migrate the VMkernel interfaces from vSwitch to DSwitch, you need to make sure that the DSwitch uplinks are configured to support the VMkernel network traffic.

How to do it...

The following procedure explains how to migrate the management network from vSwitch to DSwitch:

1. With the ESXi host selected, navigate to **Manage | Networking | Virtual switches**, and select the DSwitch and click on the migrate networking icon:

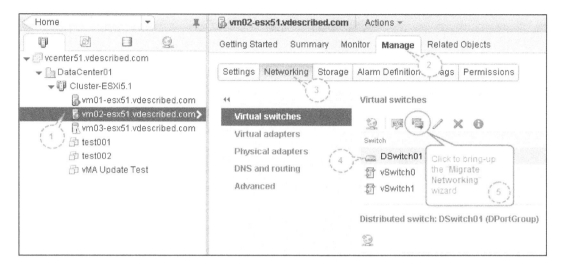

2. Since this is an existing DSwitch, the uplinks already have the physical NIC mapping. Click on **Next** to continue:

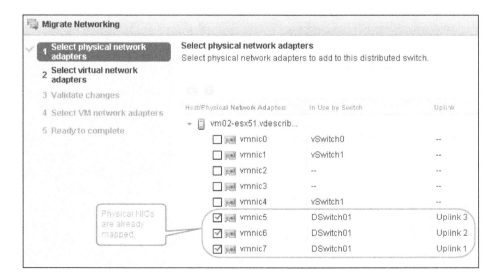

3. Select the VMkernel interface corresponding to the management network and bring up the **Select Network** window and select a destination dvPortGroup, and click on **Next**:

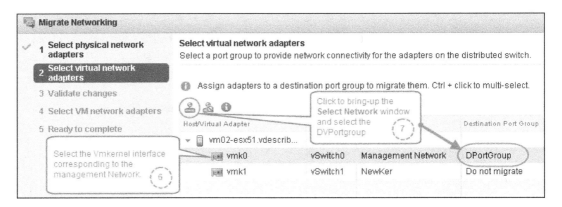

4. Review the **Validate changes** screen, and click on **Next** to continue.

5. Skip the **Select VM network adapters** wizard by not making any changes. Just click on **Next** to continue.

6. Review the **Ready to complete** screen, and click on **Finish**:

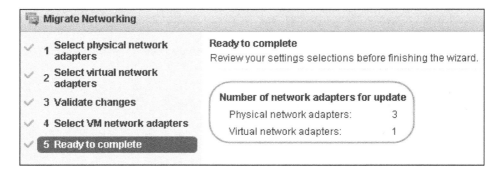

See also

More information on migrating a VMkernel interface used for the management network between standard vSwitches (VMware KnowledgeBase article 2037654) is available at `htttp://kb.vmware.com/kb/2037654`.

Creating a VMkernel interface on a vSphere Distributed Switch

As mentioned earlier, VMkernel interfaces can only be managed at the vCenter Server level. Therefore, to create a VMkernel interface, you need to modify the network configuration on a per-host basis.

How to do it...

The following procedure explains how to create a VMkernel interface on a DSwitch:

1. With the ESXi server selected, navigate to **Manage | Networking | Virtual switches**, select the DSwitch, and click on the add networking icon:

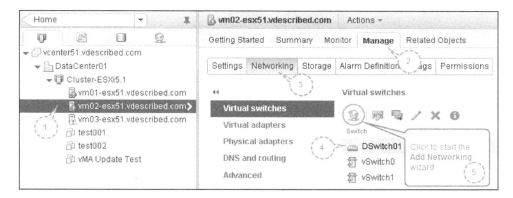

2. Select **VMkernel Network Adapter** as the connection type, and click on **Next**:

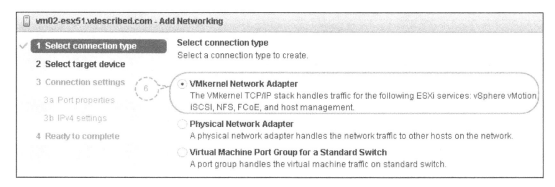

3. Navigate to and select a DPortGroup on which the VMkernel interface has to be created, and click on **Next** to continue:

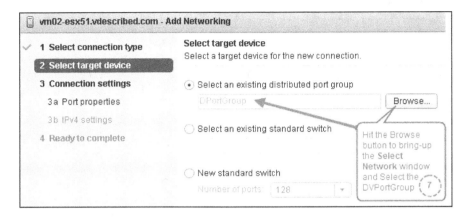

4. Select a function/service that will leverage this VMkernel interface, and click on **Next**. In this example, we will select **vMotion traffic**:

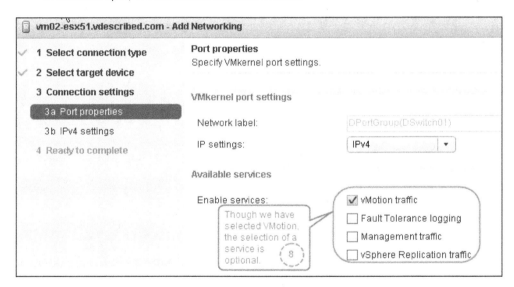

5. Supply the IP configuration for the interface, and click on **Next**:

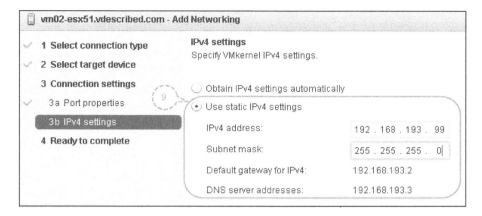

6. Review the Ready to complete screen, and click on **Finish**:

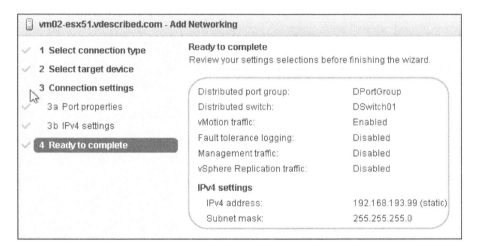

Exporting the vSphere Distributed Switch configuration

With vSphere 5.1, you now have an option to export the DSwitch configuration. Using this functionality you can now backup the DSwitch configuration when needed.

How to do it...

The following procedure explains how to export the DSwitch configuration:

1. Right-click on the DSwitch and navigate to **All vCenter Actions | Export Configuration** to bring up the **Export Configuration** dialog box.

2. Select the configuration to export. You can choose between exporting **Distributed switch and all port groups** or **Distributed switch only**. Supply an optional description if needed, and click on **OK** to export the configuration:

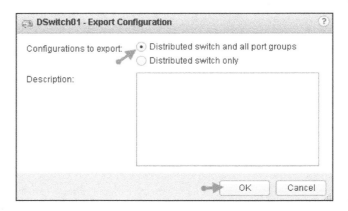

3. Click on **Yes** in the **Confirm Configuration Export** dialog box:

4. Select a location to save the exported configuration to, and click on **Save** to create a backup `.zip` archive.

How it works...

The backup taken is a snapshot of the current DSwitch configuration. The ZIP archive created will contain the DSwitch data in binary format. However, it does include a `data.xml` file with the DSwitch metadata. This backup ZIP archive can be used to restore the DSwitch configuration or to create a DSwitch in a new datacenter.

  ▸ The *Importing a vSphere Distributed Switch into the datacenter from a backup* recipe

Restoring the vSphere Distributed Switch configuration

The fact that we now can back up a DSwitch enables the ability to restore its configuration from a backup. The restore functionality is particularly useful when the changes made to a DSwitch have yielded undesired results.

How to do it...

The following procedures explain how to restore the DSwitch configuration.

1. Right-click on the DSwitch and navigate to **All vCenter Actions | Restore Configuration** to bring up the **Restore Configuration** wizard.

2. In the **Restore Configuration** wizard, click on **Browse...** to locate and select the DSwitch backup ZIP archive.

3. Choose between **Restore distributed switch and all port groups** or **Restore distributed switch only**, and click on **Next** to continue:

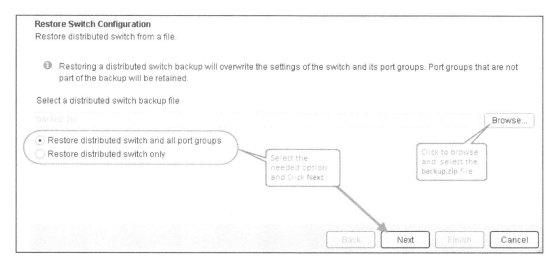

4. Review the **Import Settings** section on the **Ready to complete** screen, and click on **Finish** to initiate the restore operation.

How it works...

If the restore operation completes successfully, the changes made to the DSwitch after the snapshot (backup or export operation) will be lost.

Importing a vSphere Distributed Switch into the datacenter from a backup

It is possible to import a DSwitch into a datacenter from a configuration backup. This functionality will come in handy if the existing DSwitch configuration is corrupted or lost. Refer to the *Exporting the vSphere Distributed Switch configuration* recipe to learn how to back up the DSwitch configuration.

How to do it...

The following procedure explains how to import a DSwitch into the datacenter:

1. Right-click on the datacenter to which you intend to import the DSwitch, and navigate to **All vCenter Actions | Import Distributed Switch** to bring up the **Import Distributed Switch** wizard.

2. Click on **Browse...** to locate and select the ZIP archive.

3. If applicable, choose to **Preserve the original distributed switch and port group identifiers** by selecting the checkbox next to this option. Click on **Next** to continue.

4. Review the **Import Settings** section on the **Ready to complete** screen, and click on **Finish** to initiate the import operation.

How it works...

If we select the **Preserve the original distributed switch and port group identifiers** option and the datacenter to which the DSwitch is being imported has a DSwitch with the same name, then that DSwitch, or its port groups, is not deleted. Instead, the information from the backup file is merged and updated with the existing DSwitch.

If we do not select the **Preserve the original distributed switch and port group identifiers** option and the datacenter to which the DSwitch is being imported into has a DSwitch with the same name, then that DSwitch or its port groups are not deleted, but a new DSwitch with the configuration from the backup file is created. For example, if the datacenter had a DSwitch with the name `DSwitch01` then the new DSwitch will be called `DSwitch01 (1)`.

Enabling port mirroring on a DSwitch

Starting with vSphere Distributed Switch 5.0, you can enable port mirroring. **Port mirroring** is functionality that allows the replication of network traffic on a port (source) to another port or uplink (destination) on the DSwitch. This is particularly useful when you have a packet analyzer or **IDS** (**Intrusion Detection System**) deployed on the network. Port mirroring can only be enabled on a vSphere Distributed Switch and not on a vSphere Standard Switch.

How to do it...

The following procedure explains how to enable port mirroring on a DSwitch:

1. Select the DSwitch on which you intend to enable port mirroring, and navigate to **Manage | Settings**.
2. Under the **Settings** tab, select **Port mirroring**.
3. Click on **New** to bring up the **Add Port Mirroring Session** wizard:

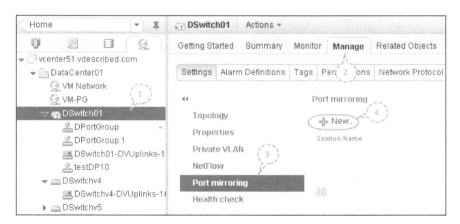

4. In the **Add Port Mirroring Session** wizard, select the desired session type, and click on **Next** to continue. In this example, we have chosen the session type to be **Distributed Port Mirroring**:

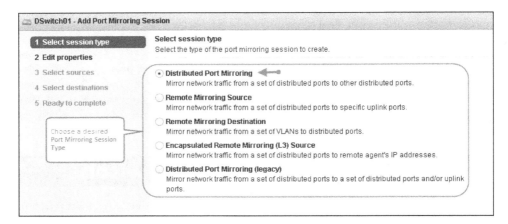

5. On the next screen, update the following details:

    ❑   Supply a name in the **Name** field

    ❑   Change the **Status** property of the session to **Enabled**

    ❑   Set **Normal I/O on destination ports** to **Allowed**, if you intend to allow other network traffic (such as RDP) on the destination ports that will be selected

    ❑   You can also choose to configure the values for **Mirrored packet length** and **Sampling Rate** if necessary

    ❑   Click on **Next** to continue

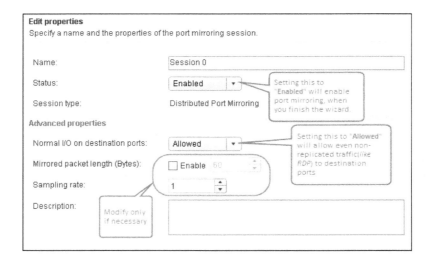

6. Add the source distributed port(s), and click on **Next**:

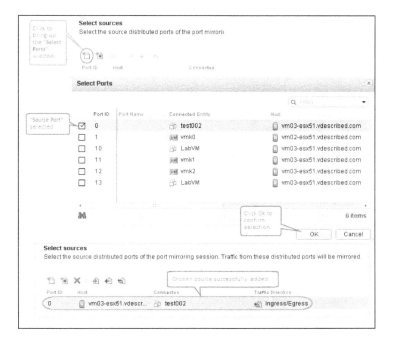

7. Add the destination distributed port(s), and click on **Next**:

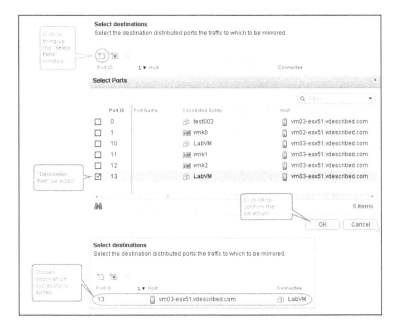

8. In the **Ready to complete** screen, review the settings, and click on **Finish** to enable port mirroring.

How it works...

Once port mirroring is enabled, all the traffic that arrives at the chosen source is mirrored (replicated) to the desired destination.

The source can be distributed ports or VLANs. The destination can be distributed ports, uplinks, or IP addresses of machines running the traffic monitoring application.

There are five mirroring session types, as follows:

- **Distributed port mirroring**: This is used for replicating network traffic from one or more distributed ports to distributed port(s) to which the vNIC(s) of the VM(s) running the packet monitoring software are attached. This session type will work only if the source and destination VMs are on the same ESXi host.

- **Remote mirroring source**: This is used when the traffic analyzer is a machine connected to one of the ports on the physical switch. This would require a configuration change on the physical switch to mirror the traffic received on a physical port, to another physical port on the same switch to which the packet analyzer machine is connected or to a port on a different switch (with the help of RSPAN VLAN).

- **Remote mirroring destination**: This is used when you want to monitor traffic in a particular VLAN by mirroring the traffic to a VM connected to a distributed port.

- **Encapsulated remote mirroring (L3) source**: This is used when the packet analyzer is on a machine on a different L3 subnet. In this case, the source will be the distributed ports and the destination will be the IP address of the packet analyzer machine.

- **Distributed port mirroring (legacy)**: This is used when we need uplinks and distributed ports as the destination.

Enabling NetFlow on a DSwitch

NetFlow is an industry standard for network traffic monitoring. Although originally developed by Cisco, it has since become an industry standard. Once enabled, it can be used to capture IP traffic statistics on all the interfaces where NetFlow is enabled, and send them as records to the NetFlow collector software. Starting with vSphere Distributed Switch 5.0, we can enable NetFlow at the DSwitch or DPortGroup level.

How to do it...

The following procedure explains how to enable NetFlow on a DSwitch:

1. Select the DSwitch on which you intend to enable NetFlow, and navigate to **Manage** | **Settings**.

2. Under the **Settings** tab, select **NetFlow**, and click on **Edit** to bring up the **Edit NetFlow Settings** window:

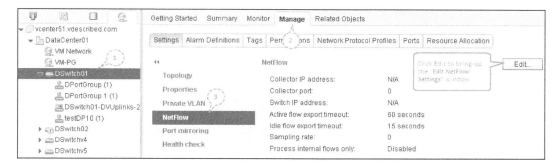

3. Specify the values for **IP address** and **Port** of the NetFlow collector machine, and then specify the value for **Switch IP address**.

4. Modify the **Advanced Settings** if necessary, and click on **OK**:

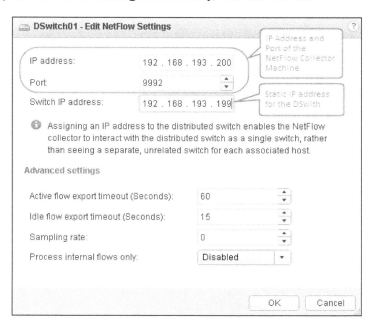

How it works...

NetFlow, once configured on the DSwitch, will allow the NetFlow collector software to capture and analyze statistics for the DSwitch. The DSwitch is identified by the NetFlow collector software using the IP address that we assigned to the DSwitch while configuring NetFlow on it. The IP assigned to the DSwitch doesn't give it a network identity. It is only used by the NetFlow collector to uniquely identify the VDS.

See also

The technical overview whitepaper from Cisco, available at `http://www.cisco.com/en/US/prod/collateral/iosswrel/ps6537/ps6555/ps6601/prod_white_paper0900aecd80406232.html`, will give you more insight into NetFlow's use cases.

Configuring private VLANs (PVLANs) on a DSwitch

VLANs provide logical segmentation of a network into different broadcast domains. **Private VLANs** (**PVLANs**) provide a method to further segment a VLAN into different private groups. We can add and configure PVLANs on a vSphere Distributed Switch. For private VLANs to work, the physical switches backing your environment should be PVLAN aware.

How to do it...

The following procedure explains how to configure PVLANs on a DSwitch:

1. Select the DSwitch on which you intend to enable private VLAN, and navigate to **Manage | Settings**.

2. Under the **Settings** tab, select **Private VLAN**, and click on **Edit** to bring up the **Edit Private VLAN Settings** window.

3. Click on **Add** under the **Primary VLAN ID** section to add a primary VLAN ID.

4. Click on **Add** under the **Secondary VLAN ID** section to add secondary VLANs of the type **Community** or **Isolated**:

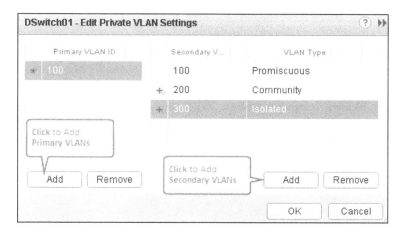

5. Click on **OK** to confirm the settings.

How it works...

Private VLANs, once configured, can be used with port groups.

The port groups can be configured to use any of the secondary PVLANs created. This is done in the **Edit Settings** window for a port group. The **VLAN** section will allow you to set the **VLAN type** to **Private VLAN**, and let you choose the secondary PVLAN IDs.

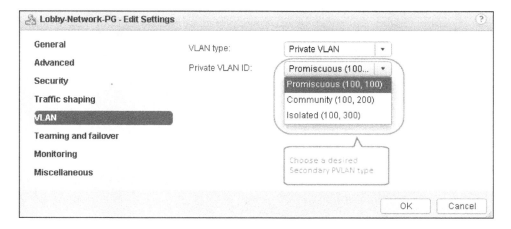

There are three types of secondary private VLANs, as follows:

- **Promiscuous PVLAN**: VMs in a promiscuous PVLAN can communicate with any VM belonging to any of its secondary PVLANs. The promiscuous PVLAN will act as a gateway for other secondary PVLANs.

- **Community PVLAN**: VMs in a community PVLAN can only talk amongst VMs in the same community PVLAN or the promiscuous PVLAN. It cannot communicate with VMs in any other secondary PVLAN.

- **Isolated PVLAN**: VMs in an isolated PVLAN are isolated from every other VM in the same isolated PVLAN. It can only communicate with the VMs in a promiscuous PVLAN. There can only be a single isolated PVLAN per primary PVLAN.

9

Creating and Managing Virtual Machines

In this chapter we will cover the following:

- ▶ Creating a virtual machine
- ▶ Creating a new hard disk for a virtual machine
- ▶ Adding an existing hard disk to a virtual machine
- ▶ Attaching RDM to a virtual machine
- ▶ Mapping a virtual machine's vNIC to a different port group
- ▶ Adding a new virtual network adapter to a virtual machine
- ▶ Creating a virtual machine snapshot
- ▶ Deleting a virtual machine snapshot
- ▶ Reverting to a current virtual machine snapshot
- ▶ Going to a virtual machine snapshot
- ▶ Consolidating snapshots
- ▶ Exporting a virtual machine

Introduction

A **virtual machine** (**VM**) is the essence of server virtualization. It is a software abstract that provides an isolated environment for an operating system. It enables the running of more than one operating system on the same physical hardware.

When virtual machines are powered on and running, the operating systems hosted inside them are not aware of the fact that they are running on a virtual machine. They operate and respond in the same manner as they would on a physical machine.

So what makes these VMs coexist on the same physical hardware? This is where the **virtual machine monitor** (**VMM**) plays its role.

The VMM virtualizes x86 architecture, which includes the instruction set, memory, interrupts, and the basic I/O operations. When a virtual machine is powered on, the VMkernel loads the VMM, and the VM executes on top of the VMM.

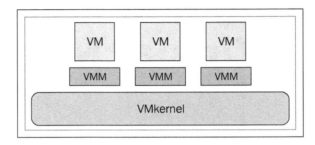

The virtual machine components

A virtual machine will have the following default virtual hardware components:

- Memory, CPUs, SCSI controller, hard disks, and network adapters
- Video card, VMCI device, CD/DVD drive, and floppy drive

Additional components can be added using the **Add Hardware** wizard. The hardware wizard presents the following components:

- Network Adapter
- Hard disk (New/Existing/RDM)
- Serial port, Parallel port, Host USB Device, USB Controller, SCSI Controller
- SCSI Device, PCI Device
- Floppy drive, CD/DVD drive

Files that back a virtual machine

Every virtual machine is backed by a set of files. The virtual machine configuration file with the extension `.vmx` holds all of the virtual machine's configuration information. For files associated with a virtual machine, see the following table:

Configuration file	File extension
The virtual machine configuration file	`*.vmx`
The virtual disk descriptor file	`*.vmdk`
The virtual disk data file	`*-flat.vmdk`
The RDM mapping file (physical compatibility mode)	`*-rdmp.vmdk`
The RDM mapping file (virtual compatibility mode)	`*-rdm.vmdk`
The virtual machine snapshot database	`*.vmsd`
The virtual machine snapshot state file	`*.vmsn`
The virtual machine snapshot delta file	`*-delta.vmdk`
The virtual machine team information file	`*.vmxf`
The virtual machine swap file	`*.vswp`
The virtual machine BIOS file	`*.nvram`

Files associated with a virtual machine

The virtual machine configuration file

The **virtual machine configuration** (**VMX**) file holds all of the configuration information for the virtual machine, which includes:

▸ The CPU and memory configuration

▸ The virtual disk drives used

▸ The virtual network card information

▸ The guest OS information

▸ The BIOS UUID of the virtual machine

▸ The vCenter Server assigned UUID of the virtual machine

The following are a few of the entries that appear in the VMX file:

▸ **numvcpus**: This entry indicates the number of processors (sockets).

▸ **cpuid.coresPerSocket**: This entry indicates the number of cores per processor.

▸ **scsiX.virtualDev**: This entry indicates the type of SCSI controller used.

▸ **ethernetX.virtualDev**: This entry indicates the type of Ethernet adapter used.

▸ **ethernetX.generatedAddress**: This entry indicates the MAC address generated by the ESXi server for that particular virtual network adapter.

▸ **guestOS**: This entry indicates the guest operating type set for the virtual machine.

▸ **uuid.bios**: This entry indicates the UUID of the virtual machine.

▸ **vc.uuid**: This is the UUID that is generated when a VM is added to the inventory using vCenter. This is not the vCenter's instance UUID.

The virtual machine BIOS file

The **virtual machine BIOS** (NVRAM) file holds the virtual BIOS (Phoenix BIOS) for a virtual machine. It can be accessed by pressing the function key *F2* during the VM boot up. This file is created when the virtual machine is powered on for the first time. All of the BIOS changes are saved to this file. If the file is manually deleted, you will lose the previous BIOS configuration, but the file is regenerated with the defaults during the next power on.

Virtual machine enhancements available with vSphere 5.1

The following are a few of the virtual machine enhancements available with vSphere 5.1:

▸ The virtual machine's virtual hardware gets an upgrade to Version 9. For more information on virtual machine hardware version, refer to the VMware KnowledgeBase article 1003746, available at `http://kb.vmware.com/kb/1003746`.

▸ A virtual machine can now support 64 vCPUs and can be configured with up to 1 terabyte of RAM.

▸ Hardware accelerated 3D graphics support.

▸ VMware has introduced a **guest OS reclamation** technique for use with VMware view, which will reduce the size of the VMDK file when files are deleted at the guest OS level. The new VMDK type, **SE Sparse** is required for the guest OS reclamation technique to work.

▸ The VMware also introduced **virtualized hardware virtualization** (**VHV**), which is used to expose more details about the CPU architecture to the virtual machine. This means that it can now expose hardware virtualization to the virtual machine and enable virtualized CPU performance counters.

▸ Another enhancement is Improved virtual machine compatibility. vSphere will now support virtual machines running older virtual machine hardware versions. You can now choose a compatibility level for a virtual machine.

Creating a virtual machine

A virtual machine can be created by either using the vSphere Web Client interface or by using the vSphere Client interface connected directly to the ESXi server. In this recipe we will learn how to create virtual machine by using the vSphere Web Client interface.

How to do it...

To create a virtual machine, we will use the **New Virtual Machine** wizard. There are many GUI locations from where the wizard can be started. However, in this recipe we will use the virtual machine inventory as a starting place.

The following procedure explains how to create a virtual machine by using the vSphere Web Client:

1. Connect to the vCenter Server as an Administrator by using the vSphere Web Client.

2. Navigate to the **VMs and Templates** view from the inventory **Home**.

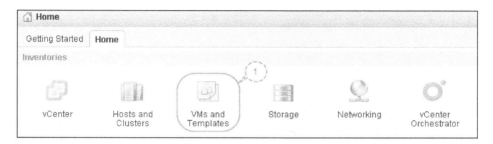

3. Navigate to and right-click on the **DataCenter**, and then click on the **New Virtual Machine...** menu item to bring-up the **New Virtual Machine** wizard.

4. At the **New Virtual Machine** wizard, select the option **Create a new virtual machine** and click on **Next**.

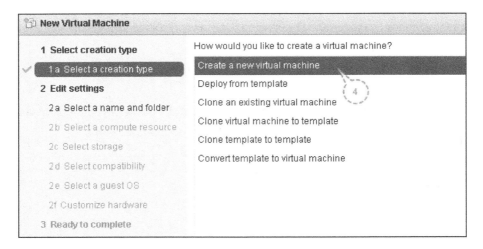

5. Provide a name for the virtual machine, choose an inventory location (datacenter), and then click on **Next**.

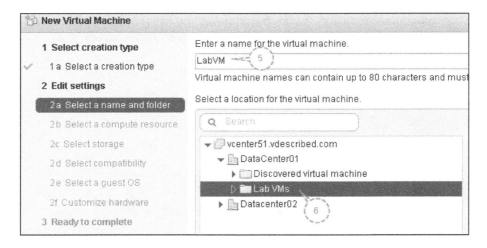

 Only folders of the type VM and Template will be listed in the **New Virtual Machine** wizard.

6. Navigate to the **Select a compute resource** (a cluster or an ESXi server) for the virtual machine, and then click on **Next**.

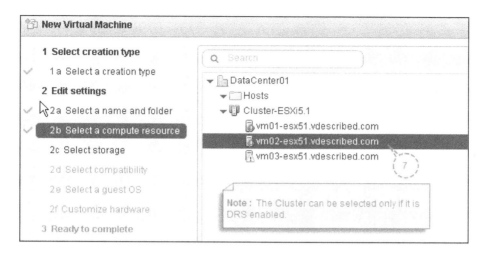

7. Choose a datastore for the virtual machine files, and then click on **Next**. At this screen we could also use **VM Storage Profile** to filter the datastores.

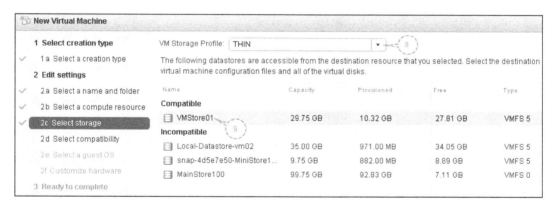

 By default, the **VM Storage Profile** option is set to **None**.

Learn more about VM Storage Profiles in *Chapter 7, Profile-driven Storage and Storage I/O Control*.

8. Select a virtual machine compatibility mode by clicking on **Select compatibility**.

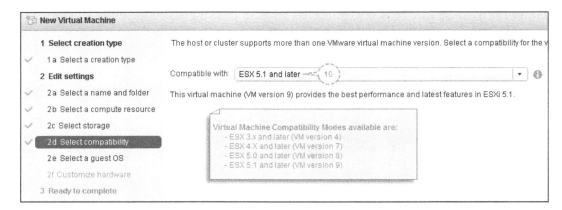

9. Select the **Guest OS Family** and **Guest OS Version** details, and then click on **Next**.

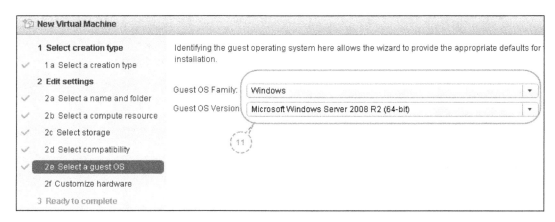

10. Customize the virtual machine's hardware if necessary, by clicking on **Customize hardware**.

11. On the **Ready to complete** screen, review the information, and then click on **Finish** to create the virtual machine.

Creating a new hard disk for a virtual machine

The need to add an additional hard drive is driven by the guest OS or the VM design requirements. As these design aspects are beyond the scope of this book, we will dive directly into the procedure of adding a hard drive to the VM. The virtual machine can be in a powered on state while we add the hard disk.

It will be beneficial to learn a few concepts before we discuss how to create a new hard disk for a virtual machine.

Virtual machine disk provisioning methods

The **virtual machine disk** (**VMDK**) can be provisioned using two different methods namely, thick provisioning and thin provisioning. Thick provisioning can be further categorized into lazy zeroed thick provisioning and eager zeroed thick provisioning.

> Zeroing is a process of writing zeroes—to the disk blocks corresponding to a VMDK, to make sure that the existing data in those blocks, if any, are not exposed via the new VMDK.

The thick provisioning methods are as follows:

- **Eager zeroed thick provisioning**: An eager zeroed thick disk, when created, will get all of the space allocation it needs, and all of the disk blocks allocated to it are zeroed out. The creation time of an eager zeroed disk, is longer as compared to a lazy zeroed or thin-provisioned disk. An eager zeroed thick disk offers better first write performance. This is due to the fact that the disk blocks corresponding to an eager zeroed disk are already zeroed out during its creation.

- **Lazy zeroed thick provisioning**: A lazy zeroed thick disk will also get all of the space allocation it needs at the time of creation, but unlike an eager zeroed disk, it does not zero out all of the disk blocks. Each disk block is zeroed out only during the first write. Although it doesn't offer the first write performance like an eager zeroed disk, all of the subsequent writes to the zeroed blocks will have the same performance.

> First write occurs when a disk block corresponding to a VMDK is accessed for the first time to store data.

A **thin-provisioned** disk will not use all of the disk space assigned to it during creation. It will only consume the disk space needed by the data on the disk. For instance, if you create a thin VMDK of 10 GB, then the initial size of the VMDK will not be 10 GB. When data gets added to it, the VMDK will grow in size to store the added data. If a 100 MB file is added to the VMDK then the VMDK will grow by 100 MB.

The performance of a thin provisioned disk is discussed in following white paper:

```
http://www.vmware.com/pdf/vsp_4_thinprov_perf.pdf
```

Virtual machine disk modes

A virtual machine disk can be in two different modes. These modes determine what operations can be performed on the VMDK:

> ▶ **Dependent disk mode**: This is the default disk mode for all virtual machine disks that you create. All the VMDK related operations can be performed while it is in dependent mode.

> ▶ **Independent disk mode**: When a virtual disk is in independent mode, no snapshot operations are allowed on it. These types of virtual disks are particularly useful for use with virtual machines in testing and development environments, when you would need to make changes and test the results, and also want to revert to a standard base line after the tests. It is also useful when you are using virtual machines to perform tests that can yield unpredictable results. These kinds of VMs are generally not backed up.

> An independent disk can have two fundamental behavioral modes:

> > ❑ **Persistent mode**: In this mode all changes made to the files on disk are written to the disk. Because these changes are immediately written to the disk, they are retained across reboots. In a test/development environment this mode is used to save changes to the test baseline.

> > ❑ **Non-persistent mode**: In this mode changes made are not immediately written to the disk and are lost when you reboot, or shutdown the virtual machine. This mode is generally used in test environments, where changes can yield unpredictable results.

How to do it...

You can add a new virtual hard disk to a VM by editing the settings for the VM.

The following procedure explains how to add a new hard disk to virtual machine:

1. Navigate to the **VM and Templates** inventory view, select and right-click on the VM to which you intend to add a hard disk, and then click on **Edit Settings...**.

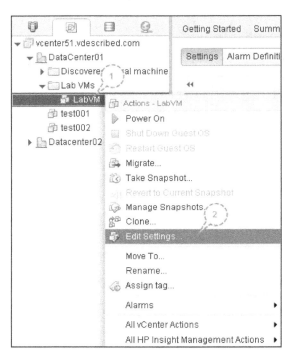

2. Use the **New device** option available in the **Edit Settings** window, select **New Hard Disk** as the device option, and then click on **Add**.

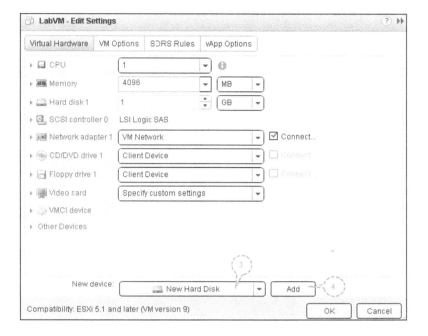

3. Once this is done, a **New Hard disk** device entry will be added to the **Edit Settings** window.

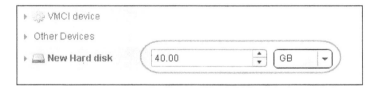

4. Click on the **New Hard disk** device entry, to expand it and reveal all of the advanced settings for that hard drive entry. Select a **Maximum Size, Location, Disk Provisioning, Virtual Device Node**, and **Disk Mode**.

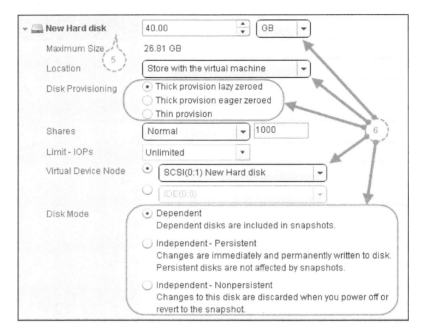

5. By default, the **Location** selected is **Store with virtual machine**. This is the recommended settings in most environments, for easier file management. For a traditional virtual machine, you would not need to modify these options.

6. Click on **OK** to confirm the settings. You should see the **Reconfigure virtual machine** task completing successfully, in the **Recent Tasks** pane.

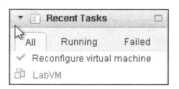

Adding an existing hard disk to a virtual machine

You can add an existing hard disk (VMDK) to a virtual machine. This is again done from the **Edit Settings** window of the virtual machine.

The virtual machine can be in powered on state while you add the hard disk.

How to do it...

The following procedure explains how to add an existing virtual hard disk (VMDK) to the VM:

1. Navigate to the **VM and Templates** inventory view, select and right-click on the VM to which you intend to add an existing virtual hard disk (VMDK), and then click on **Edit Settings.**

2. Use the **New device** option available in the **Edit Settings** window, select **Existing Hard Disk** as the device option, and then click on **Add**.

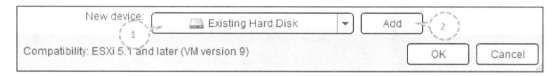

3. Browse to the location of the VMDK, select the VMDK file, and then click on **OK** to confirm the selection.

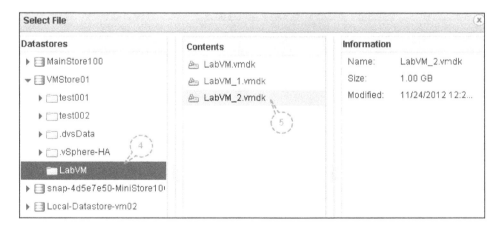

4. A **New Hard disk** entry should now be visible on the Settings page. Click on it to expand the advanced/additional settings for the virtual hard disk. Change the **Virtual Device Node** or **Disk Mode** only if necessary.

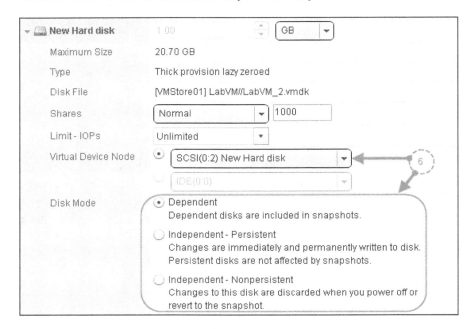

5. Click on **OK** to confirm the settings and reconfigure the virtual machine.

Attaching RDM to a virtual machine

In many environments, there will be requirements or special cases that warrant the use of **raw device mappings** (**RDM**). The use of RDMs allows the guest operating system running in a VM to create its native filesystem on a LUN device. The benefits of using RDMs have been outlined in the vSphere 5.1 Storage guide:

```
http://pubs.vmware.com/vsphere-51/topic/com.vmware.ICbase/PDF/
vsphere-esxi-vcenter-server-511-storage-guide.pdf
```

RDMs can be presented to a VM in two compatibility modes:

▶ **Physical compatibility**: In this mode all of the SCSI commands except the REPORT LUNs command is sent to the device directly. Therefore, this mode is also referred to as a Passthrough mode.

- ▶ **Virtual compatibility**: In this mode only the READ and WRITE commands are sent to the device. In this mode the RDM will be compatible with most of the tasks that can be performed on a traditional VMDK.

In this recipe of the chapter, we will learn how to attach a raw device mapping to a virtual machine.

How to do it...

The following procedure explains how to attach an RDM to a virtual machine:

1. Contact your storage administrator to present a blank/raw LUN to the ESXi server(s).

2. Navigate to the **VM and Templates** inventory view, select and right-click on the VM to which you intend to add/map an RDM LUN, and then click on **Edit Settings**.

3. Use the **New device** option available in the **Edit Settings** window, select **RDM Disk** as the device option, and then click on **Add**.

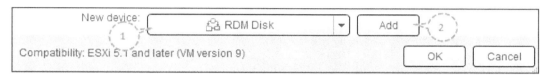

4. In the **Select Target LUN** window, select the LUN that has to be added in RDM, and then click on **OK**.

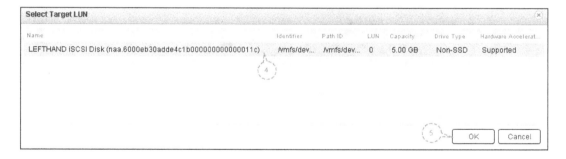

5. A **New Hard disk** entry for the RDM should now be visible on the Settings page. Click on it to expand the advanced/additional settings for the hard disk. Change the **Location**, **Virtual Device Node**, and RDM **Compatibility Mode** as needed.

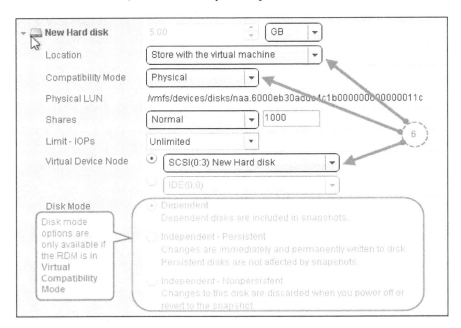

6. Click on **OK** to confirm the settings and attach the RDM.

Mapping a virtual machine's vNIC to a different port group

A virtual machine connects to the network via its virtual network adapter. The **virtual network adapter** of a VM is referred to as a **vNIC**. The vNIC connects to a port group on a vSwitch (Standard/Distributed). A vNIC cannot be directly connected to a vSwitch; it can only be mapped to any of the port groups present on the vSwitch. A port group is a set of ports on a vSwitch grouped together under a common configuration, for example, a VLAN.

If there is a need, we can reconfigure the vNIC to connect to another existing port group, or to a newly created port group. To learn more about creating and managing port groups read *Chapter 8, Configuring the vSphere Network*.

In this recipe, we will learn how to reconfigure a virtual machine to map its vNIC to different port groups.

How to do it...

The following procedure guides you through the steps required to map a VMs vNIC to different port groups:

1. Navigate to the **VM and Templates** inventory view, select and right-click on the VM, and then click on **Edit Settings**.

2. Use the drop-down box next to the **Network adapter** entry to select the port group to which the vNIC should be connected, and then click on **OK** to confirm the settings.

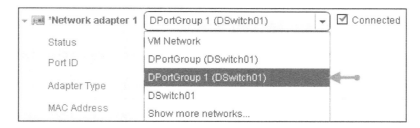

3. Click on **OK** to confirm the changes.

How it works...

Once the virtual machine's vNIC has been reconfigured to connect to a different port group, all the network I/O via vNIC will be affected by the configuration on the port group. That is, if the port group has a VLAN ID set on it, then the VM will have access to the subnet corresponding to that VLAN. The vNIC to port group mapping can be changed while the virtual machine is running.

Adding a new virtual network adapter to a virtual machine

You can add an additional virtual network adapter to a virtual machine. Such a need is dictated by the purpose of the virtual machine.

In this recipe we will learn how to add a new virtual network adapter to a VM.

How to do it...

The following procedure explains how to add an new virtual network adapter to a VM:

1. Navigate to the **VM and Templates** inventory view, select and right-click on the VM to which you intend to add a virtual network adapter (vNIC), and then click on **Edit Settings**.

2. Use the **New device** option available at the **Edit Settings** window, select **Network** as the device option, and then click on **Add**.

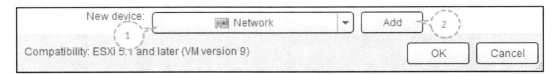

3. A **New Network** entry for the adapter is available on the settings page. Use the drop-down box next to the **New Network** to select a port group, and then click on **OK** to confirm the settings.

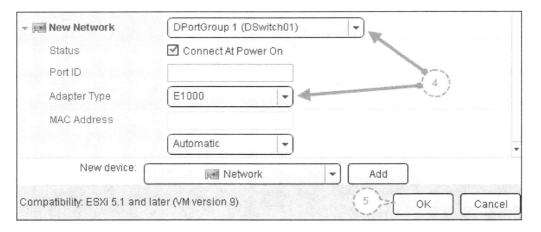

Creating a virtual machine snapshot

There are times when you need to save the current state of an application's or operating system's configuration before you experiment with a change. A real-life example would be during a system development life cycle where changes are inevitable, and you need the ability to undo a change. vSphere allows you to save the state of a virtual machine regardless of its power state.

A virtual machine snapshot can capture the following data:

- ▸ The virtual machine's memory contents
- ▸ The virtual machine's settings
- ▸ The state of the virtual disks

For you to perform snapshot operations on a virtual machine, you need to be connected to the vCenter Server either by using vSphere Web Client or vSphere Client, or by using the vSphere Client to the ESXi server hosting the virtual machine.

[💡 Snapshots cannot be created on virtual disks (VMDK) in an independent mode.]

How to do it...

The following procedure guides you through the steps required to create a snapshot on a virtual machine:

1. Navigate to the **VM and Templates** inventory view, select and right-click on the VM for which you intend to create a snapshot, and then click on **Take Snapshot...**.

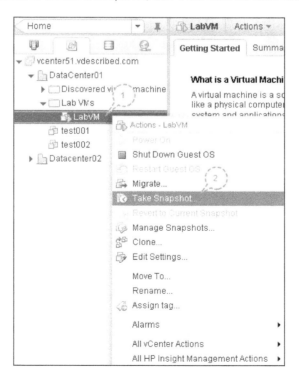

2. Provide a **Name** for the snapshot and an optional **Description**. The option **Quiesce the guest file system** requires VMware tools to be installed, and the **Snapshot the virtual machine's memory** option is selected by default for a powered on virtual machine. Click on **OK**.

3. The progress of the task can be tracked in the **Recent Tasks** pane.

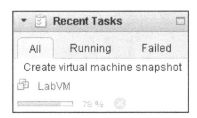

4. Once the tasks complete successfully, right-click on the VM again, and then click on **Manage Snapshots...**.

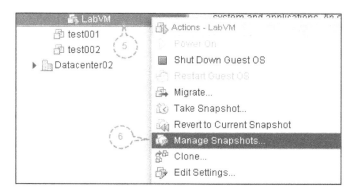

5. The **Snapshot Manager** for the virtual machine should show the newly created snapshot and its details, including the creation date and its disk usage.

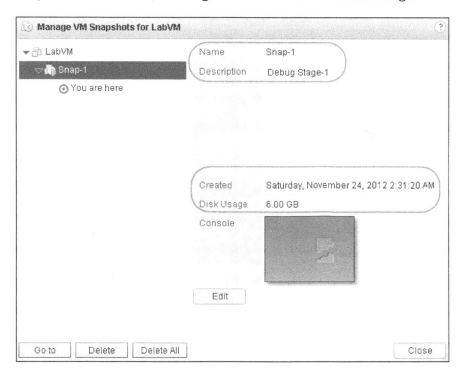

How it works...

When you create a snapshot you have options to snapshot the virtual machine's memory and to quiesce the guest filesystem.

If the memory was chosen to be included in the snapshot, then the ESXi server will flush all of the virtual machine's memory contents to disk. The flushed memory contents are stored in the virtual machine state file (*vmsn). While this is taking place the virtual machine will temporarily remain frozen or unresponsive.

 The VMSN will hold the memory, VMX, and the BIOS state information

The amount of time for which the virtual machine will continue to be in the unresponsive state depends on the amount of time that is needed to dump the memory to disk. The amount of memory that needs to be flushed and the disk performance are also contributing factors.

Once the memory is dumped to disk, subsequent disk I/O will be redirected to a snapshot difference file called the delta file.

The delta file is also a virtual disk data file, and is referenced by using a virtual disk descriptor file.

The delta file will continue to hold all of the disk I/O changes, from the time at which the snapshot was taken. For the server to do the I/O to the delta file, the virtual machine should be configured to access the delta files instead of the base virtual disk. This happens automatically when you create a snapshot.

 The delta disk cannot grow beyond the size of the original base disk.

The **virtual machine snapshot database** (**VMSD**) is also updated. The **Snapshot Manager** GUI will refer to VMSD file for displaying the snapshot information.

The snapshot chain is also updated by modifying the descriptors of the child disks.

The mode of operations and the effect on the virtual machine is the same for all of the snapshot operations (`createSnapshot/RemoveSnapshot/RemoveAllSnapshots/RevertToSnapshot/Consolidate`).

There's more...

For best practices on creating virtual machine snapshots, read the VMware KnowledgeBase article 1025279. It is available at the following link:

`http://kb.vmware.com/kb/1025279`

Also, the KnowledgeBase article 1009402, *Working with snapshot*, should also be a good read. It is available at the following link:

`http://kb.vmware.com/kb/1009402`

Deleting a virtual machine snapshot

To delete a virtual machine snapshot, you should use the virtual machine Snapshot Manager.

You can perform two types of delete operations:

- **Delete operation**: This operation will let you choose a snapshot to be deleted. When this is done, the data held by its VMSN, the changes recorded by the VMX, and the delta file, are committed (written) to its immediate parent.
- **Delete all operation**: When this operation is performed, only the contents of the current snapshot and its delta are committed to the base disk. The rest will be discarded; the VMSN and the delta files will be deleted as well.

How to do it...

The following procedure explains how to delete a virtual machine snapshot using the **Snapshot Manager**:

1. Right-click on the VM and click on **Manage Snapshots...**.

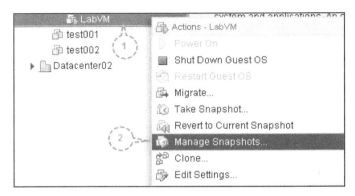

2. Select the snapshot to be deleted, and then click on **Delete**.

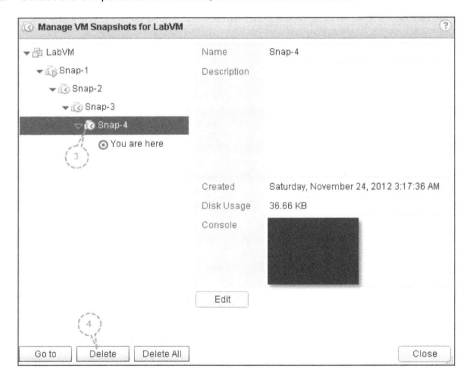

3. Click on **Yes** to confirm the delete operation.

How it works...

To explain how the delete operation works, let's use the following table for reference:

	File at the GOS	Snapshot file	Snapshot delta file
Base Disk(No snapshots)	Test		Ubuntu-flat.vmdk
Snap-1	Test	Ubuntu-Snapshot1.vmsn	Ubuntu-000001-delta.vmdk
When a new file Test1 is created, the Ubuntu-000001-delta.vmdk will hold the file Test1.			
Snap-2	Test,Test1	Ubuntu-Snapshot2.vmsn	Ubuntu-000002-delta.vmdk
When a new file Test2 is created, the Ubuntu-000002-delta.vmdk will hold the file Test2.			
Snap-3	Test, Test1, Test2	Ubuntu-Snapshot3.vmsn	Ubuntu-000003-delta.vmdk
When a new file Test3 is created, the Ubuntu-000003-delta.vmdk will hold the file Test3.			
Snap-4	Test, Test1, Test2, Test3	Ubuntu-Snapshot4.vmsn	Ubuntu-000004-delta.vmdk
When a new file Test4 is created, the Ubuntu-000004-delta.vmdk will hold the file Test4.			

A chain of four snapshots

If **Snap-4** in the preceding table is deleted then the contents of the snapshot, **Snap-4** (Test, Test1, Test2, and Test3) and the contents of the delta file Ubuntu-000004-delta.vmdk (Test4) are committed to delta of the immediate parent snapshot, **Snap-3**. So the delta Ubuntu-000003-delta.vmdk will now hold the files Test, Test1, Test2, Test3, and Test4.

However, when a delete all operation is issued, the contents of current snapshot and its delta are committed to the base disk. The rest will be discarded; the VMSN and the delta files will be deleted as well. If the current snapshot is **Snap-4** then after a delete all operation, the base disk will have the files Test, Test1, Test2, Test3, and Test4.

During the remove operations, the snapshot manager will remove the entry corresponding to the chosen snapshot from the snapshot database. This is done prior to updating the child VMDK's descriptor file with the new parent disk's Content ID (CID) value.

See also

> ▸ Refer to the *Unable to delete the virtual machine snapshot due to locked files* VMware KnowledgeBase article 2017072 at http://kb.vmware.com/kb/2017072

Reverting to a current virtual machine snapshot

The whole idea behind taking a snapshot is to save the current state of the virtual machine so that it will remain unaffected by the changes you intend to make. In a situation where you would want to discard the changes you made and return to the saved state of the virtual machine, the **Revert to Current Snapshot** operation is performed.

You will not need the **Snapshot Manager** to perform the revert operation.

How to do it...

The following procedure guides you through the steps required to revert to the current snapshot:

1. Right-click on the VM and click on **Revert to Current Snapshot**.

2. Click on **Yes** to confirm the revert operation.

How it works...

Reverting to a current snapshot will discard its delta contents. The contents of the delta file are permanently lost unless it is saved in a subsequent snapshot. That is, if the current snapshot isn't parenting a child snapshot, then its delta data is lost forever.

In our example (refer to the table from the previous recipe), the current snapshot was **Snap-4**, and its delta was saved to the file `Test4`. After the **Revert to Current Snapshot** operation, the contents of its delta file `Ubuntu-000004-delta.vmdk` are discarded and **Snap-4** will only have files `Test`, `Test1`, `Test2`, and `Test3`.

Going to a virtual machine snapshot

The **Go to** option lets you revert to a selected snapshot. This is particulary useful if you want to discard all of the changes that you have made to the virtual machine and return to an older than most recent snapshot state of the virtual machine.

This process does require using the **Snapshot Manager** for the virtual machine.

How to do it...

The following procedure explains how to perform a selective revert operation to an older snapshot in the chain:

1. Right-click on the VM and click on **Manage Snapshots...**.

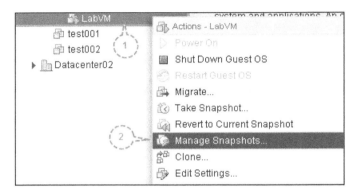

2. Select the snapshot to which you want to revert, and then click on **Go to** to perform a selective revert operation.

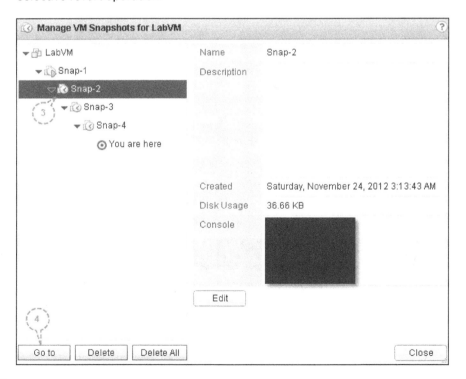

3. Click on **Yes** to confirm the Go to operation.

How it works...

When you revert to a particular snapshot, the process will discard all of the contents of its difference file (delta) and all of the subsequent snapshots. Revert to snapshot will result in the selected snapshot's state minus the contents of its delta being restored.

For example, while the VM is currently running on the delta of **Snap-4**, if we revert to **Snap-2**, this will discard the contents of the delta file Ubuntu-000002-delta.vmdk (which holds the file Test2) and the contents of all of the other snapshots that were subsequently created. So after reverting to **Snap-2**, the OS will only have the files Test and Test1.

Even though it discards the contents of its delta, it does not delete the delta file, because the snapshots that were taken subsequent to that depend on the delta of its parent. That is, **Snap-3** depends on the delta of **Snap-2**. Therefore **Snap-3** will have **Snap-2**s state and the changes recorded in **Snap-2**'s delta. So after reverting to **Snap-2**, if we go back to **Snap-3**, you will see the files Test, Test1, and Test2 in there. If we go back to **Snap-4**, you will see the files Test, Test1, Test2, and Test3.

There is a caveat that you should keep in mind when you choose to revert to snapshots. When you revert from a snapshot to an older one, the delta of the current snapshot (if it is last snapshot in the chain) will be lost. That is, if **Snap-4** is the last snapshot in the chain, then if you revert from **Snap-4** to an older snapshot up the chain this will result in the loss of the contents of the delta file Ubuntu-000004-delta.vmdk, which contains the file Test4.

 If we revert to a virtual machine snapshot that doesn't have the memory captured, it will result in the virtual machine being powered off.

Consolidating snapshots

Snapshot consolidation is a process of merging the content of all the snapshots to the base disk. We have seen snapshot consolidations fail for various reasons. For instance, a backup appliance which hot-adds the VMDK to its proxy server to back up its content, should ideally remove the hot-added VMDK and issue a delete operation on the snapshot it created. If for some reason, it fails to remove the hot-added VMDK, then all subsequent snapshot delete operations that it issues will also fail. This is because the file is in use. If this goes undetected, then you will be left with a lot of snapshot delta files, eventually using up a lot/all of the free space on the datastore. Things get worse, when the snapshot manager does not show all the left over snapshots, leaving the user/administrator with no GUI control over the situation.

Fortunately, starting with vSphere 5, you have a GUI option to consolidate the left-over snapshot files. In this recipe we will learn how to use this new feature.

How to do it...

The following procedure explains how to perform a snapshot consolidation operation:

1. Right-click on the VM and navigate to **All vCenter Actions | Snapshots**, and then click on **Consolidate**.
2. Click on **Yes** to confirm the consolidate operation.

How it works...

The consolidate operation is performed when a snapshot delete/delete all operation fails, but it also removes the snapshot information from the **Snapshot Manager**. If this happens, the VM's folder will still have the snapshot files (deltas) and the virtual machine will also be running on the snapshot disk.

Prior to the addition of the **Consolidate** option, the administrator could use several methods to consolidate snapshots. They could go through the tedious task of verifying the snapshot chain to make sure it is not broken, and then issue vmkfstools -i on the current snapshot (most recent) to clone and consolidate the delta.

See also

 ► Refer to the *Consolidating snapshots in vSphere 5.x* (VMware KnowledgeBase article 2003638) at http://kb.vmware.com/kb/2003638.

Exporting a virtual machine

A virtual machine can be packaged for transport. vSphere provides a method to do so, by exporting a virtual machine in an **open virtual machine format** (**OVF**), which is an open standard developed by the **distributed management task force** (**DMTF**) with cooperation from VMware, Citrix, IBM, Microsoft, Sun, and other companies.

There are two formats for packaging a virtual machine and its files:

- ▸ OVF (open virtualization format)
- ▸ OVA (open virtualization archive)

Read the *How it works* section of the following recipe to understand the difference between the two formats.

How to do it...

The following procedure explains how to export a virtual machine to OVA or OVF format:

1. Right-click on the VM and navigate to **All vCenter Actions | Export OVF Template...**.

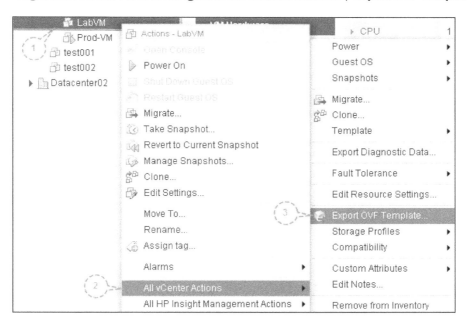

2. In the **Export OVF Template** window, provide a name for the template, choose an export folder and export format, and then click on **OK** to initiate the export.

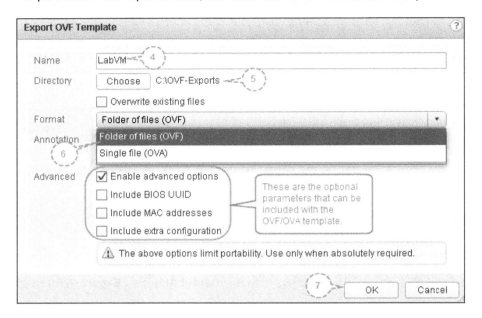

How it works...

The OVF will package all of the virtual machine files into a single folder. It will have an OVF descriptor file, which will have an extension .ovf, a manifest (.mf), the virtual disks, and certificates, if any.

The manifest file contains the SHA1 digest of all files in the package.

The OVA is simply a TAR file with the OVF folder packaged inside it.

10
Configuring vSphere HA

In this chapter we will cover the following:

- ► Enabling vSphere HA on a cluster
- ► Setting host isolation response for an HA cluster
- ► Setting the VM restart priority for an HA cluster
- ► Configuring VM monitoring
- ► Configuring datastore heartbeating
- ► Disabling host monitoring
- ► Configuring vSphere HA admission control
- ► Configuring a VM to override host monitoring and VM monitoring settings

Introduction

In this chapter we will learn how to enable and configure vSphere HA to react to host failures.

vSphere HA (High Availability) is a feature that can reduce unplanned virtual machine downtime. It does this at both the host and the virtual machine level. At the host level, it will monitor for host failures or network isolations and react accordingly. Depending on how it is configured to react, it can choose to restart or not restart the VMs that were running on a failed host. At the virtual machine level it can detect guest operating system and application failures and restart the virtual machines.

Starting with vSphere 5, HA has been completely recoded. It is also referred to as the **Fault Domain Manager**. It no longer uses Legato's AAM. The earlier concept of primary and secondary master has been relinquished as well.

With FDM, only one ESXi host among all the hosts in the cluster can become the master. The remaining hosts are slaves. During the master election process, a host with access to the largest number of datastores will be chosen as the master. If the master host fails another master is re-elected in the same fashion. FDM also introduces the concept of **datastore heartbeating**, which is used to check the liveliness of a slave host when the master host is not able to communicate with the slave over the management network. We will learn more about datastore heartbeating in the *Configuring datastore heartbeating* recipe.

Enabling vSphere HA on a cluster

vSphere HA has to be enabled on a cluster, with a minimum of two ESXi servers. Once enabled and configured correctly, in the event of a host failure, the virtual machines that were running on the failed host will be restarted on another existing host that is part of the HA cluster.

How to do it...

The following procedure describes how to enable HA on an ESXi cluster:

1. From the vCenter's **Home** inventory, navigate to the **Hosts and Clusters** view.

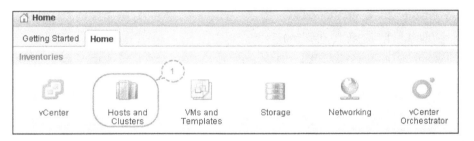

2. Select the cluster and navigate to **Manage | Settings | vSphere HA**, and click on **Edit**.

3. At the **Edit Cluster Settings** window, select the **Turn ON vSphere HA** checkbox, and click on **OK** to enable HA.

How it works...

When you enable HA on a cluster, the FDM agents available on the vCenter Server are transferred and installed on the ESXi hosts in the cluster. Then one of the ESXi hosts is selected as a master and the remaining hosts become the slave hosts.

See also

▶ The *How vSphere HA Works* section on page 11 of the *vSphere Availability* guide for vSphere 5.1 should be a good read.

▶ It also important to go through the *vSphere HA Checklist* section on page 24 of the *vSphere Availability* guide for vSphere 5.1. The guide is available via the following link:

```
http://pubs.vmware.com/vsphere-51/topic/com.vmware.ICbase/PDF/
vsphere-esxi-vcenter-server-51-availability-guide.pdf
```

Setting host isolation response for an HA cluster

The **host isolation response** setting is used by the ESXi host, which detects itself as being isolated (management-network-isolated) from the network, to decide whether to change the power state of the virtual machines running on it or to leave it unchanged.

There are three host isolation responses, as follows:

▶ **Leave powered on**: This setting will not modify the power state of the running virtual machines

▶ **Power off then failover**: This setting will hard power off the running virtual machines

▶ **Shut down then failover**: This setting will issue a graceful shutdown of the virtual machines

In this recipe we learn how to set the host isolation response on the cluster.

How to do it...

The following procedure explains how to set/modify the host isolation response settings at the cluster:

1. From the vCenter's **Home** inventory, navigate to the **Hosts and Clusters** view.
2. Select the cluster and navigate to **Manage | Settings | vSphere HA**, and click on **Edit**.
3. In the **Edit Cluster Settings** window, click on **Host Monitoring** to expand and view its additional settings.

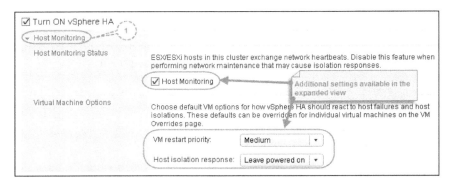

4. Click on the **Host isolation response** drop-down box to select the required isolation response.

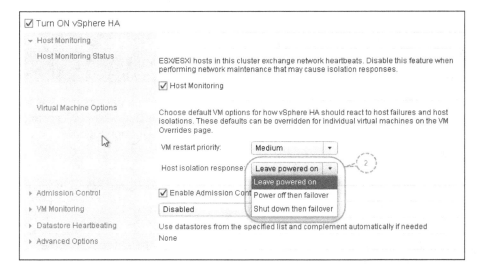

5. With a planned isolation response selected, click on **OK** to confirm the changes.

See also

The *vSphere HA Advanced Attribute*s section on page 34 of the *vSphere Availability* guide for vSphere 5.1 should be a good read. The guide is available via the following link:

```
http://pubs.vmware.com/vsphere-51/topic/com.vmware.ICbase/PDF/
vsphere-esxi-vcenter-server-51-availability-guide.pdf
```

Setting VM restart priority for an HA cluster

Setting restart priorities for individual VMs will help VMware HA to determine which VM should be restarted when an ESXi host fails.

The priorities set are relative. HA will restart VMs with the highest priority first. If the priority is set to **Disabled** for a VM, then in the event of a host failure, that particular VM will not be restarted. The priorities set are to *only* for HA to determine the restart order; they don't affect the VM monitoring.

In this recipe we learn how to configure the VM restart priority for an HA cluster.

How to do it...

The following procedure explains how to set/modify VM restart priority settings for an HA cluster:

1. From the vCenter's **Home** inventory, navigate to the **Hosts and Clusters** view.

2. Select the cluster and navigate to **Manage | Settings | vSphere HA**, and click on **Edit**.

3. In the **Edit Cluster Settings** window, click on **Host Monitoring** to expand and view its additional settings.

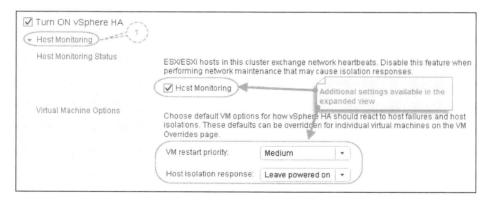

4. Use the **VM restart priority** drop-down menu to choose the **Disabled, Low, Medium,** or **High** priority setting.

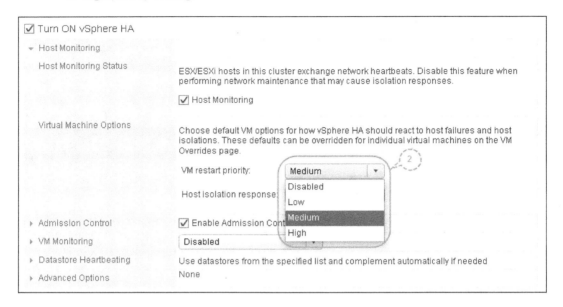

5. With the planned **VM restart priority** option selected, click on **OK** to confirm the changes.

Configuring VM monitoring

vSphere HA can be configured to monitor virtual machines, so that unresponsive VMs can be restarted (*reset*). This is achieved by enabling VM monitoring on the HA cluster.

You can also enable application monitoring. This will restart a VM if the VMware Tools application heartbeats are not received within a predefined timeout value.

How to do it...

The following procedure describes how to configure VM monitoring on an HA cluster:

1. From the vCenter's **Home** inventory, navigate to the **Hosts and Clusters** view.

2. Select the cluster and navigate to **Manage | Settings | vSphere HA**, and click on **Edit**.

3. In the **Edit Cluster Settings** window, click on **VM Monitoring** to expand and view its additional settings.

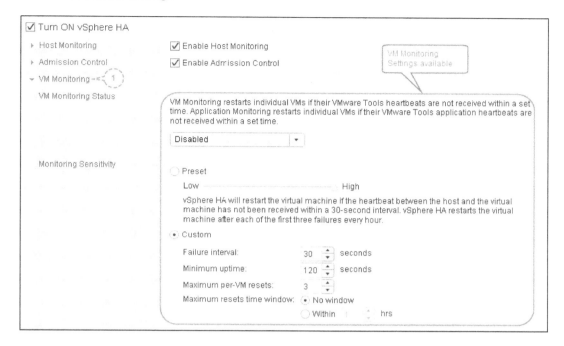

4. To enable VM monitoring, you can choose between the **Disabled**, **VM Monitoring only** and **VM and Application Monitoring** options.

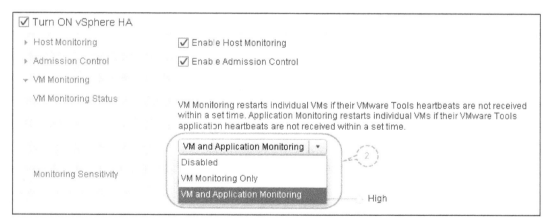

5. With the monitoring type selected, set a planned **Monitoring Sensitivity** value, and click on **OK**.

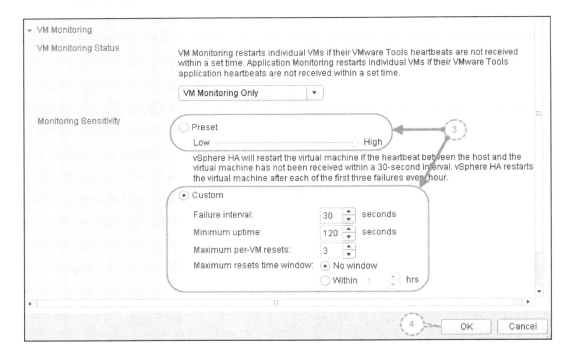

How it works...

VM monitoring is very handy when you have VMs hosting services for which you can't afford longer downtimes.

Once enabled, VM monitoring, with the help of VMware Tools installed in the VMs, will monitor for heartbeats from the VMs. Failure detection happens at different intervals of non-receipt of the VM's heartbeat. The intervals are governed by the monitoring sensitivity configured for the VM.

The default monitoring sensitivity is **High**, in which case the VM monitoring expects a heartbeat from the VM every 30 seconds. If the heartbeat is not received then VM monitoring will check for any storage or network I/O activity for the past 120 seconds (this is the default `das.iostatsInterval` value). If there are *none* then the VM is *reset*, and more importantly it is reset only three times during an hour reset-time window.

 Note that a screenshot of the virtual machine's console will be taken prior to a *reset* operation.

The **application monitoring** feature requires the use of an appropriate SDK (software development kit) or an application that is already programmed to support VMware application monitoring.

Configuring datastore heartbeating

vSphere HA uses datastore heartbeating to check the liveliness of a host if it can't be reached on the management network. This is enabled by default, but we are allowed to choose the datastore that we want to use for heartbeating.

How to do it...

The following procedure explains how to select a datastore for heartbeating:

1. From the vCenter's **Home** inventory, navigate to the **Hosts and Clusters** view.

2. Select the cluster and navigate to **Manage | Settings | vSphere HA**, and click on **Edit**.

3. At the **Edit Cluster Settings** window, click on **Datastore Heartbeating** to expand and view its additional settings.

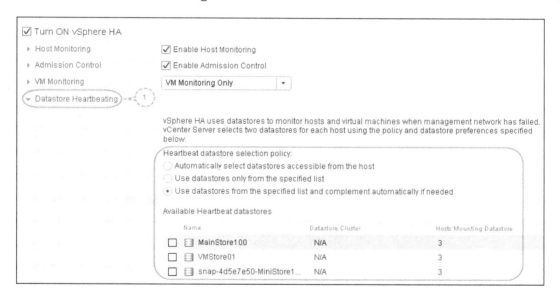

4. Choose between the **Automatically select datastores accessible from the host, Use datastores only from the specified host**, and **Use datastores from the specified list and complement automatically if needed** options. In this example, let's choose the third option and manually select the datastores. Click on **OK** to confirm the selection.

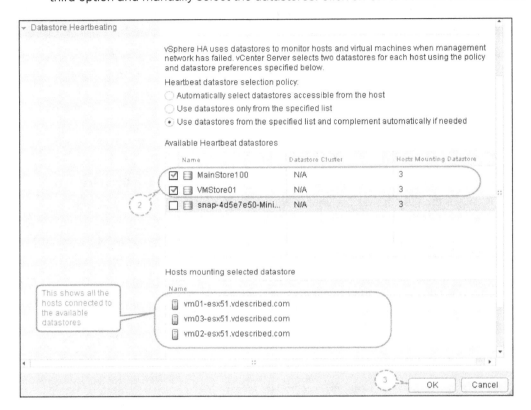

How it works...

Datastore heartbeating is enabled by default when you enable HA on an ESXi cluster. With heartbeating enabled the master host in the HA cluster can check the liveliness of a slave host if it can't be reached over the management network.

 During the election of heartbeat datastores, only datastores which are mapped to at least two ESXi hosts are considered eligible.

HA, by default, chooses two heartbeat datastores per host. This value can be modified by adding the advanced parameter das.heartbeatDsPerHost. The maximum value is **5**.

To do that, click on **Datastore Heartbeating** to expand and view its additional settings in the **Edit Cluster Settings** window. Click on **Advanced Options** to expand it, and click on the **Add** button to add the parameter.

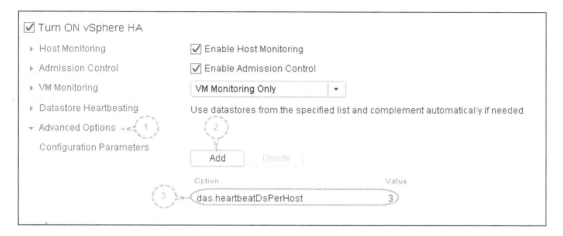

HA creates heartbeat files (`-hb`) in a directory called `.vSphere-HA` at the root of the heartbeart datastores. These files help HA to verify whether the slave host is still alive. The `-poweron` files have a list of powered on VMs on the host.

The following screenshot depicts the contents of the directory:

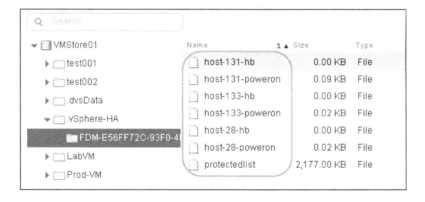

Disabling host monitoring

Host monitoring is generally disabled during network maintenance activities that would affect the host's management network connectivity. This is done to prevent unnecessary triggering of the host isolation response configured for the HA cluster. Host monitoring can be disabled by editing the cluster settings.

How to do it...

The following procedure explains how to disable host monitoring:

1. From the vCenter's **Home** inventory, navigate to the **Hosts and Clusters** view.
2. Select the cluster and navigate to **Manage | Settings | vSphere HA**, and click on **Edit**.
3. Deselect the **Enable Host Monitoring** checkbox, and click on **OK**.

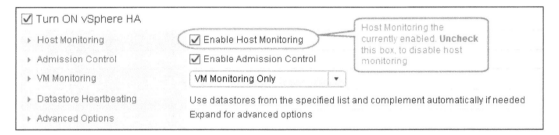

4. The runtime information for HA should now show the **Host Monitoring** value as **Disabled**.

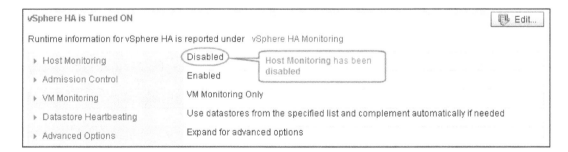

How it works...

Disabling **Host Monitoring** will not remove the HA agents from the ESXi host, hence HA will still be able to detect a host failure, but it will not restart the VMs from the failed host.

Configuring vSphere HA admission control

A well-configured HA cluster will have enough free resources to restart all of the business-critical VMs running on the hosts, in the event of host failures. This amount of free resources is referred to as the **failover capacity**.

Failover capacity determines the number of the ESXi hosts that can fail in an HA cluster, and still leave enough resources to support all of the powered-on VMs. We can use admission control to control and monitor the failover capacity.

There are three admission control methods (policies):

- Define the failover capacity by reserving a static number of hosts
- Define the failover capacity by reserving a percentage of the cluster resources
- Specify dedicated failover hosts

 Note that admission control can be disabled by selecting the **Do not reserve failover capacity** option.

Any operation that violates the resource constraints imposed by the admission control policy will not be permitted. Some of these operations include a VM power-on operation, a vMotion operation, and a change in the CPU/memory reservation of the VM.

How to do it...

We can define the failover capacity of the HA cluster by:

- Specifying a static number of hosts that will be available for failover
- Reserving a percentage of the cluster resources for failover
- Specifying dedicated failover hosts

The following procedure explains how to specify a static number of hosts for failover:

1. From the vCenter's **Home** inventory, navigate to the **Hosts and Clusters** view.
2. Select the cluster and navigate to **Manage | Settings | vSphere HA**, and click on **Edit**.
3. In the **Edit Cluster Settings** window, click on **Admission Control** to expand and view its additional settings.

4. To define a reserved failover capacity in terms of the number of hosts that will be available to failover VMs, select the **Define failover capacity by static number of hosts** option. Also choose a **Slot size policy** value for the VMs. The policy could either calculate slot size based on the powered-on VMs or you can specify a custom (fixed) slot size. Here we have selected the **Cover all powered-on virtual machines** option, as shown in the following screenshot:

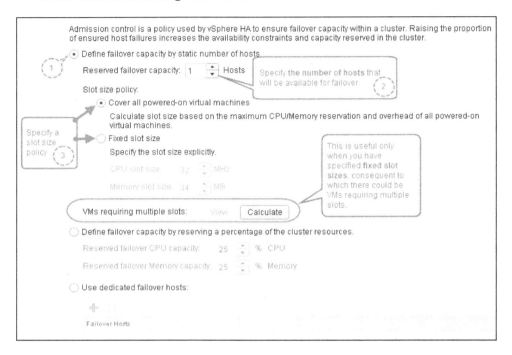

5. Click on **OK** to confirm the settings and reconfigure the cluster.

The following procedure explains how to reserve a percentage of the cluster resources (CPU and memory resources) for failover:

1. From the vCenter's **Home** inventory, navigate to the **Hosts and Clusters** view.

2. Select the cluster and navigate to **Manage | Settings | vSphere HA**, and click on **Edit**.

3. In the **Edit Cluster Settings** window, click on **Admission Control** to expand and view its additional settings.

4. Specify a failover capacity by reserving a percentage of CPU and memory resources from the cluster:

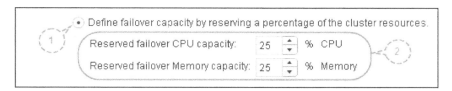

5. Click on **OK** to confirm the settings and reconfigure the cluster.

The following procedure explains how to specify the hosts that will be used as failover hosts:

1. From the vCenter's **Home** inventory, navigate to the **Hosts and Clusters** view.

2. Select the cluster and navigate to **Manage | Settings | vSphere HA**, and click on **Edit**.

3. In the **Edit Cluster Settings** window, click on **Admission Control** to expand and view its additional settings.

4. Select the **Use dedicated failover hosts** option, and click on the green **+** icon to bring up the **Add Failover Hosts** window:

5. At the **Add Failover Host** window, select the host(s) to be added as failover host(s), and then click on **OK**:

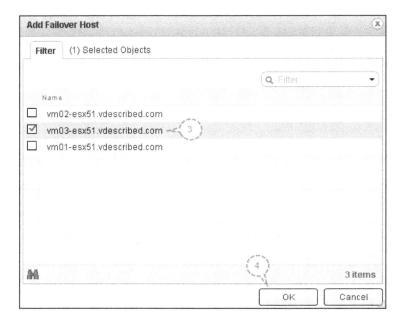

6. The **Settings** screen should now list the selected host as a failover host.

7. Click on **OK** to confirm the settings and reconfigure the cluster.

How it works...

The vSphere HA admission control is used to make sure that no operation will lower the failover capacity of the cluster, thereby preserving enough resources in the HA cluster to run VMs that are restarted in the event of a host(s) failure.

Failover capacity by static number of hosts

Any operation that would cause the failover capacity (consequent to the number of powered-on VMs and its CPU/memory reservations) to be lower than the configured failover capacity will not be permitted.

Failover capacity by reserving a percentage of the cluster resources

Any operation that would cause the current (calculated) CPU/memory failover capacity to be lower than the configured failover capacity will not be permitted.

Dedicated failover hosts

By selecting dedicated failover hosts, vSphere HA admission control will not allow any operations to be performed on those hosts.

See also

The admission control and slot calculation has been well explained in Duncan Epping's *HA Deepdive* blog. This will be a good read. It is available via the following link:

```
http://www.yellow-bricks.com/vmware-high-availability-deepdiv/
```

Configuring a VM to override host monitoring and VM monitoring settings

It is possible to configure a virtual machine to override the host monitoring and VM monitoring settings. The settings are overridden by creating **VM overrides**.

The settings that can be overridden are as follows:

  ▶ VM restart priority
  ▶ Host isolation response
  ▶ VM monitoring and monitoring sensitivity

How to do it...

The following procedure explains how to configure VM(s) to override HA cluster settings:

  1. From the vCenter's **Home** inventory, navigate to the **Hosts and Clusters** view.

2. Select the cluster and navigate to **Manage** | **Settings** | **VM Overrides**.

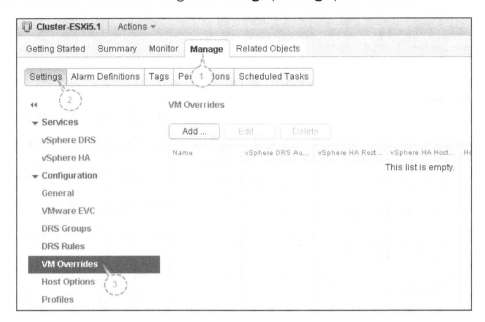

3. On the **VM Overrides** page, click on the **Add** button to bring up the **Add VM Overrides** window.

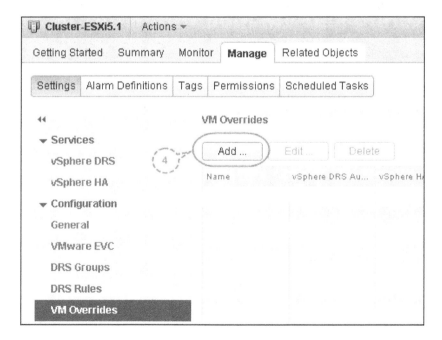

4. In the **Add VM Overrides** window, click on the green **+** icon to bring up the **Select a VM** window.

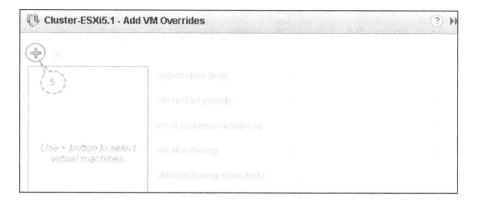

5. In the **Select a VM** window, select a virtual machine and click on **OK**.

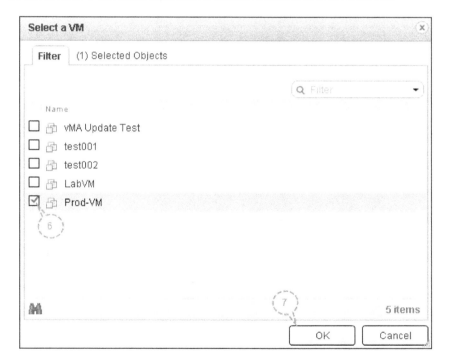

6. With the VM now added to the **Add VM Overrides** window, modify the settings for the selected VM, and click on **OK**.

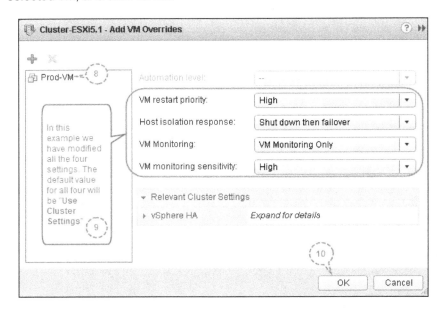

11

Configuring vSphere DRS, DPM, and VMware EVC

In this chapter we will cover the following:

- ▶ Enabling vSphere DRS on a cluster
- ▶ Choosing a DRS automation level
- ▶ Overriding the cluster automation level for a VM
- ▶ Setting a migration threshold
- ▶ Creating hosts and VM DRS groups
- ▶ Creating virtual machines to host affinity rules
- ▶ Creating "Inter-VM" affinity/anti-affinity rules
- ▶ Configuring vSphere Distributed Power Management (DPM)
- ▶ Enabling power management on a per-host level
- ▶ Configuring VMware EVC (Enhanced vMotion Compatibility)

Introduction

As you add hosts to your **vSphere Cluster**, there is definitely a need for a method to balance the utilization of computing resources. vSphere DRS is a set of algorithms designed for this. It continuously monitors resource utilization on the **ESXi hosts** and does an intelligent allocation of resources, balances the computing capacity, and also helps in reducing the power consumption in the datacenter.

Balancing the computing resources will ensure that a **virtual machine** (**VM**) gets the resources it needs thereby increasing the service levels.

VMware **DPM** (**Distributed Power Management**) can help reduce the energy consumption of a datacenter by vacating VMs from an underutilized host and leaving that host in a powered-off state.

In this chapter we will discuss how to enable and use DRS's features. We would also learn how to use VMware **EVC** (**Enhanced vMotion Compatibility**).

Enabling vSphere DRS on a cluster

You can enable the vCenter Server to distribute the virtual machines across multiple ESXi hosts based on their resource requirements. To achieve this you need to enable vSphere **Distributed Resource Scheduler** (**DRS**) on the cluster.

How to do it...

The following procedure explains how to enable DRS on a cluster:

1. From the vCenter's inventory home navigate to the **Hosts and Clusters** view.
2. Select the cluster and navigate to **Manage | Settings | vSphere DRS** and then click on **Edit....**

3. On the **Edit Cluster Settings** window, select the **Turn ON vSphere DRS** checkbox. Leave **DRS Automation**, **Power Management**, and **Advanced Options** at their defaults for now.

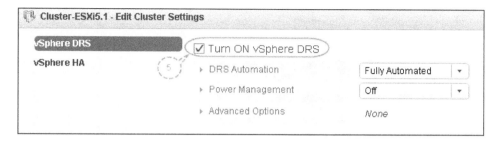

4. Click on **OK** to enable DRS.

5. The cluster's settings page should now show DRS enabled. It should read **vSphere DRS is Turned ON**.

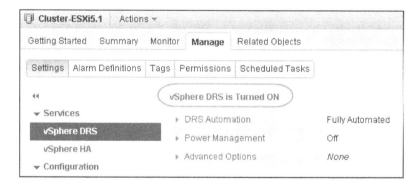

How it works...

So how does DRS really work? DRS, once enabled, will aggregate the resources from the participating ESXi hosts as cluster resources.

Its job is to load-balance the **DRS cluster** for better utilization of the cluster resources. It does so by migrating or generating migration recommendations for VMs whenever needed. It also provides initial placement for the VMs.

DRS will generate migration recommendations only when it identifies a resource imbalance in the cluster.

Resource imbalance is determined on a per ESXi basis. It does so by considering the resource reservations for all of the VMs on the ESXi host and comparing these against the total capacity of the host, and then checking whether the host can or cannot meet the cumulative resource reservations of the VMs. The result will become a deviation metric, which is then compared against the migration threshold set on the cluster. DRS does this imbalance check on every ESXi host in the DRS cluster every 5 minutes.

After DRS detects a cluster imbalance, it will check the migration threshold value set on the cluster. If the deviation calculated is more than the migration threshold then DRS will generate a migration recommendation.

DRS generates a migration recommendation by simulating the migration of each VM on the ESXi host, in order to recalculate the cluster imbalance metric, and then choose a VM which would best serve in reducing the resource crunch on the Host.

Choosing a DRS automation level

By default, DRS works at the `Fully Automated` automation level. You can however, choose to set it to `Manual` or `Partially Automated`. Although the names of the automation levels are self-explanatory, there are a few additional differences.

- **Fully Automated**: VM initial placement and migrations are done automatically
- **Partially Automated**: VM initial placement is automatic, but migration recommendations are displayed to the administrator, and are not performed until the administrator applies them
- **Manual**: Both initial placement and the migration recommendations are displayed to the administrator and requires the administrator's approval to be applied

How to do it...

The following procedure will help you modify the DRS automation level:

1. From the vCenter's inventory home, navigate to the **Hosts and Clusters** view.
2. Select the cluster and navigate to **Manage | Settings | vSphere DRS** and click on **Edit**.

3. On the **Edit Cluster Settings** page, click on **DRS Automation** to expand it and view options. Choose between any of the three automation levels available for selection.

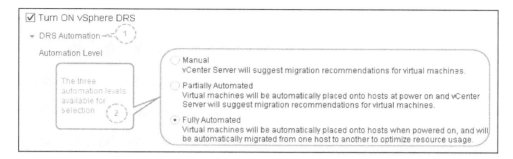

4. Click on **OK** to confirm the settings and reconfigure the cluster.

How it works...

The DRS automation level defines how DRS will react to cluster resource imbalances.

DRS can choose to apply the generated migrations/placement recommendations or present them to the administrator to choose from. If there are more than one migration recommendation then the administrator is provided with a prioritized list of recommendations to choose from.

The following table depicts how migration recommendations are dealt based on the DRS automation level configured on the cluster.

Automation Level	Virtual Machine Migrations(vMotion)
Fully Automated	VMs are automatically migrated.
Partially Automated	Migration recommendations are displayed to the administrator. The administrator has to manually apply one of the migration recommendations.
Manual	Migration recommendations are displayed to the administrator. The administrator has to manually apply one of the migration recommendations.

DRS also generates **initial placement** recommendations. Initial placement refers to the process of choosing an ESXi host from a DRS cluster to power-on or resume a virtual machine. DRS generates these recommendations by choosing an ESXi host, which has enough resources to run the virtual machine being powered-on or resumed.

The following table shows how virtual machine initial placement is determined based on the DRS automation level configured on the cluster.

Automation Level	Virtual Machine Initial Placement
Fully Automated	VM is powered-on or resumed on a suitable ESXi host automatically.
Partially Automated	VM is powered-on or resumed on a suitable ESXi host automatically.
Manual	Initial placement recommendations are displayed to the administrator. The administrator has to manually apply one of the placement recommendations.

Overriding the cluster automation level for a VM

In the previous recipe we learned how to set the cluster-wide automation levels.

In this section, we will learn how to set an automation level that is different from the DRS cluster automation level on a per VM basis. The cluster settings are overridden by creating **VM Overrides**.

How to do it...

The following procedure will help you configure a VM to override the cluster automation level:

1. From the vCenter's inventory home navigate to the **Hosts and Clusters** view.

2. Select the cluster and navigate to **Manage** | **Settings** | **VM Overrides**.

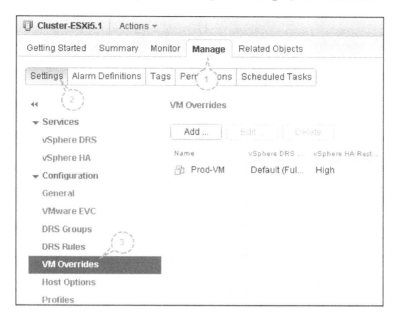

3. On the **VM Overrides** page, click on the **Add...** button to bring-up the **Add VM Overrides** window.

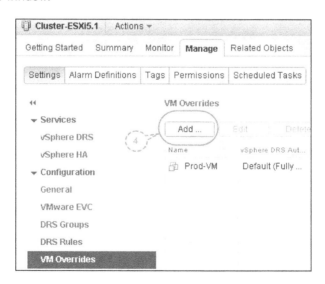

4. In the **Add VM Overrides** window, click on the green **+** icon to bring-up the **Select a VM** window.

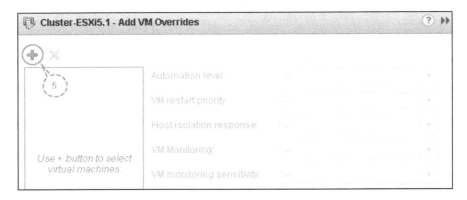

5. In the **Select a VM** window, select the virtual machine whose settings need to be overridden and click on **OK**. This should take you back to the **Add VM Overrides** window.

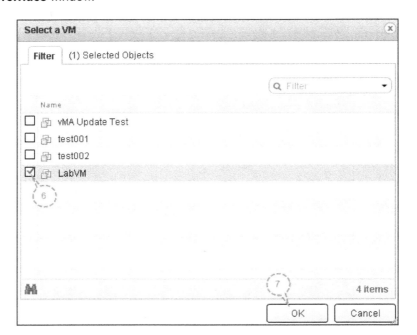

6. In the **Add VM Overrides** window, you should now see the added VM. with the VM selected. Choose the required **Automation Level** and click on **OK**.

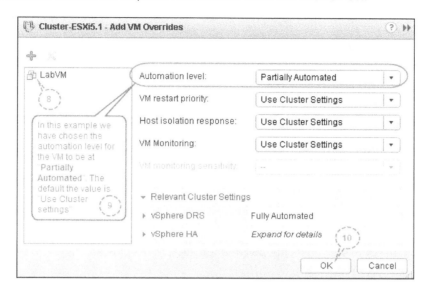

How it works...

An override (VM Override) created for a virtual machine will allow that virtual machine to have an automation level different from the cluster level settings. For instance, if the cluster's DRS automation level is Automatic then you can set an override for a particular virtual machine with a different automation level. This is particularly used for special-case virtual machines.

Let's say you need more control and awareness over the initial placement and migration activities corresponding to a specific virtual machine running a business-critical service or application. You can then create an override for the virtual machine and set its DRS automation level to Manual. Thenceforth, all placement and migration recommendations specific to that virtual machine will be displayed for the administrator's approval.

Setting a migration threshold

You can control the migration recommendations that vSphere DRS can generate or apply. Each migration recommendation generated by DRS will have a priority level associated with it, based on the level of load imbalance in the cluster.

The **migration threshold** will determine which priority recommendations are to be displayed or applied. The threshold can be modified at the cluster settings page.

How to do it...

The following procedure will guide you through the steps required to set a migration threshold:

1. From the vCenter's inventory home navigate to the **Hosts and Clusters** view.

2. Select the cluster and navigate to **Manage | Settings | vSphere DRS** and click on **Edit**.

3. At the **Edit Cluster Settings** page, click on **DRS Automation** to expand it and view the available options. Use the **Migration Threshold** slider to adjust the threshold level.

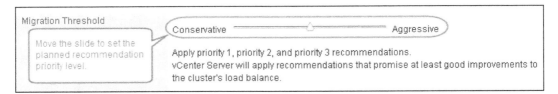

4. Click on **OK** to apply the changes and reconfigure the cluster.

How it works...

Setting a migration threshold will not stop DRS from generating recommendations. Recommendations are generated, but before they are "displayed" (*if manual/partially automated*) or "applied" (*if fully automated*), the priority level associated with it will be compared against the migration threshold set for the cluster. If the migration threshold doesn't cover the priority of the recommendation then it is ignored; else it is displayed or applied.

The following are the available threshold levels:

▶ Conservative Level: This will display/apply only priority 1 recommendations

▶ Conservative Level +1: This will display/apply only priority 1 and priority 2 recommendations

▶ Mid-level (default): This will display/apply priority 1, priority 2, and priority 3 recommendations

▶ Aggressive Level -1: This will display/apply priority 1, priority 2, priority 3, and priority 4 recommendations

▶ Aggressive Level: This will apply all recommendations

Creating host and VM DRS groups

DRS provides an option to segregate virtual machines and ESXi hosts into their own groups. The groups are used with **VM-Host Affinity Rules**. These rules do not address individual VMs/hosts. These groups are created using the **DRS Groups Manager**.

The creation of DRS hosts/VMs groups is a pre-requisite for creating the affinity rules.

How to do it...

The following procedure will help you create host/VM DRS groups:

1. From the vCenter's inventory home navigate to the **Hosts and Clusters** view.
2. Select the cluster and navigate to **Manage | Settings | DRS Groups** and click on **Add...** to bring-up the **Create DRS Group** window.

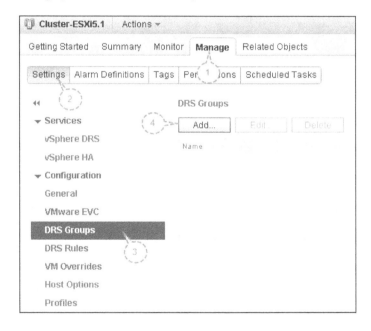

3. In the **Create DRS Group** window supply a name for the group, choose the type as **Host DRS Group**, and click on the **Add** button to bring-up the **Add DRS Group Member** window.

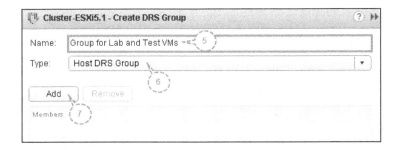

4. In the **Add DRS Group Member** window, select the hosts that should be added to the group and click on **OK**.

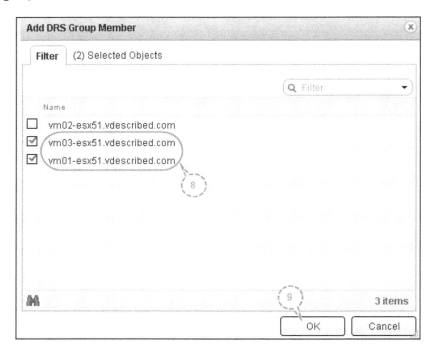

5. The **Create DRS Group** window should now list all of the hosts added as the to-be members of the group. Click on **OK** to create the group.

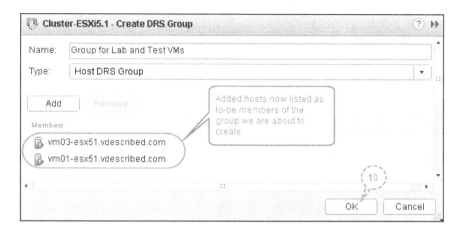

6. Repeat the steps (1) and (2), and at the **Create DRS Group** window, supply a name for the group, choose the type as **VM DRS Group**, and click on the **Add** button to bring-up the **Add DRS Group Member** window.

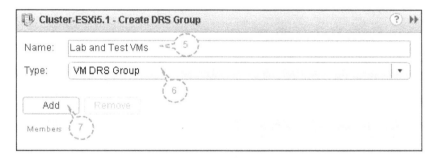

7. In the **Add DRS Group Member** window, select the VMs that should be added to the group and click on **OK**.

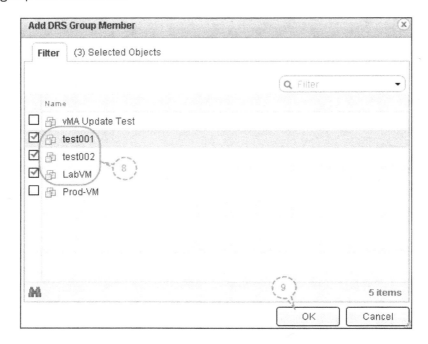

8. The **Create DRS Group** window we should now list the virtual machines that have been added to be members of the group. Click on **OK** to create the group.

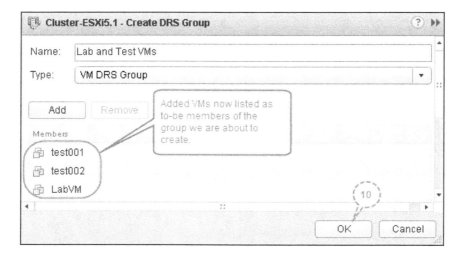

Note that the steps 1 to 5 are the steps required to create a host DRS group. Steps 6 to 8 are the steps required to create a VM DRS group.

Creating virtual machines to host affinity rules

We can create rules that will determine VM-Host DRS placement rules. This is done by creating "virtual machines to hosts" affinity rules. The rules determine whether a group of virtual machines can run on a group of chosen ESXi hosts.

The creation of VMs to hosts affinity rules requires DRS hosts/VMs groups to be created. Read the recipe *Creating host and VM DRS groups* for instructions.

How to do it...

The following procedure will help you create a virtual machines to hosts affinity rule.

1. From the vCenter's inventory home, navigate to the **Hosts and Clusters** view.

2. Select the cluster and navigate to **Manage | Settings | DRS Rules** and click on **Add...** to bring-up the **Create DRS Rule** window.

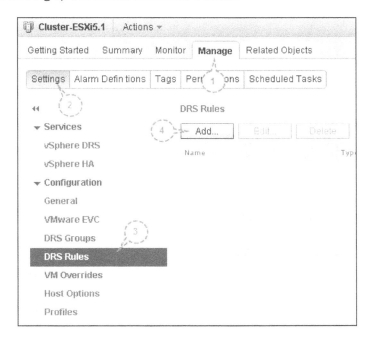

3. At the **Create DRS Rule** window, supply a name for the rule, choose the rule type as **Virtual Machines to Hosts**. Select a **VM Group**, a rule and a **Host Group** and click on **OK** to create the rule.

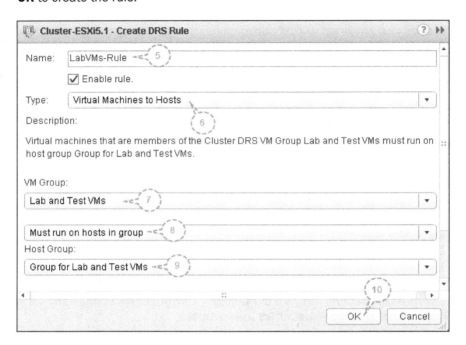

How it works...

The rule can indicate either a requirement or a preference.

The "must" rules dictate a requirement and the "should" rules specify a preference.

Must rules:

- ▶ Must run on hosts in group
- ▶ Must not run on hosts in group

Should rules:

- ▶ Should run on hosts in group
- ▶ Should not run on hosts in group

The "must" rules should be mandatorily met and the "should" rules would just state the preference (the VMs can run on other hosts).

The VM-Host Affinity Rules are generally used to meet the specific requirements for the virtual machines. The requirements could be of any nature, such as licensing or hardware.

> Note that vSphere HA, DRS, and DPM will not violate the "must" rules.

Creating "Inter-VM" affinity/anti-affinity rules

Unlike the VM-Host affinity rules, the inter-virtual machine (VM-VM) affinity rules can work between individual VMs.

How to do it...

The following procedure will help you create an Inter-VM affinity/Anti-affinity rule.

1. From the vCenter's inventory home, navigate to the **Hosts and Clusters** view.
2. Select the cluster and navigate to **Manage | Settings | DRS Rules** and click on **Add...** to bring up the **Create DRS Rule** window.

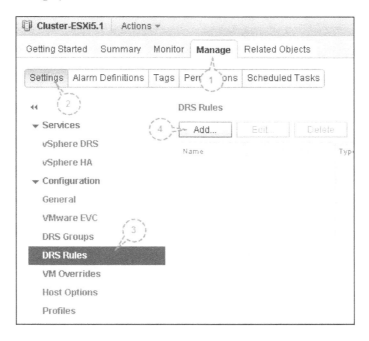

3.   In the **Create DRS Rule** window, supply a name for the rule, and choose the rule type. In this example, we have selected the rule **Separate Virtual Machines**. If you intend to keep the VMs together then select the rule **Keep Virtual Machines Together**.

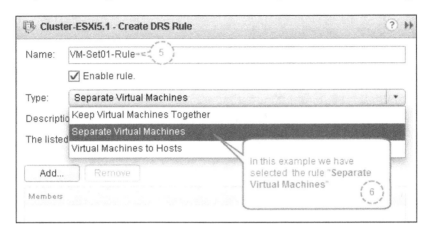

4.   With the rule selected, click on the **Add...** button to bring-up the **Add Rule Member** window.

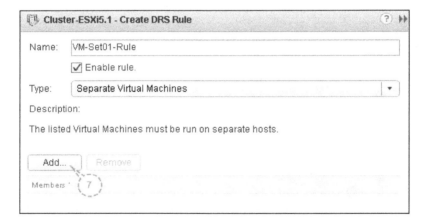

5. In the **Add Rule Member** window, select the VMs to be added and click on **OK**.

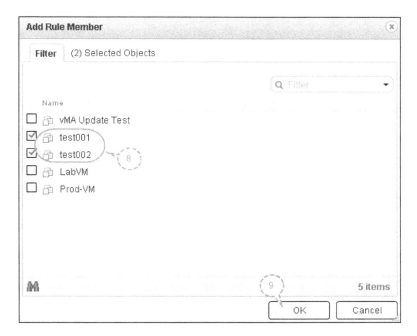

6. The **Create DRS Rule** window should now list the VMs added as to-be members which would participate in the rule. Click on **OK** to create the rule.

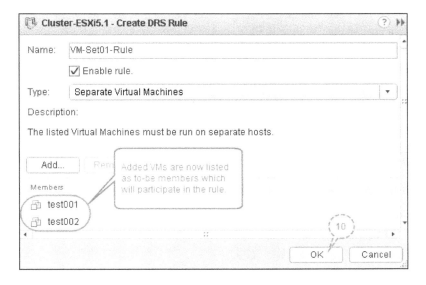

How it works...

An inter-VM rule determines whether the VMs participating in the rule should or should not run on the same ESXi hosts.

Keep virtual machines together:

When this rule is set, the DRS will try to keep the participating VMs on the same ESXi host.

Separate virtual machines:

When this rule is set, the DRS will try to make sure that none of the participating VMs run on the same host as the other participating VMs.

 When there is a conflict between rules, the oldest rule takes preference and the others will be disabled by DRS.

Configuring vSphere Distributed Power Management (DPM)

A DRS cluster can be configured to change the power state of the selected hosts, in order to reduce the power consumption by the cluster. This feature is called the vSphere Distributed Power Management and is configurable only if the cluster is DRS-enabled.

 DPM is disabled by default. You will need to edit the DRS cluster settings to enable DPM.

How to do it...

The following procedure will help you enable and configure DPM on a DRS enabled cluster:

1. From the vCenter's inventory home, navigate to the **Hosts and Clusters** view.

2. Select the cluster and navigate to **Manage | Settings | vSphere DRS** and click on **Edit**.

3. On the **Edit Cluster Settings** page, click on **Power Management** to expand it and view the sub-settings. Note that the default setting is **Off**. Select either **Manual** or **Automatic** automation level.

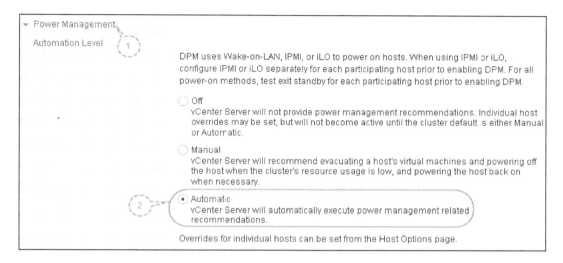

4. Modify the **DPM threshold** if necessary and click on **OK**.

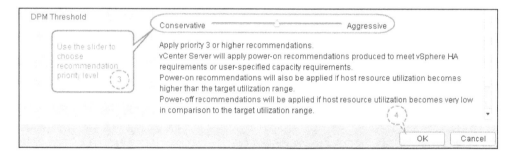

5. Click on **OK** to acknowledge the warning and enable power management.

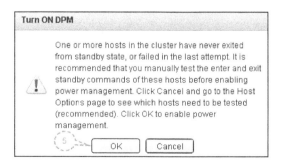

How it works...

Once enabled, power management (vSphere DPM) will analyze the cumulative resource requirement (current usage and reservations), verify the HA requirements, and determine the number of hosts required to meet them. Thenceforth DPM will selectively put ESXi host/hosts into standby mode. Prior to putting an ESXi into standby mode, DPM will leverage DRS's ability to distribute the VMs running on the selected ESXi host to the other ESXi hosts in the cluster.

[Although a host is said to be put in standby mode by DPM, it is actually powered-off. "Standby Mode" is kind of a misnomer.]

DPM requires hardware support for power management and can use the following protocols:

- Intelligent Platform Management Interface (IPMI)
- Hewlett-Packard Integrated Lights-Out (HP iLO)
- Wake-On-LAN (WOL)

DPM can operate in three modes:

- `Off`: DPM is disabled
- `Manual`: DPM recommendations are displayed for the administrator to choose and confirm
- `Automatic`: DPM recommendations are automatically executed

The DPM threshold, much like DRS's migration threshold will display/apply recommendations based on the priority assigned to the recommendation.

Enabling power management on a per-host level

Power management can be modified on a per-host level. The settings at the host level will override the cluster-level DPM settings.

Power management is set at the host level by modifying the DPM's automation level on each host.

How to do it...

The following procedure will help you set the DPM automation level on a host:

1. From the vCenter's inventory home, navigate to the **Hosts and Clusters** view.

2. Select the cluster and navigate to **Manage | Settings | Host Options**.

3. Select a host and click on **Edit** to bring-up the **Edit Host Options** window.

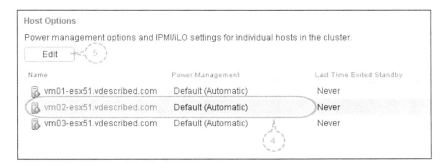

4. In the **Edit Host Options** window, change the DPM power mode to the desired automation level and click on **OK**. Ignore the BMC fields as they are not required for setting host level DPM automation.

5. The **Host Options** page should now show the configured **Power Management** for the host.

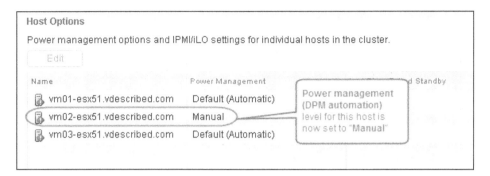

Configuring VMware EVC (Enhanced vMotion Compatibility)

Although unusual, you might end up having hosts in a cluster with same make CPUs but with uncommon feature-sets. For vMotion to work, the underlying CPU features on the cluster hosts should be identical. With EVC you can now present a common CPU feature-set across the hosts to the virtual machines.

EVC should be enabled from the cluster settings page.

How to do it...

The following procedure will help you configure EVC on an ESXi cluster:

1. Connect to the vCenter Server and migrate all the VMs to another host which is not in the cluster.

2. From the vCenter's inventory home, navigate to the **Hosts and Clusters** view.

3. Select the cluster and navigate to **Manage | Settings | VMware EVC** and click on **Edit...** to bring-up the **Change EVC Mode** window.

4. In the **Change EVC Mode** window, select an EVC mode. You get to choose from two options:

   ❑ **Enable EVC for AMD Hosts**

   ❑ **Enable EVC for Intel Hosts**

   Click on **OK** if the validation succeeds.

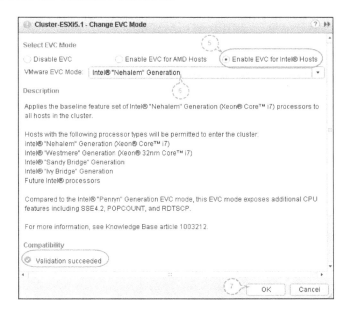

5. Power-off the migrated VMs, move them back to the EVC cluster, and power them back ON.

How it works...

All that EVC does is present a common baseline (CPU feature-set) to the VMs running on the ESXi hosts in the EVC enabled cluster. We do have more than one baseline available to choose from, for both AMD and Intel Processors. Setting a baseline that has more CPU features than the current one doesn't require evacuating the running VMs, but keep in mind that the VM needs to be power-cycled to see the new features.

If you are downgrading to a lower baseline (a lower feature set when compared to the current baseline), then you will need to power-off the VMs.

See also

The following KnowledgeBase articles will be a good read.

- ▶ EVC and CPU Compatibility FAQ (KnowledgeBase article 1005764) at `http://kb.vmware.com/kb/1005764`
- ▶ Enhanced vMotion Compatibility (EVC) processor support (KnowledgeBase article 1003212) at `http://kb.vmware.com/kb/1003212`

12
Upgrading and Patching using vSphere Update Manager

In this chapter we will cover the following:

- ▶ Preparing a database for vSphere Update Manager
- ▶ Installing the vSphere Update Manager
- ▶ Installing vSphere Update Manager plugin
- ▶ Adding a download source
- ▶ Creating a baseline
- ▶ Importing ESXi Images
- ▶ Creating a host baseline group
- ▶ Creating a VM and VA baseline group
- ▶ Remediating a host or a cluster
- ▶ Remediating a VM or a VA
- ▶ Staging patches
- ▶ Installing the Update Manager Download Service (UMDS)
- ▶ Configuring UMDS and downloading data
- ▶ Creating a shared repository
- ▶ Using a shared repository

Introduction

Updating and patching of your vSphere Environment is part of a periodic maintenance routine. Although the update/upgrade/patching can be done manually, it becomes a tedious process when dealing with a large environment. vSphere Update Manager (VUM) provides a method to manage patching and the upgrade process with ease. In this chapter, we will learn how to install and configure update manager and also how to use it to perform the patching or upgrades tasks.

Preparing a database for vSphere Update Manager

Before you install **vSphere Update Manager**, you need to decide whether to use an existing database server or use the installer-packaged SQL Express.

If you choose to use an existing database server then you will need to create a separate database for vSphere Update Manager.

The database user should have a `sysadmin` or `db_owner` role for SQL.

For a list of compatible databases with vSphere Update Manager, you can use the **VMware Product Interoperability Matrixes**.

> For more details, visit `http://www.vmware.com/resources/compatibility/sim/interop_matrix.php`
> Select **Solution/Database Interoperability**. In step 1, select the product as **VMware vCenter Update Manager** Version 5.1 and in step 2, the **Add Database** step, add **Any**.

How to do it...

The following instructions will help you to create a new SQL database and configure ODBC connectivity to it.

1. Connect to the **Microsoft SQL Server Management Studio** and right-click on the `Databases` folder item and click on **New Database**.

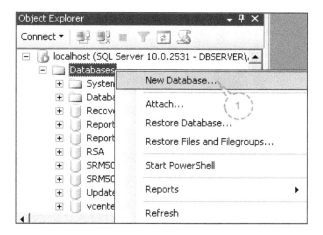

 If the SQL Server Management Studio is not installed then you can download it from Microsoft's website. I have included the download URL for **Microsoft® SQL Server® 2008 Management Studio Express** at the following URL:

`http://www.microsoft.com/en-in/download/details.aspx?id=7593`

2. Supply a name for the database and click on **OK**. Do not modify any other options.

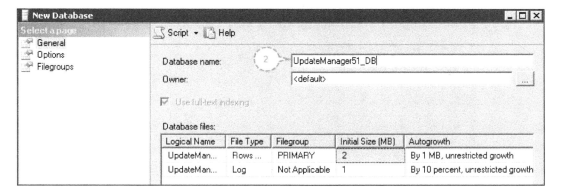

3. You need to create a 32-bit **System DSN** for the Update Manager Database. Go to **Windows**, then navigate to **Start | Run** and execute the following file:

```
c:\Windows\SysWOW64\odbcad32.exe
```

[Note that the DSN should be created on a vCenter Machine or on the machine on which you plan to install vSphere Update Manager.]

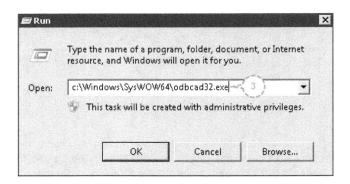

4. In the **ODBC Data Source Administrator** window, navigate to the **System DSN** tab and click on **Add...** to bring up the **Create new Data Source** window for the DSN.

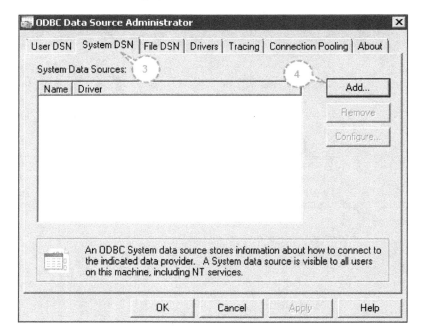

5. In the **Create New Data Source** window, scroll down to the end of the list and select the **SQL Server Native Client 10.0** item from the list.

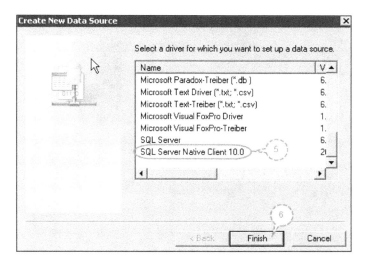

 Some systems may not have the SQL Server Native Client installed. If that is the case then you can download and install the client from Microsoft's website. It is available from the following URL:

`http://msdn.microsoft.com/en-us/sqlserver/`
`ff658533.aspx`

6. Supply a **Name** for the DSN, choose the **SQL Server** you would like to connect to, and click on **Next**.

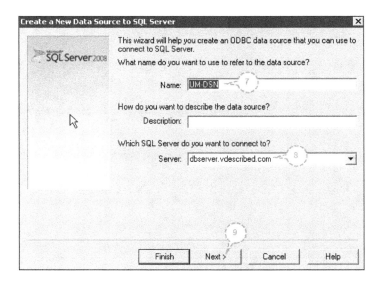

7. Select the authentication type to be either **Windows Authentication** or **SQL Server Authentication** and click on **Next**.

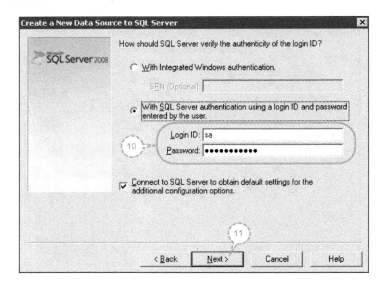

 In this example, since SQL Server is running on a different machine, we have used SQL authentication.

8. Change the default database to the one we created for the Update Manager and click on **Next**.

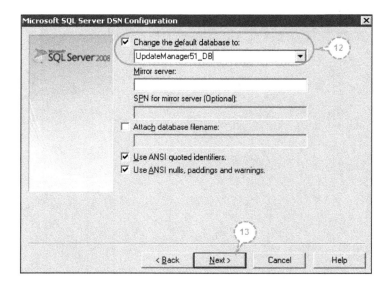

9. On the next screen, click on **Finish**, click on **Test Data Source**, and click on **OK** to create the DSN.

How it works...

The 32-bit System DSN that was created is used during the Update Manager Installation. Note that even though Update Manager can only be installed on a 64-bit machine, it is a 32-bit application and hence it needs a 32-bit DSN for database connectivity.

Update Manager can use the vCenter Database for its tables, but it's always a best practice to have a separate database. The Update Manager installer can install a **SQL Express database** for smaller deployments not exceeding 5 hosts and 50 virtual machines. For a larger environment, you will need a separate SQL Server or Oracle DB Server.

See also

Use the **Sizing Estimator** for vSphere Update Manager 5.1 to determine the minimum amount of free space per month for database usage.

The Sizing Estimator for vSphere Update Manager 5.1 is available at the vSphere Update Manager documentation site:

```
http://www.vmware.com/support/pubs/vum_pubs.html
```

Installing vSphere Update Manager

The Update Manager was used to patch both the ESXi hosts and **VM Guest Operating Systems**. Starting with the Update Manager 5.x, patching VM Guest Operating Systems is no longer supported. The Update Manager can be installed on the same machine running vCenter Server. The Update Manager 5.1 can only be installed on a 64-bit machine.

Here are the compatible operating systems:

- Windows 2003, Windows 2003 R2 [all 64-bit and SP 2 is a requirement]
- Windows 2008, Windows 2008 SP2, Windows 2008 R2, Windows R2 SP1 [all 64-bit]

> With the release of vSphere Update Manager 5.1—Update1 on 25-April-2013, VMware have added support for Windows Server 2012 64-bit. For further details, visit the following link:
>
> `http://www.vmware.com/support/vsphere5/doc/`
> `vsphere-update-manager-51u1-release-notes.html`

You need the following information handy in order to install vSphere Update Manager:

- The vCenter Server's IP address or FQDN
- The vCenter Server's administrator username and password

You also need to make the following decisions before you begin the installation:

- Choose between using an existing DB Server or the installer-packaged SQL Express.
- Ports and proxy settings if needed.
- Location for the patch store. Recommended size is 120 GB.
- A compatible Windows version, if you are installing this on a different physical machine than the vCenter Server.

How to do it...

The following instructions will guide you through the installation of vSphere Update Manager:

1. At the **vSphere 5.1 Installer** welcome window, select **VMware vSphere® Update Manager** and click on **Install** to start the installation wizard.
2. Click through the initial wizard screens, accept the license agreement, and click on **Next**.
3. You can choose to download the updates from the default upgrade/patch sources before you proceed. In this example, we will choose to download the updates by selecting the **Download updates from default sources immediately after installation checkbox**.

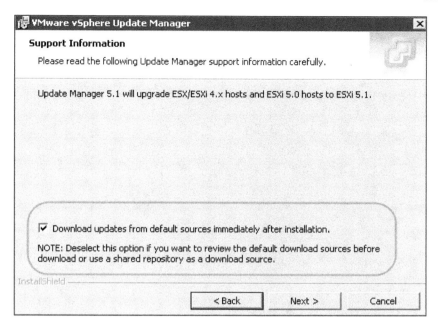

4. Supply the **vCenter Server Information** and click on **Next** to continue.

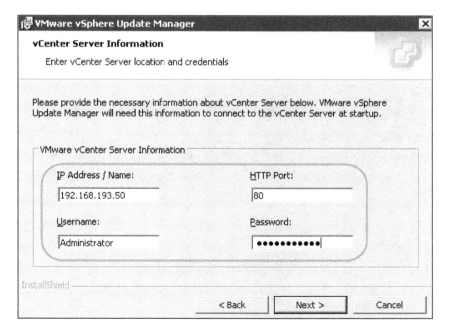

5. You can choose to install SQL Express, but since we already have a database created, select the option **Use an existing supported database** and choose the System DSN which we created for the Update Manager database and click on **Next**.

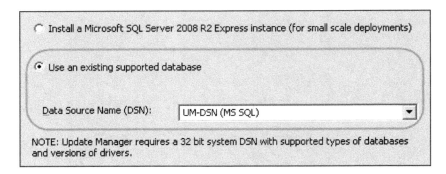

6. Supply the database credentials and click on **Next**.

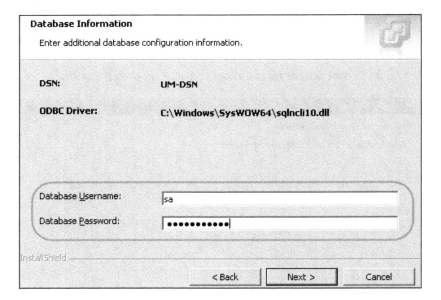

 Although, I have used the sa user, it is not a good practice to do so. It would be best to create a service account and assign dbo permissions.

7. Choose how the Update Manager is identified on the network. This can be done by using either the IP address or FQDN of the machine it is installed on. If the server requires proxy information to get to the Internet then you can configure the proxy on the wizard screen by selecting the option **Yes, I have Internet connection and I want to configure proxy settings now**.

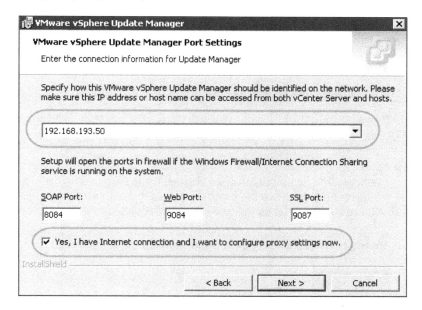

8. On the next screen, supply the proxy details and click on **Next** to continue.

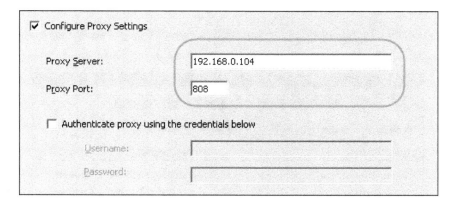

9. Modify the vSphere Update Manager install location and patch store location, if needed, and click on **Next**.

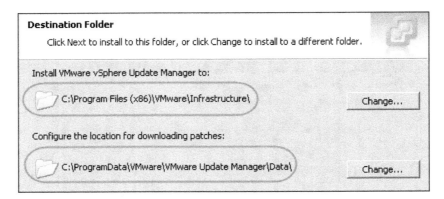

 Although the default patch store location is the system drive (C:), it is recommended to have the patch store on a different drive to reduce the chances of using up all the free space in the system drive.

10. On the **Ready to Install** screen, click on **Install** to initiate the installation.

How it works...

The installer will use the DSN to connect to the new database that was created and initialize it. On finishing the installation, the Update Manager will download the latest patch definitions to the data directory.

The location of the directory is at C:\ProgramData\VMware\VMware Update Manager\Data.

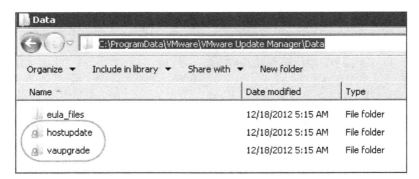

Installing the vSphere Update Manager plugin

For you to be able to manage and configure the Update Manager, you need to install a plugin for use with vCenter Server and enable it.

 The vSphere Update Manage plugin is not supported with vSphere 5.1 Web Client. This might change in the future releases, but for now we need to use the vSphere Windows Client.

How to do it...

The following procedure will help you install and enable the Update Manager plugin for the vSphere Client:

1. Connect to the vCenter Sever and navigate to **Plug-ins** | **Manage Plug-ins...**.

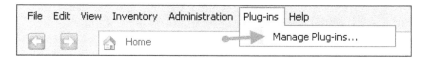

2. At the **Plug-in Manager** window, you will see **VMware vSphere Update Manager Extension** under **Available Plug-ins**. Click on **Download and Install...** to install the plugin.

3. Run through the wizard to finish the plugin installation.

4. If the installation completes successfully, you should see the plugin listed under **Installed Plug-ins**.

5. The vCenter's home inventory should list the **Update Manager** under **Solutions and Applications**.

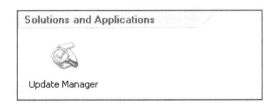

Adding a download source

The vSphere Update Manager downloads patch definitions and notifications from online download sources.

By default, there are three download sources: ESXi updates, Cisco, and Virtual appliances.

You can also add a custom download source. This becomes necessary if your hardware vendor has system specific updates.

How to do it...

The following procedure explains how to add a download source:

1. Connect to the vCenter Server as an administrator, using the vSphere Client.
2. Go to **Home | Update Manager**.
3. Navigate to the **Configuration** tab and then to **Download Settings**.
4. Click on **Add Download Source**.

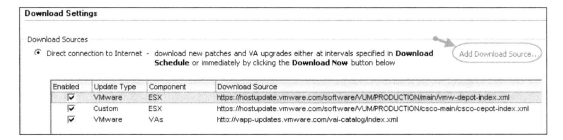

5. In the **Add Download Source** window, enter the **Source URL** and click on **Validate URL**. If the validation completes successfully then click on **OK**.

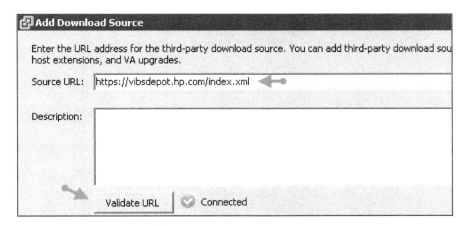

6. Once the custom source has been added to the list, click on **Apply** to save this configuration.

How it works...

The vSphere Update Manager will periodically download the update/patch definitions based on the configured **Download Schedule**. However, you also have the option to initiate a download manually at any point in time. This can be done on the **Download Settings** page by clicking on the **Download Now** button.

By default, the download frequency is **Daily**, at a specified start time. This can be modified by clicking on the **Edit Download Schedule** link on the **Download Schedule** screen.

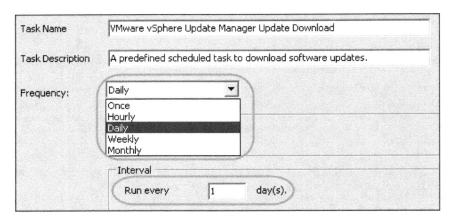

You can also choose the **Interval** and the **Start Time** at the same screen.

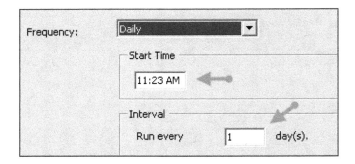

The notifications are also checked periodically. By default the frequency is **hourly**. The schedule can be modified on the **Notification Check Schedule** screen, which can be reached from the left pane on the **Configuration** tab.

For both path definitions and notifications, a scheduled download can be disabled by unchecking the **Enable scheduled download** option on their respective screens.

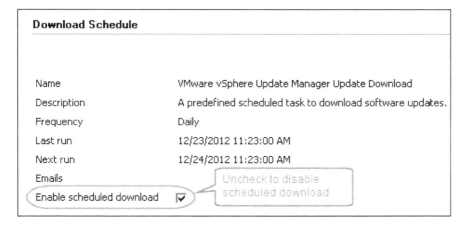

Creating a baseline

A **baseline** is a list of patches that can be used to check the ESXi hosts or **virtual appliances** for compliance. By default, there are two sets of baselines that are predefined:

- ▶ Critical host patches (dynamic)
- ▶ Non-critical host patches (dynamic)

The other baselines are:

- ▶ VMware tools upgrade to match host (dynamic)
- ▶ VM hardware upgrade to match host (dynamic)
- ▶ VA upgrade to latest (dynamic)

You can manually create a new custom baseline, which can be used to check the ESXi hosts for compliance.

How to do it...

The following procedure will guide you through the steps required to create a baseline:

1. Connect to the vCenter Server as an administrator, using the vSphere Client.
2. Go to **Home** | **Update Manager**.

3. Navigate to the **Baselines and Groups** tab, select the **Hosts** view and click on **Create**.

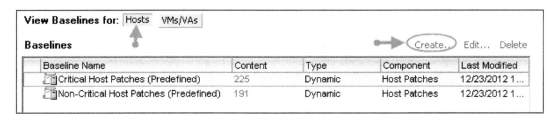

4. Enter a name for the baseline and select the **Baseline Type**. The selections available are:

   ❑ Host Patch, Host Extension and Host Upgrade

   ❑ VA Upgrade

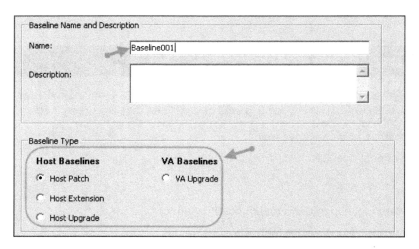

5. Select the baseline type to be either **Fixed** or **Dynamic** and click on **Next**.

6. Specify a criterion by choosing the **Patch Vendor**, **Product**, **Severity**, and **Category**, and click on **Next**. By default the **Severity** and **Category** is set to **Any**.

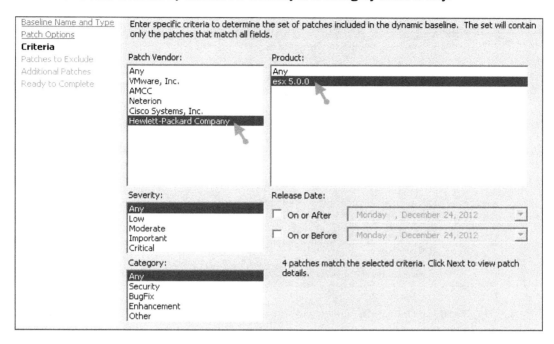

7. Choose to exclude any patches if needed. This can be done by highlighting the patches that needs to be excluded and moving them to the exclusion list (the **Patches to Exclude** pane) by clicking on the blue down-pointing arrow button. Once done, click **Next** to continue.

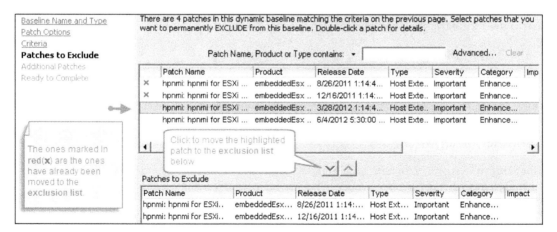

8. The next screen will list the patches that don't meet the criteria. You can choose to include any of these patches by highlighting and moving them to the inclusion list (the **Fixed Patches to Add** pane).

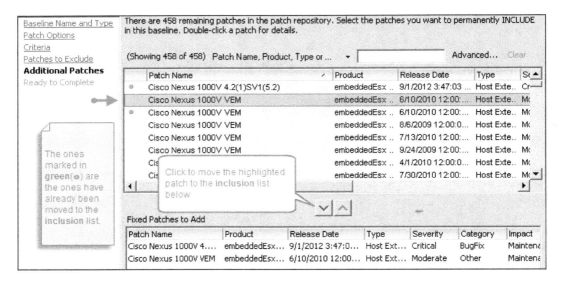

9. The **Ready to Complete** screen will summarize the options selected. Click on **Finish** to create the baseline.

Creating a baseline is a method of creating a reference container for a set of patches that you would like to have installed on a host or a group of hosts.

There are four different types of baselines:

1. Host Patch
2. Host Upgrade
3. Host Extension
4. VA Upgrade

Host Patch will include security patches, bug fixes, enhancements, and other general patches.

Host Upgrade will only include ESXi Images, which will be used to upgrade the ESXi host to a new updated version.

Host Extension refers to the software updates pushed by the hardware vendor, which includes hardware driver updates, updates that enable additional features, CIM providers, updates that enable supportability, and updates that improve performance.

VA Upgrade refers to the upgrades available for the virtual appliances.

 Unlike the other baseline types, a Host Patch baseline can be of type "fixed" or "dynamic".

A fixed baseline type will not poll the patch repository for updates. You will have to manually modify the patch list.

A dynamic baseline type will get updated when new patches meeting the criterion arrive at the patch repository.

 All predefined Host Patches are dynamic in type. The **New Baseline** wizard also defaults to dynamic when creating a Host Patch baseline.

Importing ESXi Images

For you to be able to create a Host Upgrade baseline or a baseline group, you need to have ESXi Images imported to the Update Manager server's repository.

How to do it...

The following procedure will help you import an ESXi Image into Update Manager's repository.

1. Connect to the vCenter Server as an administrator, using the vSphere Client.
2. Go to **Home** | **Update Manager**.
3. Navigate to the **ESXi Images** tab and click on **Import ESXi Image** to bring up the **Import ESXi Image** wizard.
4. At the **Import ESXi Image** wizard, browse to add an ESXi Image and click on **Next**.
5. It will upload and import the image.

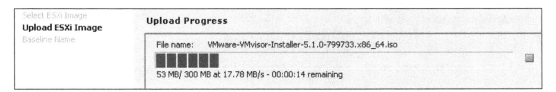

6. Once the upload is complete, the wizard will display the image details.

7. Subsequently, the wizard will prompt you to create an upgrade baseline. Enter a baseline name and click on **Finish**. At this screen you can choose not to create a baseline by unchecking the **Create a Baseline using the ESXi Image** checkbox.

How it works...

When you import an ESXi Image by using the **Import ESXi Image** wizard, the wizard actually copies the ESXi Image contents to a folder at the following location:

```
C:\ProgramData\VMware\VMware Update Manager\Data\host_upgrade_
packages
```

The folder will contain the contents of the ISO image.

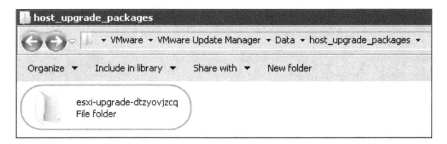

Creating a host baseline group

Host baseline groups are useful when you have to perform an upgrade and post upgrade you need to install patches that were released at a later date than the host upgrade or an extension (for example, a driver upgrade) that will make the server hardware compatible with the newer upgrade.

It is a requirement that you already have the required ESXi Image imported. Read the recipe *Importing ESXi Image* for instructions.

How to do it...

The following procedure will help you create a host Baseline group.

1. Connect to the vCenter Server as an administrator, using the vSphere Client.
2. Go to **Home | Update Manager**.
3. Navigate to the **Baselines and Groups** tab and click on the **Create** link corresponding to the baseline groups.

4. At the **New Baseline Group Wizard**, select the baseline group type as **Host Baseline Group**, supply a name for the baseline group and click on **Next** to continue.

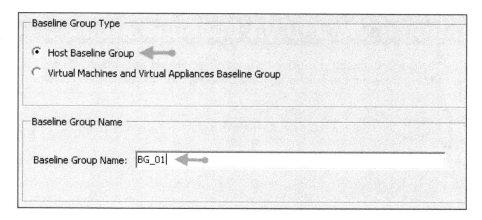

5. Choose an existing Host Upgrade baseline with the correct image or choose to **Create a new Host Upgrade Baseline** from this screen. With the required baseline selected, click on **Next** to continue.

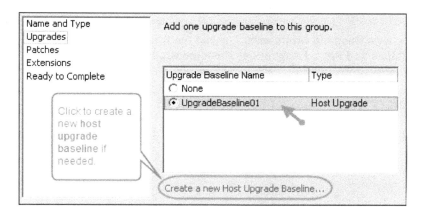

6. Select an existing Host Patch baseline or create a new one with the required criteria, and click on **Next**.

7. The **Ready to Complete** screen will summarize the options selected. Review the information provided and click on **Finish** to create the baseline group.

Creating a VM and VA baseline group

VM and VA baseline groups are useful when upgrading a **virtual appliance** (**VA**) and its dependent VMs. It uses the predefined upgrade baselines for a virtual machine (VM).

[Note that you cannot create a custom VM upgrade baseline.]

How to do it...

The following procedure will help you create a VM and VA Baseline groups:

1. Connect to the vCenter Server as an administrator, using the vSphere Client.

2. Go to **Home | Update Manager**.

3. Navigate to the **Baselines and Groups** tab and click on the **Create** link corresponding to the baseline groups.

4. At the **New Baseline Group** wizard, select the **Baseline Group Type** as **Virtual Machines and Virtual Appliances Baseline Group**. Enter a group name and click on **Next** to continue.

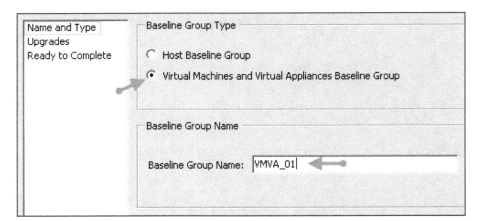

5. Select a **VA Upgrades** baseline, a **VM Hardware Upgrades** baseline, a **VMware Tools Upgrades** baseline, and click on **Next** to continue.

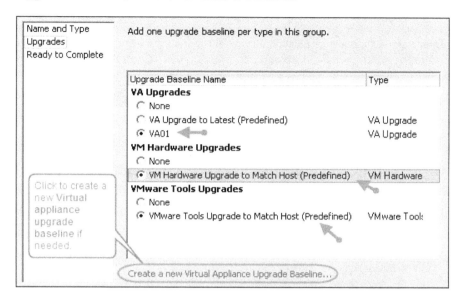

6. The **Ready to Complete** screen will summarize the options selected. Review the information provided and click on **Finish** to create the baseline group.

Remediating a host or a cluster

We learned how to create baselines and baseline groups. The purpose of creating these is to remediate an ESXi server. In this recipe, we will learn how to remediate an ESXi server or a cluster of ESXi hosts. Remediation refers to the process of installing the chosen patches or upgrades on the ESXi server.

How to do it...

The following procedure will guide you through the steps required to remediate an ESXi server.

1. Select an ESXi server or ESXi cluster from the inventory and navigate to the **Update Manager** tab and click on **Attach...** to bring-up the **Attach Baseline or Group** window.

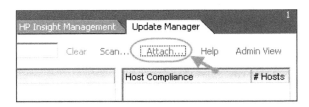

2. In the **Attach Baseline or Baseline Group** window, select a baseline or baseline group and click on **Attach** to tag it to the ESXi server.

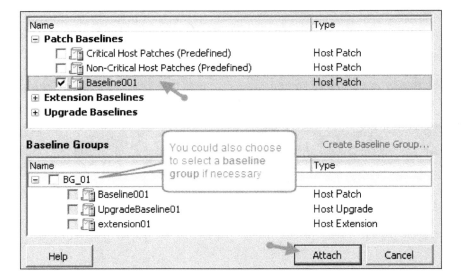

3. Once a baseline has been attached, click on **Scan** to scan for compliance.
4. The scan completes and displays the non-compliance details, if any.

5. Click on **Remediate** to bring up the **Remediate** wizard.

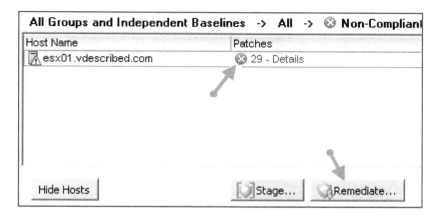

6. On the **Remediate** wizard screen, you will be shown the baselines selected. If multiple baselines were attached to the host then you can choose to deselect individual baselines as well. Click on **Next** to continue.

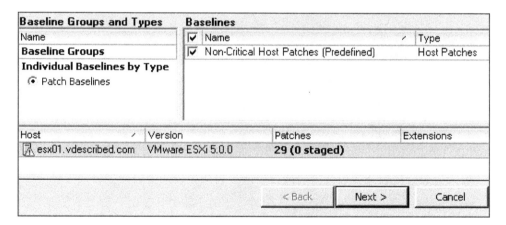

7. The next screen lists all of the applicable patches. Deselect patches that you do not intend to install on the ESXi server, and click on **Next** to continue.

8. You could either run the remediation **Immediately** or schedule it to run at a specified time and click on **Next** to continue.

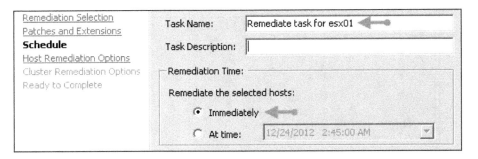

9. Set the **Host Maintenance Mode Options**. Make sure that you disable any removable media. This is important because, when a host tries to enter maintenance mode, the VMs on it are migrated (vMotion) to the other hosts in the cluster. VMs with removable media attached to them cannot be migrated using vMotion, hence preventing the host from entering the maintenance mode. Select the **Disable any removable media devices connected to the virtual machines on the host** checkbox and click on **Next** to continue.

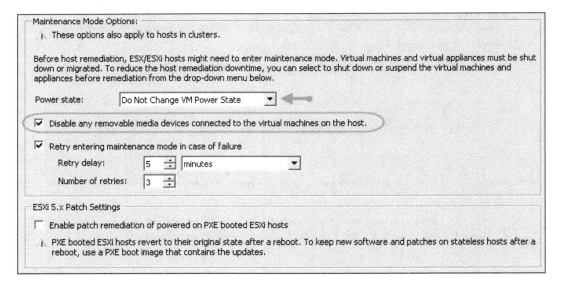

10. Set the **Cluster Remediation** options. You can disable High Availability admission control and Fault Tolerance (FT) to increase the chances of the host entering maintenance mode, without any issues. You can also generate a report to see the recommendations.

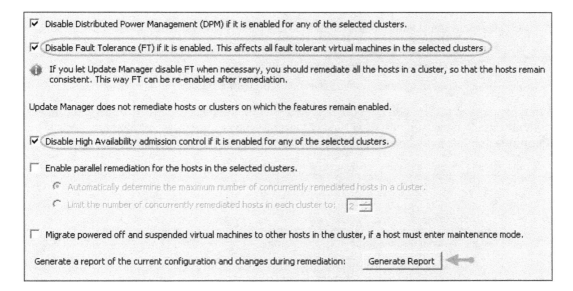

11. The **Ready to Complete** screen summarizes the selected options. Review the information provided and click on **Finish** to start the remediation or create the remediation schedule.

12. Once the remediation completes, scan the host for compliance again. It should then show the host/cluster as compliant to the baseline.

How it works...

Attaching a baseline to an ESXi host or a cluster of ESXi hosts is a way to inform Update Manager about the patches that you would like to have installed on the selected hosts/cluster.

Once a baseline/baseline group is attached to an entity, the entity needs to be scanned for compliance with the attached baseline. When you select a cluster to be scanned for compliance, it will scan all the ESXi hosts in the cluster.

Non-compliant hosts/clusters can be remediated. The remediation process will put the host in maintenance mode. By default, the VMs on the host will be migrated. If a cluster is chosen for remediation then hosts in the cluster are remediated sequentially.

Here is what happens in a five host cluster:

1. The first host in the cluster is put into maintenance mode. The VMs on it will be migrated to the remaining ESXi hosts with the help of DRS.

2. The first host is remediated.

3. Once the remediation completes, the host exits maintenance mode.

4. Once the first host is available in the cluster for hosting VMs again, the second host is put into maintenance mode for remediation.

5. This process continues until all five hosts are remediated.

What happens to the VMs on the host being put into maintenance mode by Update Manager can be controlled by using the **ESXi Host/Cluster Settings** under the Update Manager's **Configuration** tab. You can choose to **Power Off** or **Suspend virtual machines** as well.

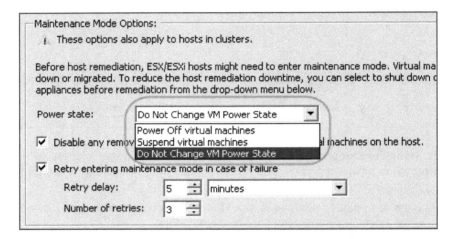

You can also choose to enable parallel remediation of hosts in the cluster. This can be done at the **ESXi Host/Cluster Settings** under the Update Manager's **Configuration** tab or at the remediation wizard.

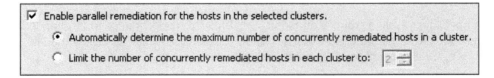

Host maintenance mode options for remediation

The host maintenance mode options can help you to reduce the downtime required to remediate an ESXi host, by either choosing to power-off or to suspend the VMs running on it. Choosing to power-off/suspend will cut down the time otherwise required to vMotion the VMs off that host. But keep in mind that we are gaining time at the expense of virtual machine downtime.

A host entering maintenance mode can fail at times. You can configure the number of retries the Update Manager will attempt and the time interval between each retry. It is recommended that you choose to disable any removable devices connected to the VM, as this can prevent vMotion.

Cluster maintenance mode options for remediation

When you remediate a cluster, it is recommended that you disable the DPM and enable the EVC (if required). If you generate a report, it will post the same recommendations.

It is a best practice to disable the High Availability admission control and FT, in order to increase the chances of the host entering the maintenance mode successfully.

You can also choose to migrate the powered-off/suspended VMs to other hosts in the cluster, so that if the remediated host fails to boot for some reason, then you are not left with VMs that needs to be manually re-added to the inventory

Enabling parallel remediation will reduce the amount of time needed to remediate the entire cluster, as it would concurrently remediate more than one host. Unless you want to limit the concurrency leave it as automatic.

Remediating a VM or a VA

Virtual machines can be remediated by using one of the following two predefined baselines:

- ▸ VMware tools upgrade to match host
- ▸ VM hardware upgrade to match host

A virtual appliance (VA) can be remediated by either using the predefined baseline VA Upgrade to Latest or by using a custom baseline.

 Remediating a VM or a virtual appliance can't be done from the host and clusters inventory view. Make sure you change to view to **VMs and Templates**.

How to do it...

The following procedure will help you remediate a VM or a virtual appliance:

1. At the vCenter Server, change the inventory view to **VMs and Templates**.

2. Select the VM to be remediated and navigate to its **Update Manger** tab.

3. Click on **Attach** to bring up the **Attach Baseline or Group** window.

4. In the **Attach Baseline or Group** window, select the VM Upgrade baselines or a baseline group and click on **Attach**.

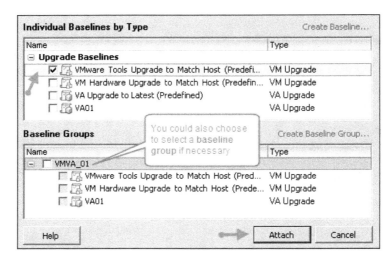

5. Scan the VM for compliance with the baseline.

6. Click on **Remediate** if the VM is non-compliant.

7. On the **Remediate** wizard screen, you can see the baselines selected. If multiple baselines were selected then you can choose to deselect individual baselines as well.

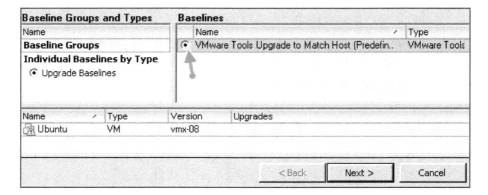

8. Enter a task name and schedule the upgrade at a specific time for powered-on, powered-off, and suspended VMs, and click on **Next**.

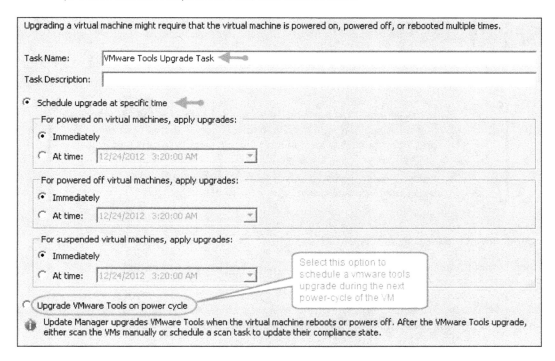

9. Choose the rollback options for the VM. This is achieved with the help of virtual machine snapshots. Select **Take a snapshot of the virtual machines before remediation to enable rollback**. You can optionally specify a snapshot name and also choose to snapshot the virtual machine memory.

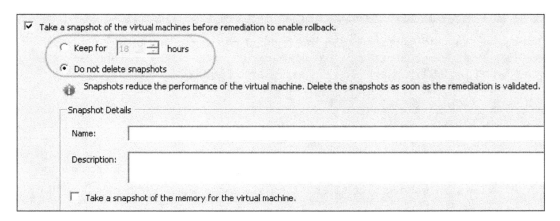

10. The **Ready to Complete** screen summarizes the settings. Review and click on **Finish** to start remediating at the scheduled time.

How it works...

When you remediate Windows VMs, it requires a downtime during the reboot after the VMware tools upgrade, but no downtime for the virtual hardware upgrade.

 With vSphere 5.1 the downtime (reboot) required for a VMware tools upgrade has been reduced. Read the section *Reduced downtime upgrade for VMware tools* in the *What's New in VMware vSphere 5.1* whitepaper, which is available at:

http://www.vmware.com/files/pdf/products/
vsphere/vmware-what-is-new-vsphere51.pdf

For Linux, Netware, and Solaris VMs you will not need a downtime for tools upgrade, but will need a downtime for a virtual hardware upgrade.

Keep in mind that the VMs need to be in the powered-on state for remediation. Power-off/suspended VMs will be powered-on/resumed for remediation.

It is a best practice to take snapshots of the VMs that will be remediated. Once the VMs are validated for proper functioning after remediating, delete the snapshots.

 Note that the steps involved in remediating a VA is exactly the same, the only difference being that you will be attaching a VA upgrade baseline instead of a VM upgrade baseline.

Staging patches

The remediation time is the *cumulative time* required to download and install patches on the ESXi server. The update manager can download the patches to the ESXi and perform a remediation at a later date/time. This process is called **Staging**.

How to do it...

The following procedure will help you stage patches for remediation:

1. Attach a baseline to a host/cluster, and then click on **Scan** to scan for compliance.
2. If the scan reports non-compliance then click on the **Stage** button to bring-up the **Stage** wizard.

3. At the **Stage** wizard, make sure that the correct baseline is selected and click on **Next**.

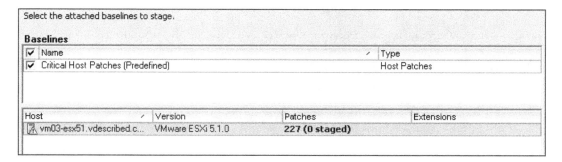

4. The next screen shows all the patches that will be staged. You can exclude patches by deselecting them, if needed.

5. On the **Ready to complete** screen, review the options and click on **Finish** to stage the patches.

How it works...

The staging process copies the patches to be installed onto the ESXi host. It is not required for the host to be in maintenance mode while the patches are being staged, hence saving a considerable amount of downtime for the ESXi server. The VMs can still continue to run while the patches are being staged.

Unlike remediation, staging cannot be scheduled. Once staging completes, remediation can be scheduled.

Installing the Update Manager Download Service (UMDS)

The **Update Manager Download Server** comes in handy when the Update Manger server doesn't have access to the Internet to download patches.

In this section we will learn how to install the Update Manager Download Service.

UMDS 5.1 should be installed on a 64-bit machine only. It cannot be installed on the same machine running the Update Manager and it is only compatible with the Update Manager 5.1.

If UMDS 5.1 is being installed on a machine running an older version of UMDS (UMDS 4.x or UMDS 5.x) then the older version should be uninstalled before installing UMDS 5.1.

How to do it...

The following procedure will help you install the Update Manager Download Service:

1. Locate the `VMware-UMDS.exe` under the `DVD ROM` in the `\umds` folder.

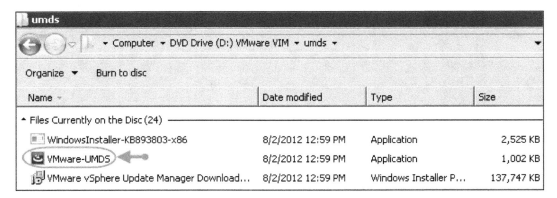

2. Create a new database for UMDS and a DSN, as we did for the Update Manger. Refer to the recipe *Preparing a database for vSphere Update Manager* for instructions.

3. Go through the installation wizard and make sure that you select the DSN for UMDS. We have created a new database `UMDS-Database` and 32-bit System DSN `UMDS51-DSN`.

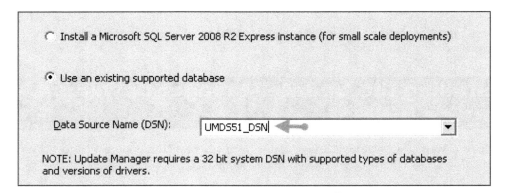

4. Configure the proxy settings if necessary, and click on **Next** to continue.

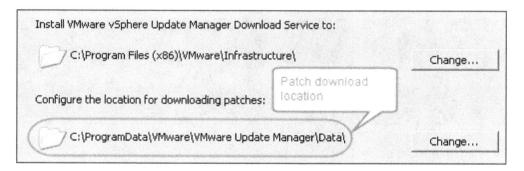

5. Configure the patch download location if necessary, click on **Next**, and then click on **Install** to start the installation.

Configuring UMDS and downloading data

UDMS can be configured to download and export patches to a shared repository. The entire configuration is done via the Windows command line.

How to do it...

The following procedure will help you configure UMDS and download data:

1. Locate the vm-umds.exe under the following directory:

   `C:\Program Files (x86)\VMware\Infrastructure\Update Manager`

2. By default, the UMDS will only download patches and notifications for hosts. To configure it to download even the VA upgrades, you should run the following command:

```
vmware-umds -S --enable-host --enable-va
```

```
c:\Program Files (x86)\VMware\Infrastructure\Update Manager>
vmware-umds -S --enable-host --enable-va
[2012-07-30 22:29:16:495 '' 4968 ALERT] [logUtil, 265] Product = VMware Update
Manager, Version = 5.0.0, Build = 432001
Setting up UMDS configuration
Host update downloads: Enabled
Virtual appliance upgrade downloads: Enabled

c:\Program Files (x86)\VMware\Infrastructure\Update Manager>_
```

3. If you need to change the patch repository location (optional) then issue the following command:

Syntax:

```
vmware-umds -S --patch-store your_new_patchstore_folder
```

Example:

```
vmware-umds -S --patch-store C:\Data_Here
```

```
c:\Program Files (x86)\VMware\Infrastructure\Update Manager>
vmware-umds -S --patch-store c:\Data_Here
[2012-07-30 22:36:19:013 '' 4824 ALERT] [logUtil, 265] Product = VMware Update
Manager, Version = 5.0.0, Build = 432001
Setting up UMDS configuration
Directory for storing downloaded updates: c:\Data_Here
Directory C:\ProgramData\VMware\VMware Update Manager\Data\ is no longer used as
 the patch store. You may want to delete its contents or move it to the new loca
tion c:\Data_Here

c:\Program Files (x86)\VMware\Infrastructure\Update Manager>_
```

4. You can add a patch download source by using the following command:

Syntax:

```
vmware-umds -S --add-url https://host_URL/index.xml --url-type
HOST
```

Example:

```
vmware-umds -S --add-url http://vibsdepot.hp.com/index.xml --url-
type HOST
```

```
c:\Program Files (x86)\VMware\Infrastructure\Update Manager>
 vmware-umds -S --add-url http://vibsdepot.hp.com/index.xml --url-type HOST ◀━
[2012-07-30 22:45:07:770 '' 6124 ALERT]  [logUtil, 265] Product = VMware Update
Manager, Version = 5.0.0, Build = 432001
Setting up UMDS configuration
[2012-07-30 22:45:07:801 'DownloadMgr' 6124 DEBUG]  [downloadMgr, 319] Maximum

[2012-07-30 22:45:09:205 'HostUpdateDepotManager' 6124 INFO]  [vendorIndexParser
, 36] vendor index contains 1 vendors.
Added HOST URL http://vibsdepot.hp.com/index.xml ◀━

c:\Program Files (x86)\VMware\Infrastructure\Update Manager>_
```

5. To initiate a download from the patch download sources, issue the following command:

   `vmware-umds -D`

Creating a shared repository

We can export downloaded patch data from the repository used by the UMDS to a shared location so that the Update Manager server can be configured to use this shared location.

How to do it...

To export the downloaded patch data to a shared repository, issue the following command:

Syntax:

`vmware-umds -E --export-store repository_path`

Example:

`vmware-umds -E --export-store C:\PatchRep`

`vmware-umds -E --export-store \\vcenter51\atvc`

How it works...

The command copies the data from the patch store to the shared repository. You have to periodically export the patch data to keep the shared repository up to date. The shared repository folder should have full permissions (everyone) over the network.

Using a shared repository

In scenarios where the Update Manager server cannot be provided with access to the Internet, you can configure the Update Manager server to access a shared repository containing patch data. For instructions on how to create a shared repository, read the recipe *Creating a shared repository*.

How to do it...

The following the procedure will help you to configure access to a shared repository:

1. On the UMDS server, set the shared repository folder as the "export store". Read the recipe *Creating a shared repository* for instructions.

2. Once a shared repository has been created, connect to the vCenter Server by using the vSphere Client and navigate to **Home | Update Manager** and then navigate to the **Configuration** tab and then to **Download Settings**. Select the **Use a shared repository** option to specify a shared repository and click on **Validate URL**.

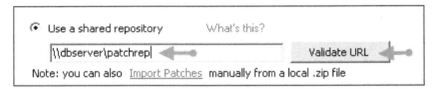

3. Once the URL is validated, click on **Apply** and then **Download** to download patches from the shared repository.

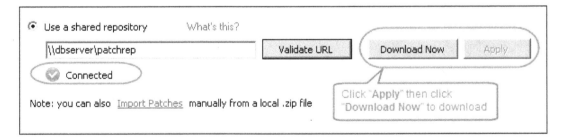

4. You should see a dialog box indicating that a new download task has been added to the **Recent Tasks** pane.

13

Using vSphere Management Assistant (vMA 5.1)

In this chapter we will cover the following:

- ▶ Deploying the vMA appliance
- ▶ Preparing the vMA for first use
- ▶ Configuring vMA to join an existing domain
- ▶ Adding vCenter to vMA with AD authentication
- ▶ Adding vCenter to vMA with fastpass (fpauth) authentication
- ▶ Adding an ESXi host to vMA
- ▶ Reconfiguring an added target server
- ▶ Running CLI commands on target servers

Introduction

The **vSphere Management Assistant** (**vMA**) is a virtual appliance that can be used to run remote commands or scripts on an ESXi host.

The vMA virtual machine runs an SLES 11 based operating system with the vSphere CLI (command line interface) packaged with it. It is generally used by administrators to run commands/scripts without the need to authenticate every attempt.

Deploying the vMA appliance

The vMA appliance will be deployed as an appliance VM on an ESXi server. Download the vMA appliance from the following website:

`https://my.vmware.com/web/vmware/details?downloadGroup=VSP510-vMA-510&productId=285#product_downloads`

The vMA appliance can be deployed on an ESXi server by using vSphere Client or by using the vCenter Server.

vMA 5.1 can be deployed on the following systems:

▸ vSphere 4.1 or later

▸ vCenter 5.0 or later

vMA 5.1 can be used to target operations on vSphere 5.0 and later, and vSphere 4.1 and later systems.

How to do it...

The following procedure will help you deploy the vMA appliance using the **vSphere Web Client interface**.

1. Download and extract the appliance ZIP bundle to a location accessible to the vSphere Web Client.

2. At the vSphere Web Client interface's inventory home, navigate to **Hosts and Clusters**.

3. Right-click on the ESXi cluster and then click on **Deploy OVF Template**.

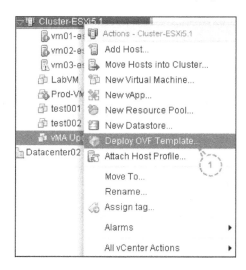

4. At the **Deploy OVF Template** wizard, select the **Local File** option and then click on the **Browse...** button.

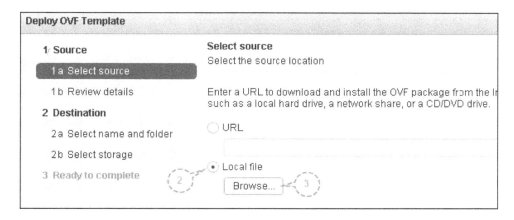

5. Browse and select the OVF file from the extracted location and then click on **Next** to continue with the wizard.

6. Review the details of the OVF file and then click on **Next** to continue.

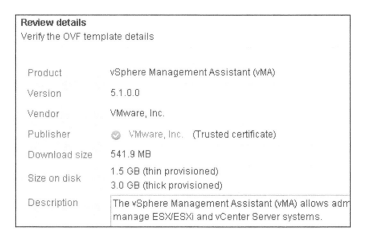

7. Accept the license agreement and then click on **Next**.

8. Choose an inventory location for the appliance VM and then click on **Next**.

9. Choose a datastore for the VM and then click on **Next**.

10. Choose a port group to which the vNIC will be mapped. Set the **IP allocation** policy and **Protocol Settings** and then click on **Next**.

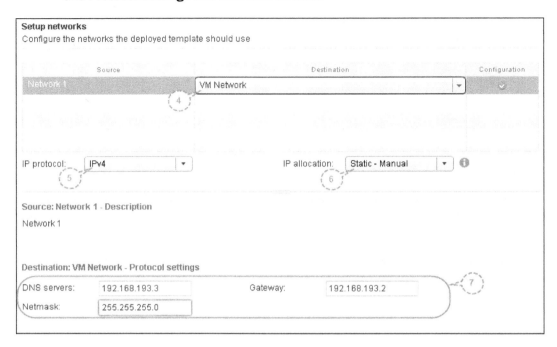

11. Specify an IP address for the VM's NIC and then click on **Next**.

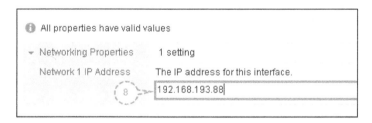

12. Review the **Ready to complete** screen and then click on **Finish** to deploy the appliance.

 Note that it doesn't matter what IP allocation policy you choose or what IP address you specify; you will need to choose between a DHCP and a static configuration when you configure the appliance after the first boot.

How it works...

Once you finish the wizard, it will deploy the vMA appliance onto one of the ESXi hosts in the cluster. The inventory should now list a virtual machine with the name **vSphere Management Assistant (vMA)**. The appliance, however, is not ready for use yet. The appliance needs to be manually configured before its first use. Read the recipe *Preparing vMA for first use* for instructions on how to prepare the vMA appliance for first use.

Preparing vMA for first use

A vMA deployed appliance will need to go through a few manual configuration steps before you can begin using it. The configuration is done at the appliance's guest operating system level.

 The vMA appliance runs **SUSE Linux Enterprise Linux** (**SLES**) 11 SP1 as the guest operating system.

How to do it...

The follow procedure will help you prepare the vMA VM for first use:

1. Power on the vMA VM and wait for the VM to boot-up and display the network configuration main menu.

```
Starting network configuration ...

Main Menu

 0)      Show Current Configuration (scroll with Shift-PgUp/PgDown)
 1)      Exit this program
 2)      Default Gateway
 3)      Hostname
 4)      DNS
 5)      Proxy Server
 6)      IP Address Allocation for eth0
Enter a menu number [0]: _
```

2. Enter 6 to select **IP Address Allocation for eth0** and supply the static configuration and then enter y to confirm the configuration.

```
Enter a menu number [0]: 6  ←
Type Ctrl-C to go back to the Main Menu

Configure an IPv6 address for eth0? y/n [n]: n
Configure an IPv4 address for eth0? y/n [n]: y
Use a DHCPv4 Server instead of a static IPv4 address? y/n [n]: n
IPv4 Address []: 192.168.193.88
Netmask []: 255.255.255.0
IPv4 Address:    192.168.193.88  ←
Netmask:         255.255.255.0

Is this correct? y/n [y]: _
```

3. Enter 2 to set the **Default Gateway**. Although, I have supplied an IPv4 address in this example, you can supply an IPv6 address instead. This step is completely dependent on your network infrastructure.

```
Enter a menu number [0]: 2  ←

Warning: if any of the interfaces for this VM use DHCP,
the Hostname, DNS, and Gateway parameters will be
overwritten by information from the DHCP server.

Type Ctrl-C to go back to the Main Menu

0)        eth0
Choose the interface to associate with default gateway [0]: 0
Gateway will be associated with eth0
IPv4 Default Gateway []: 192.168.193.2  ←
IPv6 Default Gateway []: _        Hit "ENTER" to skip
```

4. Enter 4 and supply the **DNS Server** details. Although I have supplied a single DNS sever address in this example, most environments will have a secondary DNS server.

```
Enter a menu number [0]: 4  ←

Warning: if any of the interfaces for this VM use DHCP,
the Hostname, DNS, and Gateway parameters will be
overwritten by information from the DHCP server.

Type Ctrl-C to go back to the Main Menu

DNS Server 1 []: 192.168.193.3  ←        Hit "ENTER" to skip
DNS Server 2 (optional) [192.168.193.3]: _
```

5. Enter 3 and supply a **hostname**.

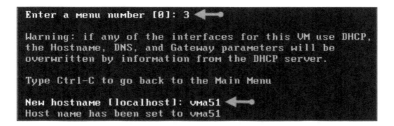

```
Enter a menu number [0]: 3 ←

Warning: if any of the interfaces for this VM use DHCP,
the Hostname, DNS, and Gateway parameters will be
overwritten by information from the DHCP server.

Type Ctrl-C to go back to the Main Menu

New hostname [localhost]: vma51 ←
Host name has been set to vma51
```

6. Enter 5 and supply the **Proxy Server** information.

```
Enter a menu number [0]: 5 ←
Type Ctrl-C to go back to the Main Menu

Is an IPv4 proxy server necessary to reach the Internet? y/n [n]: y
Proxy Server (http:// will be auto prepended) []: 192.168.0.104 ←
Proxy Port []: 808_ ←
```

7. Enter 0 to view the current IP configuration of the appliance.

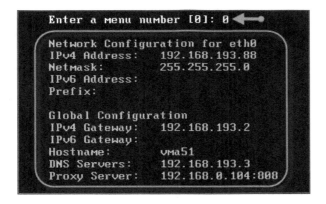

```
Enter a menu number [0]: 0 ←

Network Configuration for eth0
IPv4 Address:      192.168.193.88
Netmask:           255.255.255.0
IPv6 Address:
Prefix:

Global Configuration
IPv4 Gateway:      192.168.193.2
IPv6 Gateway:
Hostname:          vma51
DNS Servers:       192.168.193.3
Proxy Server:      192.168.0.104:808
```

8. Enter 1 to exit the network configuration program and start the password configuration program.

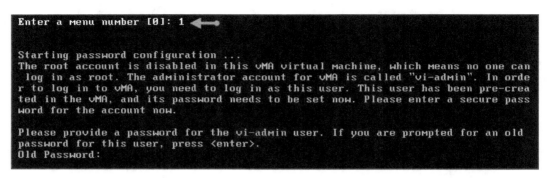

9. Press the *Enter* key at the old password prompt, and then enter a new password. The new password must at least contain *nine* characters, including one upper case, one lower case, one numerical character, and one printable ASCII symbol.

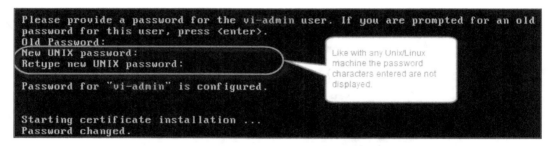

10. The appliance with continue with loading the guest OS of the appliance, and will reach the main page.

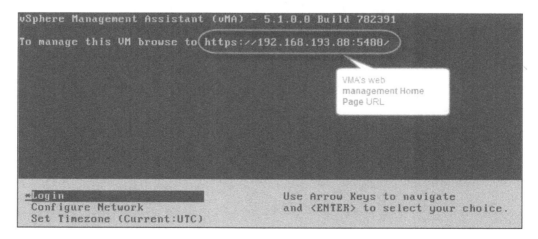

How it works...

Once the appliance has been configured for first use, you can perform various operations from the console of the appliance and its management home page.

When you log in using the `vi-admin` user, at the vMA appliance's management home page you get options to reconfigure the network, the time-zone, and to check for appliance updates.

The following tasks can be performed:

- ▸ From the console, you can perform the following tasks:
  - ❑ Add vCenter Servers or ESXi servers to vMA
  - ❑ Issue commands from the vMA console against the added servers
  - ❑ Configure the vMA's network and proxy settings
  - ❑ Configure the time-zone settings.

- ▸ From the Web UI, you can perform the following tasks:
  - ❑ Configure the vMA's network and proxy settings
  - ❑ Configure the time-zone settings
  - ❑ Update vMA

 The `root` user account on the appliance is not enabled. For tasks requiring root privileges, use the `vi-admin` user and `sudo` to get privileges.

Configuring vMA to join an existing domain

The `vi-user` account can't be used to run commands against the **Active Directory** targets. To be able to run command on an AD target, you should either use the `vi-admin` account or log in to the vMA appliance using an AD user. To be able to log in to the vMA appliance using an AD user, the appliance first needs to be added to the AD. In this section we will learn how to do that.

How to do it...

The following procedure explains how to configure a vMA appliance to join an existing AD domain.

1. Log in to the vMA console or SSH to it as the `vi-admin` user.

2. Issue the following command to add the vMA appliance to the domain:

   Syntax:

   ```
   sudo domainjoin-cli join <domain-name> <domain-admin-user>
   ```

   Example:

   ```
   sudo domainjoin-cli join vdescribed.com Administrator
   ```

   ```
   vi-admin@localhost:~> sudo domainjoin-cli join vdescribed.com Administrator
   vi-admin's password:
   Joining to AD Domain:   vdescribed.com
   With Computer DNS Name: localhost.localdom

   Administrator@VDESCRIBED.COM's password:
   Warning: System restart required
   Your system has been configured to authenticate to Active Directory for the
   first time.  It is recommended that you restart your system to ensure that all
   applications recognize the new settings.

   SUCCESS
   vi-admin@localhost:~> _
   ```

3. Reboot the vMA appliance by issuing the command `sudo reboot`.

4. Verify whether the domain login was successful by issuing the following command:

   ```
   sudo domainjoin-cli query
   ```

   ```
   vi-admin@vma51:~> sudo domainjoin-cli query
   Name = vma51
   Domain = VDESCRIBED.COM
   Distinguished Name = CN=VMA51,CN=Computers,DC=vdescribed,DC=com
   vi-admin@vma51:~> _
   ```

Adding vCenter to vMA with AD authentication

You can add vCenter Servers to vMA with AD authentication.

How to do it...

The following procedure explains how to add the vCenter Server to the vMA by using AD authentication.

1. Log in to the vMA console or SSH to it as the `vi-admin`.

2. Issue the following command:

```
vifp addserver <vCenter>   --authpolicy adauth --username
<domain>\\<domain admin>
```

Example:

```
vifp addserver vcenter5x.vdescibed.com  --authpolicy adauth
--username vdescribed.com\\Administrator
```

3. Issue the command `vifp listservers` to verify that the server has been added.

```
vi-admin@localhost:~[vcenter5x.vdescribed.com]> vifp listservers
vcenter5x.vdescribed.com          vCenter  ⬅
vi-admin@localhost:~[vcenter5x.vdescribed.com]> ▮        ⬈
```

How it works...

When executing this command make sure that you specify the username in the <DOMAIN>\\<DOMAIN ADMIN> format. Else, the authentication will be verified against the local credentials on the vCenter Server.

 Note that we should be using two backward slashes. This is because on a Linux Shell two backward slashes (\\) is an escape sequence for a single backward slash (\).

If the adauth value is not specified by using the authpolicy switch then the default fpauth mechanism will be used.

Once configured correctly, you can issue vSphere CLI command on ESXi hosts managed by the added vCenter without a prompt for authentication.

Adding vCenter to vMA with fastpass (fpauth) authentication

You can add vCenter Servers to vMA with the standard/default fastpass authentication (fpauth). vMA's fastpass authentication method provides a mechanism to cache the target server's credentials, on the vMA machine, so that you don't have authenticate every time you run a command against the target server.

How to do it...

The following procedure explains how to add the vCenter Server to the vMA by using fastpass Authentication.

1. Log in to the vMA console or SSH to it as the `vi-admin` user.

2. Issue the following command:

   ```
   vifp addserver <vCenter>   --authpolicy fpauth
   ```

   Example:

   ```
   vifp addserver vcenter5x.vdescribed.com   --authpolicy fpauth
   ```

```
vi-admin@localhost:~> vifp addserver vcenter5x.vdescribed.com  ←
--authpolicy fpauth
Enter username for vcenter5x.vdescribed.com: Administrator
Administrator@vcenter5x.vdescribed.com's password:
This will store username and password in credential store which is a security ri
sk. Do you want to continue?(yes/no): yes  ←
vi-admin@localhost:~[vcenter5x.vdescribed.com]> ▌
```

3. Issue the command `vifp listservers` to verify that the server has been added.

How it works...

Unlike AD authentication, the fastpass mechanism stores the username and password information in a local credential store.

The `vi-admin` credentials are stored in the following XML file:

`/home/vi-admin/vmware/credstore/ vmacredentials.xml`

By default the added server is set as the target. You can issue the following command to verify the same:

```
vifptarget -d
```

Adding an ESXi host to vMA

Instead of adding a vCenter Server to vMA, it is possible to add just the individual ESXi hosts. This is particularly useful if a single vCenter is used to manage multiple Data Centers and you don't want to expose all of the ESXi hosts managed by the vCenter to the vMA appliance.

How to do it...

The following procedure explains how to add an ESXi server to the vMA appliance.

1. Log in to the vMA console or SSH to it as the `vi-admin` user.

2. Issue the following command:

   vifp addserver <ESXi_server_name>

   Example:

   vifp addserver esx51-01.vdescribed.com

3. When prompted, specify the root password for the ESXi host.

4. Issue the `vifp listservers` command to verify that the ESXi host was added.

How it works...

When you add an ESXi server to vMA, unlike adding a vCenter Server, vMA doesn't store the `root` password in its credstore.

Instead, it will create two users on the target ESXi server:

► `vi-admin` with administrator privileges
► `vi-user` with read-only privilege

On the ESXi server, the `/etc/passwd` should show both the users have been created.

```
~ # cat /etc/passwd
root:x:0:0:Administrator:/:/bin/sh
daemon:x:2:2:System daemons:/:/sbin/nologin
nfsnobody:x:65534:65534:Anonymous NFS User:/:/sbin/nologin
dcui:x:100:100:DCUI User:/:/sbin/nologin
vpxuser:x:500:100:VMware VirtualCenter administration account:/:/bin/sh
vi-admin00:x:1000:1000:ESXID=52186596-e95f-429f-7dff-3e44eb5754ab;VIMAID=420948F7-3
0FC-0FED-7133-779C591A0E9F;:/:/bin/sh
vi-user00:x:1001:1001:ESXID=52186596-e95f-429f-7dff-3e44eb5754ab;VIMAID=420948F7-30
FC-0FED-7133-779C591A0E9F;:/:/bin/sh
~ #
```

> vi-admin and vi-user entries

In the credstore on the vMA, you will see a `vi-admin` password entry for the ESXi server.

```
vi-admin@localhost:~> cat /home/vi-admin/.vmware/credstore/vmacredentials.xml
<?xml version="1.0" encoding="UTF-8"?>

<viCredentials>
    <version>1.0</version>
    <passwordEntry>
        <host>vc51-01.vdescribed.com</host>
        <username>Administrator</username>
        <password>r7+qxZeJia+vr6+9gp2mtqrfh6G2ur+vr6+LqMn4Ct16uopKSAwYyNhrbft
7S4haWe34iFmYaH24DWi4iilJm/xYGrhZiChaXY3bq6hNmZvJvertvp+Bh4m8gNuK7u6ims+b35GH
sXt2VgiDPgjrGocoHX7LF1WK7uZc3b8=</password>
    </passwordEntry>

    <passwordEntry>
        <host>esx51-01.vdescribed.com</host>
        <username>vi-admin00</username>
        <password>sKC12oiWlrCwsLWhoYGZiImruJ2hpKCwsLCwiLLeh7TJvbKV2p2en4KU2se1k
rOT1d61oaCGqYGfl6e5poiFxbK53py215fCxLK3mb+L3sKHxISEpLewo5mch6WJhd6/v7mEvcG8ocSn
qbqY2pjIkKaAo7yUoMzM8fGdiyYTw+U=</password>
    </passwordEntry>

</viCredentials>
vi-admin@localhost:~>
```

> Entry corresponding to the added ESXi server

To remove a server (ESXi/vCenter), issue the following command:

`vifp removeserver <servername>`

Examples:

`Vifp removeserver vcenter5x.vdescribed.com`

Reconfiguring an added target server

An added target server can be reconfigured for a change in the authentication policy, a change in the users authenticating the target or to recover a `fastpass` user in the event of a local credstore corruption.

How to do it...

The follow procedures will guide you through the steps required for the following:

- ▶ Changing the authentication policy
- ▶ Changing or recovering a user

Changing the authentication policy

The following procedure will help you change the authentication policy of a target that has already been added to vMA:

1. Issue the following command:

   ```
   vifp recover <servername>  --authpolicy <authpolicy type>
   ```

   Example:

   ```
   vifp recover vcenter5x.vdescribed.com  --authpolicy fpauth
   ```

2. When prompted, supply the credentials.

Changing or recovering a user

The need to recover a user may arise if the login credentials corresponding to a user has changed or if vMA's credential store is corrupted. The following procedure will help you recover a target that has already been added to vMA:

1. Issue the following command:

   ```
   vifp recover <servername>
   ```

   Example:

   ```
   vifp recover vcenter5x.vdescribed.com
   vifp recover esx01.vdescribed.com
   ```

2. When prompted, supply the credentials.

How it works...

When you are switching over from `adauth` to `fpauth` or if you are reconfiguring a fastpass target, it will prompt you only for a password. Whereas, if you are reconfiguring an AD target, it will prompt you only for a username. If the intended target is not the default target then you will have to use the `vifptarget -s` command to set the required target.

Running CLI command on target servers

In this recipe we will learn how to issue commands on the added target servers.

How to do it...

The following procedures explain how to set a target server to direct commands to it. We will discuss all three methods.

Method 1 – Issue commands on the default target

1. Set the intended server as the default target for all commands.

   Command:

   ```
   vifptarget -s <servername>
   ```

   Example:

   ```
   vifptarget -s esx01.vdescribed.com
   vifptarget -s vcenter5x.vdescribed.com
   ```

2. Similar to the CLI commands you would run at an ESXi host's console.

   Example:

   ```
   esxcli network nic list
   ```

Method 2 – Issue commands by specifying a target server

1. Issue the command specifying the server name.

   Example:

   ```
   esxcli –server esx01.vdescribed.com iscsi adapter list
   vifptarget -s esx01.vdescribed.com
   ```

2. Supply the username and password when prompted.

Method 3 – Issuing commands against a vCenter Server added as the target

1. Issue the command specifying the vCenter Server and ESXi server:

   Command:

   ```
   esxcli --server <VC_server> --vihost <esx_host> network nic list
   ```

   Example:

   ```
   esxcli -server vcenter5x.vdescribed.com -vihost esx02.vdescribed.
   com network list
   ```

2. Supply the vCenter username and password when prompted.

 Note that this method will ONLY prompt you for the vCenter's username and password. It will not prompt you for the ESXi host's root password.

Index

Thank you for buying
VMware vSphere 5.1 Cookbook

About Packt Publishing

Packt, pronounced 'packed', published its first book "*Mastering phpMyAdmin for Effective MySQL Management*" in April 2004 and subsequently continued to specialize in publishing highly focused books on specific technologies and solutions.

Our books and publications share the experiences of your fellow IT professionals in adapting and customizing today's systems, applications, and frameworks. Our solution-based books give you the knowledge and power to customize the software and technologies you're using to get the job done. Packt books are more specific and less general than the IT books you have seen in the past. Our unique business model allows us to bring you more focused information, giving you more of what you need to know, and less of what you don't.

Packt is a modern, yet unique publishing company, which focuses on producing quality, cutting-edge books for communities of developers, administrators, and newbies alike. For more information, please visit our website: www.PacktPub.com.

About Packt Enterprise

In 2010, Packt launched two new brands, Packt Enterprise and Packt Open Source, in order to continue its focus on specialization. This book is part of the Packt Enterprise brand, home to books published on enterprise software – software created by major vendors, including (but not limited to) IBM, Microsoft and Oracle, often for use in other corporations. Its titles will offer information relevant to a range of users of this software, including administrators, developers, architects, and end users.

Writing for Packt

We welcome all inquiries from people who are interested in authoring. Book proposals should be sent to author@packtpub.com. If your book idea is still at an early stage and you would like to discuss it first before writing a formal book proposal, contact us; one of our commissioning editors will get in touch with you.

We're not just looking for published authors; if you have strong technical skills but no writing experience, our experienced editors can help you develop a writing career, or simply get some additional reward for your expertise.

**VMware ThinApp 4.7
Essentials**

VMware ThinApp 4.7
Essentials

Learn how to quickly and efficiently virtualize your applications
with ThinApp 4.7

Peter Björk   [PACKT] enterprise 🎗

VMware ThinApp 4.7 Essentials

ISBN: 978-1-84968-628-0   Paperback: 256 pages

Learn how to quickly and efficiently virtualize your applications with ThinApp 4.7

1. Practical book which provides the essentials of application virtualization with ThinApp 4.7

2. Learn the various methods and best practices of application packaging and deployment

3. Save money and time on your projects with this book by learning how to create portable applications

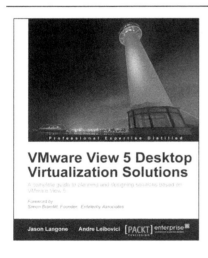

VMware View 5 Desktop
Virtualization Solutions

A complete guide to planning and designing solutions based on
VMware View 5

Foreword by
Simon Bramfitt, Founder, Entelechy Associates

Jason Langone   Andre Leibovici [PACKT] enterprise 🎗

VMware View 5 Desktop Virtualization Solutions

ISBN: 978-184968-112-4   Paperback: 288 pages

A complete guide to planning and designing solutions based on VMware View 5

1. Written by VMware experts Jason Langone and Andre Leibovici, this book is a complete guide to planning and designing a solution based on VMware View 5

2. Secure your Visual Desktop Infrastructure (VDI) by having firewalls, antivirus, virtual enclaves, USB redirection and filtering and smart card authentication

3. Analyze the strategies and techniques used to migrate a user population from a physical desktop environment to a virtual desktop solution

Please check **www.PacktPub.com** for information on our titles

Citrix XenDesktop 5.6 Cookbook

Gaspare A. Silvestri

Citrix XenDesktop 5.6 Cookbook

ISBN: 978-1-84968-504-7   Paperback: 354 pages

Implement a fully featured XenDesktop 5.6 architecture in a rich and powerful VDI experience configuration

1. Real-world methodologies and functioning explanations about the XenDesktop 5.6 architecture and its satellite components used to perform a service-oriented architecture

2. Learn how to publish desktops and applications to end user devices, optimizing their performance and increasing the general security

3. Step-by-step guide on how to install and configure the XenDesktop 5.6 architecture to access and use the published virtual resources

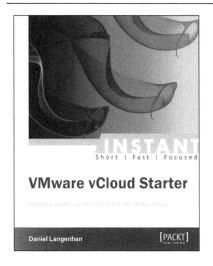

VMware vCloud Starter

Short | Fast | Focused

Daniel Langenhan

Instant VMware vCloud Starter

ISBN: 978-1-84968-996-0   Paperback: 76 pages

A practical, hands-on guide to get started with VMware vCloud

1. Learn something new in an Instant! A short, fast, focused guide delivering immediate results.

2. Deploy and operate a VMware vCloud in your own demo kit

3. Understand the basics about the cloud in general and why there is such a hype

4. Build and use templates to quickly deploy complete environments

Please check **www.PacktPub.com** for information on our titles

www.ingramcontent.com/pod-product-compliance
Lightning Source LLC
LaVergne TN
LVHW062300060326

832902LV00013B/1980